A PATH THROUGH THE TREES

A PATH THROUGH

THE TREES

Mary Sutherland

FORESTER, BOTANIST *&* WOMEN'S ADVOCATE

Vivien Edwards

ISBN 978-0-9941494-4-2

Every effort has been made to contact copyright owners to obtain permissions.
Please make contact with any queries or information about rights holders.

Title page: Mary Sutherland in Kaingaroa Forest, 1932. SCION
Facing page: Kauri tree. ALEXANDER TURNBULL LIBRARY

Grateful thanks to the Stout Trust and the New Zealand Institute of Forestry
Foundation for making the publication of this book possible.

Thanks to Dr Colin Bassett, Roger Steele and Julia Millen for editorial assistance.
Map illustrations: Emma Muirhead

Printed by Quorum Print Services, United Kingdom

Book design & production: Writes Hill Press
www.writeshillpress.co.nz

The Mary Sutherland memorial plaque in Whakarewarewa Forest, Rotorua, 2009. VIVIEN EDWARDS

FOREWORD

Mary Sutherland is a name familiar to many members of the New Zealand Institute of Forestry, although the details of her involvement in New Zealand forestry are not so well known. Author Vivien Edwards has filled this gap, spurred on by a chance encounter with a plaque in the Redwood Grove in Whakarewarewa Forest, Rotorua, that commemorates Mary as the first woman in the world to graduate with a degree in forestry. Vivien's diligent research has uncovered details of the life and work of a remarkable woman for her time. Her book is a valuable contribution to the history of New Zealand forestry and the New Zealand Institute of Forestry (NZIF).

In 1916 during World War One, Mary Sutherland graduated from the University College of North Wales, Bangor. Thus began a career that took her through two world wars, economic depressions and redundancy, and brought her to New Zealand to work for the fledgling State Forest Service. The skills she acquired also led her into the fields of botany and farm forestry, and Vivien has woven Mary's personality, and personal and community life into this professional record.

Mary's years at the Forest Service were during the time of a massive afforestation scheme — an exciting time for a forester. Timber supplies from indigenous forests were predicted to run out in thirty years, so to provide an alternative supply, from 1920 to 1933 state plantation forest increased from 15,000 to 142,000 hectares with a corresponding increase in the private sector. Mary was involved in a range of activities from analytical studies and research to public education and authorship. She travelled widely to investigate nursery and plantation operations, measure sample plots and conduct other field work. She was also an inaugural and active member of the New Zealand Institute of Foresters (now the New Zealand Institute of Forestry: Te Pūtahi Ngāherehere o Aotearoa Incorporated), and in 1930 designed the official seal that is the basis of the institute's logo today. Mary served as a councillor for 1935–36 and vice president for 1941–42, and she left a bequest to the institute that seeded the annual Mary Sutherland Scholarship.

The tensions and prejudices underlying the official reports Vivien Edwards describes were still present when I joined the Forest Service in 1962: tensions associated with professional women working in a male-dominated profession, particularly in fieldwork; tensions between university-qualified and technically-trained staff (could the latter be full members of NZIF?); and tensions between the conservancies and head office when conservators reported to the head of the Forest Service and resented receiving instructions from head office. The profession also remained resolutely male. Although there were Schools of Forestry at both the Auckland and Canterbury university colleges during the 1920s and '30s, I found only one woman student, Millicent Mary Brooke, who studied for a Bachelor of Forestry Science at Auckland from 1927 to 1929, but she appears to have not completed the fourth year. When the School of Forestry at Canterbury was re-established in 1970, the first woman to graduate was Heather McKenzie in 1974, almost sixty years after Mary Sutherland "trampled the first path through the trees for other women foresters to follow".

~ Andrew McEwen, ONZM, FNZIF
    Chair, New Zealand Institute of Forestry Foundation
    President, New Zealand Institute of Forestry, 2008–2014

Helen (Nellie) and David Sutherland with their children, Helen (Nell), Mary on her mother's knee, Catherine (Kate), and Margaret (Daisy) in front, 1893. SUTHERLAND/GRAY FAMILY

CONTENTS

Mary Sutherland, 1930. SUTHERLAND/GRAY FAMILY

INTRODUCTION

Just over a hundred years ago Mary Sutherland changed the status of women working in forestry when she graduated from the University College of North Wales. She was the first woman forestry graduate in the world. It was daring to take up a male-only career in 1916, and an amazing achievement that she was successful in a climate of two world wars and economic depression, and when society generally disregarded women's contributions. Her path was not easy.

Mary's story is not just about overcoming gender bias, it is also an important thread in a worldwide tale of attempts to redress forest exploitation caused by our insatiable need for wood, which at the time was used in almost every form of construction. The huge demand for timber meant scientific forestry needed to develop to grow the best species for each product, achieve maximum tree growth, and harvest the largest amount of useful timber from each log. Men who learned their craft on the job felt challenged by a woman in their midst, especially one with a university degree who also had practical skills.

I first became aware of Mary Sutherland when I saw a memorial plaque for her among the redwoods in Whakarewarewa Forest, Rotorua. I wondered how a woman became a forester during that era. What encouraged her to take up her chosen career? How did the men cope with a woman in forestry? Did they accept her? What job did she do? Was she working in the forest or typing and making the tea? What happened before Mary came to New Zealand and later after she left the State Forest Service? My curiosity was aroused, so I decided to find out.

Mary lived through major social and economic upheaval, and lost her job on two occasions due to the cost-cutting recommendations of national economic reports.[1] During World War One she supervised gangs of women in British forests, and then worked on a baronet's estates in Scotland and for the British Forestry Commission in England and Wales. In 1923, at the age of 29, she came to New Zealand and was employed by the State Forest Service; later at the Dominion Museum, Wellington, she worked as a botanist, and after the second world war was appointed by the Department of Agriculture as its first farm forestry officer.

Yet there was more to Mary's life than forestry and botany; she contributed much to society, professionally and personally. While on military service during World War Two she worked as an assistant and then supervisor of the Young Women's Christian Association's Woburn hostel for women mobilised for war work.[2] She was an inaugural and lifelong member of the New Zealand Institute of Foresters (NZIF) and designed its official seal, which was later adapted for use as the current logo. Mary served on the NZIF council in 1935, the New Zealand Forestry League council in 1936, and was vice president of NZIF from 1941 to 1942. Furthermore, she was an advocate for women's causes, particularly access to higher education, and served on the Federation of University Women (FUW) national executive and Wellington committees.

Considerable detail exists for some of her life. Her work for the State Forest Service is well documented, thanks to the people who recognised the importance of historical records and kept memos and reports. Personal information during her time at the State Forest Service is sparse, but is available for other years through the Sutherland and Gray family records. Weaving the different information together to tell Mary's story has proved a challenge.

Not everyone who crossed paths with Mary could be identified from material published when formal address was the usual practice. If there are any errors or omissions in the names we have identified we would be grateful to receive corrections. And not all readers will be foresters or botanists so the common names of plants and trees are used, and a glossary of their taxonomy is included at the back. Happy reading.

~ Vivien Edwards

NOTES
- Metric conversions are approximate.
- The maps of Mary's journeys are conceptual.
- Full image credits and acknowledgements are supplied in the end matter.

ABBREVIATIONS
FUW	Federation of University Women
NZIF	New Zealand Institute of Foresters/Forestry
RSPCA	Royal Society for the Prevention of Cruelty to Animals
SOSBW	Society for the Oversea Settlement of British Women
WFS	Women's Forestry Service
YWCA	Young Women's Christian Association

SHIPS
HMS	Her/His Majesty's ship	RFA	Royal fleet auxiliary
MS	Motor ship	RMS	Royal mail ship
MV	Motor vessel	SS	Steamship

CHAPTER I

FORESTRY in BRITAIN

Birth of a woman forester

Most British foresters in 1912 learned forest management on the job from their predecessors. Scientific training was available at the University of Oxford, but only for men, and teaching was largely based on experience gained in the Indian Forest Service. A forestry career was considered unsuitable for women. So when a dark-haired young woman, Mary Sutherland, chose forestry as a degree course at the University College of North Wales, Bangor,[1] she would have faced surprise. The university's principal, Sir Harry Reichel, was a forward-thinking man, not averse to higher education for women,[2] so around forty percent of the first students in 1884 had been female. Mary started her studies in July 1912. It is possible she initially enrolled to read agriculture and while studying found her greater passion to be trees. She was an industrious and conscientious student and accepting her into the forestry programme part way through her studies seems more likely than at the outset. At the time, agriculture and forestry were inextricably linked as both industries were overseen by the British Board of Agriculture and Fisheries.

Who was Mary Sutherland? Mary, sometimes called Mare, was born at the family home, 145 Osbaldeston Road, Stoke Newington, on 4 May 1893.[3] She was the fourth daughter of Scottish parents. Her father David was a wine merchant and her mother Helen (Nellie) was a teacher, who like other women of her time gave up her career when she married. Mary's older sisters were Catherine (Kate), Helen (Nell) and Margaret (Daisy). Anne (Nancy) was born five years after Mary. The Sutherlands were a happy family and the girls had a religious upbringing, worshipping at the United Free Church. They enjoyed the outdoors and spent summer holidays at Bridge House in Torphins, Aberdeenshire, which David purchased in 1900.

No doubt because she was a teacher, Nellie Sutherland wanted her daughters to be well educated. They all attended the City of London School for Girls. Mary was an able student and passed the London University matriculation examination,

Birthplace of
Mary Sutherland,
145 Osbaldeston Road,
Stoke Newington.
SUTHERLAND/GRAY FAMILY

Mary, aged 16, 1909.
SUTHERLAND/GRAY FAMILY

Bridge House, Torphins, Scotland, which was purchased in 1900 by Mary's father for £870.
SUTHERLAND/GRAY FAMILY

and obtained a Higher Certificate from the Oxford and Cambridge Schools Examination Board.[4] At least three of Mary's sisters earned university degrees. When Mary began studying at Bangor, Nell had just graduated from the University College of Wales, Aberystwyth, with a BA(Hons) in Classics.[5]

Mary's choice of forestry as a career came from her love of the outdoors, which was nurtured by her parents. The University College of North Wales was the only option available for women in Britain to study for a scientific degree in forestry, and Bangor, separated by the narrow Menai Strait from Anglesey Island and bordered by the mountains of Snowdonia National Park, was considered to be a suitable environment to be educated. The college opened in an old coaching inn, the Penrhyn Arms, twelve years after the University College of Wales was established.[6] Forestry education began in 1904 when Fraser Story was appointed as an assistant lecturer in the university's Department of Agriculture, and an adviser to local farmers and landowners. By the end of 1907 forestry was an independent academic department and Story was a permanent lecturer.[7] Mary's other tutors included assistant lecturer Thomas Thomson, who had studied forestry in Germany and held a first class honours degree in chemistry.[8]

Mary took the Applied Science in Agriculture course for the 1914–15 and 1915–16 academic years, studying soils, manures, crops and agricultural chemistry. For part of the latter year she held a government scholarship from the Board of Agriculture and Fisheries to research the influence of heredity on the growth of forest trees. Years later she recalled carrying out seed testing for Story while at the university, but whether it was part of her scholarship is unclear.[9]

Mary was halfway through her studies when Britain declared war on Germany in August 1914. Across Britain, men were encouraged to enlist, which affected the delivery of university courses as students left to join the armed services and staff were expected to use their expertise to contribute to war work. The war caused a forestry crisis. Deforestation of ancient stands had been occurring over centuries, and instead of renewing and developing resources Britain had been importing cheap timber from Europe and the Empire. These imports ceased because of the war, and the military's increasing demand for timber soon led to a national emergency.[10] During these years Story's advisory work expanded throughout Wales. He worked with the government-appointed Forestry Subcommittee, better known as the Acland Committee, to purchase home-grown timber,[11] and informed the university's senate that Thomson's full-time services were also required for this work. Only seven students remained at the department, three were studying forestry, and although teaching was suspended, Story continued to tutor Mary and the two diploma students. Mary sat her examination and graduated in July 1916.[12]

Mary (second left) as a confident teenager, with her sister Nancy (far right) and friends.
SUTHERLAND/GRAY FAMILY

The family at Bridge House celebrating Helen (Nellie) and David Sutherland's silver wedding anniversary, 1909. Mary, Nell and Daisy are at the rear, Kate is next to her mother and Nancy is in front. SUTHERLAND/GRAY FAMILY

Graduation day, July 1916.
SUTHERLAND/GRAY FAMILY

Because the entire staff was engaged in war work, the Forestry faculty remained closed until 1919, but either before or soon after graduating Mary was employed on the university's farm at Abergwyngregyn, which she called Aber farm. It was situated west of the present-day research farm at Henfaes. She worked there as a general farm hand, as evidenced by the interests listed on her curriculum vitae: riding, driving, care of horses, general farm-work, milking, butter making and motorcycling. She would have learned these skills at Aber.

Mary reported to Robert White, who taught her agricultural science, and because of her academic interest in forestry she was put in charge of raising tree seedlings for the Board of Agriculture and Fisheries. It is likely Story instigated the work; he was by then in charge of timber supply operations in nine counties. White was a technical adviser to the board's department of food production and was establishing co-operative cheese schools for the war effort, so he needed to trust Mary to get on with the job. Her role at the nursery was to supervise seedbed workers and handle their hostel accommodation needs, which she did from July to December 1916.[13] Impressed with her efforts, White wrote a reference recommending her for similar posts. He described her as a steady and persevering worker, with a pleasant temperament, who would get on well with all whom she had to deal.[14] Sir Harry Reichel also wrote her a reference, describing Mary as an excellent student who exercised a wholesome influence on fellow students and had a strong and vigorous personality rendered attractive by sincerity, refinement, and a frank and pleasing manner. He recommended her for any responsible forestry post that required scientific training, practical capacity and personal trustworthiness.[15] But while her tutors were pleased with her efforts, Mary was yet to prove her capabilities beyond the university confines.

Women work the forests

The social norms of the early 20th century suggest starting a career as the first professional woman forester would have posed a challenge for Mary had World War One not removed a large number of men from the workforce. Two years into the war, Britain's forests were badly neglected and the nation was drastically short of timber. In 1916, Rosamund Crowdy began to organise women to work in forestry, and in December that year Mary was at Crown Woods in the Forest of Dean, Gloucestershire, labouring with a gang of women, planting, pruning and thinning trees.[16]

The Women's Land Army was set up in January 1917 to rejuvenate Britain's rundown farms and address the country's food shortage. The army was divided into three sections: agriculture, forage and timber. Crowdy retained charge of the timber section[17] and Mary continued to work with her gang in the Forest of Dean, taking on a supervisory role.[18] When new recruits signed on for twelve months they were given a free uniform of a pair of breeches, a knee-length overall tunic with a button-fastened integrated belt, two pairs of short or high boots per year, a mackintosh, a jersey and a soft felt hat. Harrods advertised the land outfit for sale at twenty-five shillings. Mary would have dressed in similarly suitable clothing, which she may have purchased as she was already working in the forest.

Forestry training camps were set up around the country and recruits with no experience were trained for four to six weeks. The well-educated women learned how to measure trees. The timber cutters were taught how to cut trees down and stack them, how to load and transport timber, operate a sawmill, produce

While the men were away fighting World War One, women worked in forestry to supply Britain with the wood required at home and for the war effort. Mary worked with a gang of women in the Forest of Dean. © IMPERIAL WAR MUSEUM

Nellie Wright (left) with friends dressed in Women's Forestry Service uniforms. Nellie was in the service from 1917 to 1918. She worked in a timber yard in Moreton in the Marsh, and later at Shab Hill, Birdlip, near Cheltenham. Her armlet stripes depicted proficiency and service length. WAYNE FINCH

pit props and timber products for the war (such as ammunition boxes and duck boards for the trenches), as well as carry out afforestation tasks such as tree nursery cultivation and planting. Farm and estate owners were at first reluctant to employ the women and many refused, believing the opposite sex incapable of doing the physical work. But later, after seeing the quality of the women's work, they often changed their minds.

However, Britain's lack of timber supply remained critical, so in 1917 the Board of Trade's timber supply department set up an independent body, the Women's Forestry Service (WFS), to address the labour shortage. By August 1917 WFS had over two thousand employees, and while employers were still initially sceptical that women could fulfil men's forestry roles, work was available for all who volunteered.

The women were given white smocks, khaki breeches, leggings and a badge, and underwent training to become either a timber measurer or a cutter. Measurers needed to be competent in mathematics, so most were university graduates or secondary school teachers. They marked trees for felling, did stocktaking, filled out wage sheets, consigned wood to stations and sawmills, and dealt with large contract orders.

The new Forestry Service was in addition to the Women's Land Army, which by January 1918 had four hundred women foresters.[19, 20] The services worked in close co-operation; the Land Army recruited for the Forestry Service, and its county organisers worked for both.[21]

When Mary's father was appointed as Justice of the Peace for Kincardine O'Neil,[22] Mary took a position in Scotland. Unlike England, where deforestation had occurred with little or no replacement for centuries, Scottish aristocracy had been planting for over two hundred years for hunting and to improve their estates. The Scottish Arboricultural Society, which later became the Royal Scottish Forestry Society, encouraged landowners to establish plantations, often on marginal land, to provide local timber and work for people.[23] Sir John Stirling-Maxwell, 10th Baronet, employed Mary to oversee the women foresters on his estates, Pollock in Renfrewshire and Corrour in Inverness-shire. His ancestors were heavily involved in arboriculture, and Pollock had been in his family since the mid-thirteenth century; his father, 9th Baronet Sir William Stirling-Maxwell (dean of faculties and later chancellor at Glasgow University) had planted considerable woods.[24] Death duties had forced many estate owners to sell their lands, and in 1878 the Pollock estate was 10,800 acres (4370 hectares); in 1917 when Mary was there it would still have covered several thousand acres. Sir John purchased the Corrour estate of 70,000 acres (28,330 hectares) around 1891. Its original shooting lodge was reputably the highest house in the Highlands, and almost inaccessible. Mary was fortunate to gain forestry experience at Corrour as Sir John had been planting upland forest there on a commercial scale for some years. He trialled many species to determine their ability to withstand high altitude, and compared various planting techniques. When she revisited in 1952, Mary reminisced that she had supervised the planting of two square plantations by Loch Ossian, and fires always started just before the bridge in the adjacent Fersit plantation near Loch Treig.[25]

In his book *Loch Ossian Plantations* Sir John recorded that Mary Sutherland's squad of girl foresters planted noble fir (*Abies nobilis*) on the turfs in the middle of compartment v of the Boathouse plantation in 1917. The entire compartment was 26.4 acres (11 hectares): it faced north, overlooked the loch and ranged in altitude from 1275 to 1510 feet (388 to 460 metres). The size of the area Mary and the women planted is not recorded. In compartment vi of the same plantation, which had an altitude of 1410 to 1680 feet (430 to 512 metres), they planted noble fir and Engelmann spruce (*Picea engelmannii*) in two long hollows drained and left unplanted since 1915 through lack of labour.[26]

Women had worked in forestry for years, carrying out nursery and planting work, but their employment ceased when societal attitudes changed and men took over the permanent roles. The war reversed this trend. While working for Sir John, Mary conducted research comparing the performance of men and women during planting and nursery work. The tasks were typical for afforestation in many parts of Scotland: the women sorted, counted and bundled larch seedlings; they lined-out, and pit and notch planted on both peat and rocky ground; men did the heavy spadework, while women placed the plants and helped to fill in the earth. The women also pruned in the nursery lines and young plantations, and removed double leaders and growth liable to snow damage. They thinned and weeded. It took six women four and a half days to thin and clear 4 acres (1.6 hectares) of a 15-year-old larch plantation. Mary reported that women withstood severe weather conditions, took more care and were faster than men when sorting and counting seedlings, but in heavy operations, such as felling, their work took longer, making their labour alone uneconomic.[27]

Mary's work was under head forester Simon Cameron's direction, so she would have had more contact with him than Sir John, who was preoccupied with politics and issues concerning Britain's timber shortage. It is probable Sir John was appointed to the Acland Committee in 1916 on the basis of his experimental work. The committee recommended creating a forestry commission separate from the Board of Agriculture and Fisheries to conserve and develop woodland and forestry resources and alleviate the pressure on Britain's remaining ancient forests. The severe wood shortage increased demands on Scotland's timber supplies to feed into the war effort, mines and railways. Sir John, as chairman of the Scottish Landowners' Co-operative Society, proposed to its four hundred members that they accept the recommendations of the Acland Report, and warned that timber would be needed for reconstruction at the end of the war.[28]

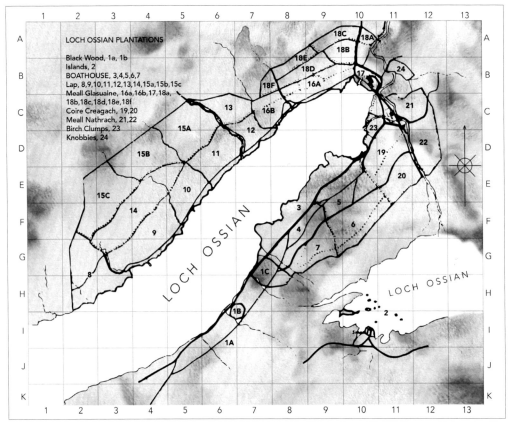

LOCH OSSIAN PLANTATIONS

Black Wood, 1a, 1b
Islands, 2
BOATHOUSE, 3,4,5,6,7
Lap, 8,9,10,11,12,13,14,15a,15b,15c
Meall Glasuaine, 16a,16b,17,18a,
18b,18c,18d,18e,18f
Coire Creagach, 19,20
Meall Nathrach, 21,22
Birch Clumps, 23
Knobbies, 24

The Loch Ossian plantations, Corrour Estate: In 1917 Mary and her 'squad of girl foresters' planted an area in the Boathouse plantation, compartment 5 with *Nobilis fir* on turfs and compartment 6 with *Abies nobilis* and *Picea englemannii* on turfs. ADAPTED FROM 'LOCH OSSIAN PLANTATIONS'

Thinnings from Scots pine near the Boathouse plantation, 1934. The trees were planted circa 1895 under the supervision of estate forester John Boyd. Note the profile of the butts of some of the stacked wood indicating laying in with axe and felling with handsaws.
© CROWN COPYRIGHT
FORESTRY COMMISSION

Sir John's expertise in Highland forestry was recognised with his appointment as the assistant controller (Scotland) to the Board of Trade's timber supply department. Mary also had a new job; she was to help conduct England's statistical forest survey for the Board of Agriculture and Fisheries' forestry branch. The role developed her analytical skills and provided another opportunity to research women's labour in forestry. Mary's findings agreed with her research in Scotland, and in an article published in the *Transactions of the Royal Scottish Arboricultural Society*, she confirmed that employing women in heavy work, such as trenching, was not profitable. Women required great physical strength to fell trees and were undertaking not just light felling, but also much of the big timber felling, which took them longer and was not economical forestry. It would increase the profitability of wood if women did the lighter work of tending to the growing trees and men did the heavier work. Mary pointed out that given good conditions and reasonable hours, women's work in nurseries and plantations would be valuable for Britain's forestry, and if paid equally for their work, the rise in profits would return the added expenditure.[29]

In 1918 an Interim Forest Authority began operating and Mary was appointed as an assistant inspector. Having proved her capabilities during the statistical forest survey, she oversaw a statistical survey party working in England and Wales, and was made chief instructor in charge of training women forestry supervisors at the Forest of Dean crown woodmen's school and nurseries.[30] Few records of her work there remain, but a letter sent to James Simpson at Delamere Forest[31] says Roy Robinson[32] had arranged for Mary to visit: "… this lady has been engaged in training forewomen for nursery work. I understand she will stay at Delamere a few days and help Miss Cousins and Miss Stansfield with the general arrangements of nursery work."[33] Mary's task was to organise women forestry workers, and she wrote to Robinson saying she was arranging for Miss Hodge and Miss Wainwright to go to Delamere as Mr Osmaston had not yet obtained the six [women] he required for the gang.[34]

When the Forestry Act 1919 established the Forestry Commission, Sir John became one of the eight commissioners to serve on the board, and Mary transferred to its experimental and research branch where, as assistant to the experimental officer, she was in charge of the Windsor Crown Woods experimental nursery.

Facing retrenchment

It is unlikely Mary participated in overseas field trips during the war, but in 1920 she was given the opportunity to inspect French forests with a group of Professor Robert Troup's students. While students who studied at the Imperial Forestry Institute at Oxford were all men, the students Mary accompanied could have been women, as Troup may also have provided training for the Women's Forestry Service. Mary and her group visited the pineries at the Landes forest, France,[35] where sand dune reclamation had converted wasteland into prosperous forestry through drainage and planting marram grass and maritime pine forests. The lumber and pine resin, which was used to manufacture turpentine, provided local income.

Britain experienced a heatwave in 1921. Mary used the experience to investigate the effects of drought on species of trees in the nursery. She researched the timing of seed sowing, the effect of pretreatment on germination, and how ground conditions, watering and shelter affected growth. Only one species, Scots pine, withstood the drought. Her research appeared in the *Quarterly Journal of Forestry*.[36]

Three years after the war had ended Britain's economy was still suffering, and the Committee on National Expenditure, led by Sir Eric Geddes, was established to look into ways to cut £130 million of government expenditure. Its 1921 report, known as the Geddes Axe, recommended that afforestation cease and the Forestry Commission be disbanded. The commission was saved largely through the efforts of Simon Fraser, 16th Lord Lovat, who chaired the Acland Committee, but afforestation was suspended and in 1922 Mary and other skilled foresters lost their jobs. However, her work on the use of women's labour in forestry had been heeded: an item in the *Auckland Star* noted that the *Gentlewoman,* a weekly illustrated newspaper for women, reported light forestry work was being arranged for women in England.[37, 38]

Despite her wealth of forestry experience, Mary was unable to find another suitable position; unemployed returned servicemen were given priority for available work, whether or not they were qualified. Mary's sister Kate was now married and living in New Zealand, and as their parents had died, Mary wondered about employment with the recently set up New Zealand State Forest Service. She had been out of work for nearly a year when she approached the Society for the Oversea Settlement of British Women (SOSBW) about emigrating.[39] It is also likely she wrote to the State Forest Service before leaving Britain.[40]

Through her work during and after the war, Mary developed lasting friendships with the women she supervised and worked alongside, and she earned great respect from influential people. John Sutherland, assistant commissioner for the Forestry Commission in Scotland, wrote to the prime minister of New Zealand, William Massey, informing him that Mary Sutherland had given good service in connection with timber work during the war and through her Forestry Commission employment: "She is capable and enthusiastic about whatever work she has to undertake and would be excellent as an instructress." Sutherland also told Massey that he and Mary were not related.[41]

Harold Dale, assistant secretary of the now Ministry of Agriculture and Fisheries, also wrote on Mary's behalf to the assistant director of New Zealand's Department of Agriculture, Frederick Pope.[42] Miss Sutherland impressed him as being practical and sensible; she was leaving Liverpool next day on the SS *Paparoa,* due in New Zealand 15–19 August 1923. Dale enclosed Mary's curriculum vitae and noted she had published technical articles in the *Journal of the Board of Agriculture, Transactions of the Royal Scottish Arboricultural Society* and the *Quarterly Journal of Forestry*. Not yet added was she had recently inspected Swiss forests at Zurich and Lucerne. Pope replied to Dale's letter saying Miss Sutherland might make a valuable assistant to the professor when a school of forestry was established in a few years. There was little prospect of employment in the Department of Agriculture, but if she communicated with him, he would do everything he could for her.[43]

A flock of sheep (left) and figure of a man (right) emphasise the size of these kauri in New Zealand. Early European settlers discovered vast kauri forests of over a million hectares from the northern part of the North Island down to 38°S. Explorers and whalers exploited the trees for their long, straight boles, which they used to replace broken masts and spars. The spar trade continued from 1790 to 1840 when most kauri forests had been depleted.[44] Settlers had a massive need for wood for fuel and domestic, infrastructural and commercial construction. This led to the exploitation of other indigenous forests,[45] but kauri attracted the greatest attention due to its knot-free timber and fine grain. The first export load of kauri spars was shipped in 1820. For more than a century it was the only indigenous species exported on a large scale. ALEXANDER TURNBULL LIBRARY

CHAPTER 2

FORESTRY in NEW ZEALAND

Forests of men

The ss *Paparoa* left Liverpool in 1923 with 280 passengers; 224 were assisted-passage emigrants for New Zealand, including Mary who by now was 30 years old. The weather was fair for the Atlantic crossing. In Panama they refuelled with coal, which turned out to be poor quality, and subsequent bad weather and the inferiority of the coal slowed the vessel, so instead of a planned morning stop at Pitcairn Island the ship sailed past during the night to make up time.[1] When the passengers awoke the next day, they were disappointed they had missed the opportunity for the islanders to bring their wares out to the ship so they could shop; Mary among them, for she liked to buy interesting things.

The ship was now due to arrive in Auckland on the morning of 24 August, but off the coast of New Zealand it ran into a strong westerly and so arrived ahead of expectation at midnight on 23 August 1923. It was to continue its journey to Wellington, but was not due there for another week, so Mary probably travelled on the 'extra' main trunk express provided for the 150 southbound passengers. The train also carried passengers from the RMS *Niagara,* which had arrived the previous day.[2] This vessel was blamed for bringing the 1918 influenza epidemic to New Zealand after twenty-eight crew members were admitted to Auckland Hospital, infecting nearly eighty percent of the staff members.[3] Controversy over whether infected passengers were allowed to disembark because the prime minister (William Massey) and minister of finance (Sir Joseph Ward) were on board led to a Royal Commission inquiry.[4] The epidemic is now considered to have been brought into the country by soldiers returning from World War One.[5]

Mary travelled on to Nelson to reunite with her sister Kate and brother-in-law Dr Theodore Gray, known to the family as Dory, and to meet their children. Theodore jnr (Ted) was almost five years old, David was three, and Helen was eighteen months. Kate was expecting their fourth child. Dory was in charge of the Nelson Mental Hospital and Stoke Farm, which was situated on 800 acres

(324 hectares) obtained from the Department of Education; it later became Ngawhatu Psychiatric Hospital. His aim was to establish a facility entirely of villas housing patients according to diagnosis, and with female and male patients in separate cottages. Dory campaigned to change public attitudes to mental illness, presented a series of lectures to Red Cross members, which were published in the newspapers,[6] and hosted patients at his home.[7] He considered outdoor work to be therapy for some patients, and parts of the grounds were used for gardening, crops and 'farmsteading'.[8]

Three months after arriving and still with no job, Mary was restless. Her article published in the National Council of Women's (NCW) newsletter[9] says she had just arranged work in an orchard—disbudding, thinning, picking and packing—paying the minimum wage for the district of eight shillings when she was offered a temporary position with the New Zealand State Forest Service.

The director, Leon Macintosh Ellis, had been employed in 1920 to set up the service, which began in 1922. He was a forestry graduate from the University of Toronto and had spent six years with the Pacific Railways Company in Canada. From 1916 to 1919 he served in France as a captain and assistant chief forest officer of the 242nd Overseas Battalion of the Canadian Forestry Corps. He oversaw the Canadian exploitation of French forests for war purposes, working to rules governing tree cutting and the maximum quantities allowed from state and communal forests. Post-war, Ellis worked in Scotland with the Board of Agriculture and Fisheries, and then the Forestry Commission alongside Colonel John Sutherland, who had sent the reference for Mary to Prime Minister Massey.[10] It is likely Sutherland personally informed Ellis about Mary's forestry experience, which raises a question about why he contacted Massey; perhaps the State Forest Service needed extra finance to hire her?

Mary started work at head office in Wellington on 10 November 1923 as an engineer's assistant in the forest products branch.[11] Her role for the first few weeks was initially clerical, which gave her time to learn about New Zealand's forest operations and indigenous trees and timber.

The forest products branch was responsible for determining the properties of various timbers to best utilise New Zealand's forest resources. Alex Entrican (Pat) was in charge of the branch. He was a University of Auckland graduate with a background in hydraulics, electric tramways and civil engineering.[12] Entrican discovered a news item in a 1924 *Australian Forestry Journal* that claimed an American, Estella Florence Dodge of Portland, was the only woman forestry graduate in the world.[13] He wrote to the editor on Ellis's behalf saying the New Zealand State Forest Service employed Miss Sutherland, an earlier graduate from the University College of North Wales.[14] This prompted Mary to offer the article published in the NCW newsletter to the

Imperial Colonist, which printed extracts.[15] Since her graduation, seven more women had graduated or undergone technical forest training in the United Kingdom. "Qualified male foresters in Britain are confined chiefly to the Indian service," she wrote. "Forestry as a women's profession was unthought of, although an occasional German or Austrian woman landowner studied at a forest school so as to have a personal say in how her forests were managed."

The State Forest Service's main focus was to manage and utilise native forests, develop plantation forestry and maintain forest health and protection.[16] New Zealand relied heavily on native timbers, so investigations were being carried out on red and black beech for building and general industrial purposes. Auckland University College was testing New Zealand manufactured plywood and veneers. There were cross arm tests on southern rata (*Metrosideros umbellata*), pole tests on silver pine (*Dacrydium colensoi*) and kawaka (*Libocedrus plumosa*), and studies to prevent sapstain in kahikatea (*Podocarpus dacrydioides*) as a mould that occurred in New Zealand butter was traceable to the sapstain fungus. Other studies tested timber suitability for manufacturing brush backs, bobbins and spools; tanekaha (*Phyllocladus trichomanoides*) was being tested for deep-sea fishing rods, and beech (*Nothofagus sp.*) for milk crates. The tannin value of kamahi (*Weinmannia racemosa*) was being investigated in conjunction with the Woolston Tannery in Christchurch.[17]

Experimental forestry stations were being set up around the country, and each region incorporated the state forests in that province. Auckland covered the whole of the north; Rotorua the central North Island; and Palmerston North managed Wellington. The South Island regions were Nelson, Canterbury and Otago/Southland. Its staffing structure was hierarchical, and seniority and pay scales were important. Each region's conservator was responsible for administering, conserving and utilising the timber. When Mary was transferred to the silviculture branch in 1924 she was appointed as a temporary forest assistant.[18] Under her were forest rangers, classed as grade one or two depending on seniority, and below them the forest guards who may have had a greater role in forest health and protection. The work of rangers and guards often overlapped in day-to-day operations and supervising labour, although rangers likely had more administrative responsibilities.[19]

Leon McIntosh Ellis would have sought Entrican's opinion on Mary's capabilities, and it is clear from State Forest Service records that Ellis planned to use her skills. Both a Dominion-wide survey of forest resources and a lumber industry economic survey had been completed. The total area of state plantations was over 51,800 acres (20,900 hectares), and 7500 acres (3035 hectares) of new plantations were established in Rotorua, Hanmer Springs, Balmoral, and Tapanui by April 1924. In Hokitika 140 acres (57 hectares) had been planted in cutover bush land. But timber was being consumed at an alarming rate and Ellis realised New Zealand would run out of millable timber by the 1960s. To develop his national forestry

In 1928 the State Forest Service in the Rotorua district planted 100,000 acres (40,470 hectares) and employed 400 people — 300 on unemployment relief work. Tree stock at the Whakarewarewa nursery totalled 34 million. Trees were exported to Australia, as well as supplying farmers and local bodies. Top left: 1. A nursery worker. 2. Looking across the plantation to the Green Lake. 3. A ranger on the lookout for fires. 4. A view of the Whakarewarewa nursery. 5. A fire lookout station. 6. A firebreak through the plantation. 7. Maori women weeding young trees. 8. A crate of seedlings ready for the market. AUCKLAND LIBRARIES HERITAGE COLLECTIONS

plan, he needed information on the nursery and plantation methods used in the different regions, as well as greater knowledge of the various timber species. He believed Mary was capable of gathering the necessary data.

In Britain Mary mainly worked alongside women, whereas New Zealand's forestry workforce was totally male. Ellis understood the men were likely to feel threatened by a woman and her presence could foster resistance. Mary was not just a woman intruding in a male-run organisation, she was also a university graduate who possessed practical forestry experience, whereas most foresters had learned forest management on the job without tertiary education, and many forest labourers lacked skills. Mary was also aware she faced challenges to develop a co-operative working relationship with men in a country new to her, with a culture not quite the same as in Britain.

Two weeks before she transferred to the silviculture branch, Ellis wrote to Halbert Goudie, the Rotorua conservator, to inform him Miss Sutherland would be proceeding north to undertake a co-ordination study and nursery plantation research.[20] Goudie, though not university educated,[21] was highly skilled. Prior to the State Forest Service, he ran a government forest nursery and was the superintending nurseryman for the North Island. Ellis described Mary's proposed work as "a complete analytical study of methods, practice, procedure, philosophy and the cost of every nursery and plantation operation, from seed collection to thinning. Where Miss Sutherland cannot access the work, she will interrogate and examine to secure the necessary data. The work is important, and I know Miss Sutherland will secure your full and hearty co-operation, and that of all your officers." He put the onus on Goudie to see that his staff stepped up, but also let him know he could use the information Mary collected for his proposed nursery and plantation practice bulletin. The staff newsletter, *Te Karere o Tane*, reported that Miss Sutherland would be in Rotorua compiling a history of the region's plantations and nurseries, and the data would be of great value to future foresters.[22]

After Mary arrived in Rotorua she received a postcard from a fellow passenger on the *Paparoa*, Miss E M Waller,[23, 24] saying she was going to be in town and intended staying at Mrs Tapper's guest house, The Bungalow,[25] and asking Mary to join her on Sunday. It is uncertain whether they met, but lacking female company it is likely Mary seized the opportunity. However, for most of the week, work took priority. Goudie had little choice but to follow Ellis's directive and ensure co-operation with Mary, but this must have been a challenge, for besides being a woman and a graduate she no doubt was perceived to be a spy for head office. Ellis's persuasion and Mary's ability to observe and extract information won out and she successfully carried out the study. When she finished her report, Goudie wanted to immediately send her to Hanmer Springs to conduct her next co-ordination study,[26] but Ellis informed him that he was to retain Miss Sutherland productively in his region until after the rangers instruction course at Whakarewarewa in July. She could then proceed to Hanmer Springs.[27]

To ensure Goudie knew what work she had done in his region, Mary sent her report to Ellis through him. She had inspected all nursery processes, gathered information on methods, and analysed costs for the various operations using actual practice or nursery records. She also inspected planting operations and carried out time analyses on the Kaingaroa Plains work. She collected data on thinning procedures in Waiotapu, looked at sample tree-research plots and discussed them with ranger John Rodgerson. Her article 'Experimental methods in forestry' was published in *Te Karere o Tane*.[28] It covered forestry methods and seeding experiments at Rotorua, including statistical analyses and the treatment of exotic plantations. Ellis complimented Mary on the general layout and comprehensiveness of her report, but noted she had made no recommendations, nor criticised work methods. He asked her to submit a supplementary report direct to him rather than through the local conservator. A similar supplementary report would be required for the South Island. She could proceed there after the rangers school where she was to assist the chief inspector, Arnold Hansson, who was in charge of the course.[29] Hansson was a graduate from the University of Königsberg, and he had a Master's degree from Yale University.[30]

The rangers school would have been Mary's first opportunity to meet many of the field staff from around the country. Though she encountered a wall of male prejudice and conservatism in the state forests, Frank Hutchinson's memory of meeting Mary at the school[31] was that she was "quiet and unassuming, with a good Scots heritage of doggedness and common sense, and she possessed a sound biological grounding". Hansson arrived a week before the school began, along with Frank Foster, a forest assistant who like Mary was based in head office.[32]

Twenty rangers attended the school and camped in the nursery paddock. They slept on straw mattresses with their own bedding and had their own cook.[33] For the sake of propriety, Mary was not allowed to camp with the men, but having just completed the Rotorua co-ordination study she was already staying at the Geyser Hotel. Hansson made good use of her instruction skills as a useful 'lab boy'. He instructed the rangers on sample plots, Foster lectured on tree biology, and Goudie covered nursery practice and eucalypts identification. Mary accompanied the rangers on field trips to Whakarewarewa Forest and to view planting operations on the Kaingaroa Plains.[34] Hutchinson wrote that she ignored the men's bad language, and wore an off-white leather jacket, riding breeches and high boots — kit that became an integral part of her personality. He classed her dress as British Forestry Commission, and from photographs it appears similar to the land outfit advertised by Harrods at the time Mary was working for the Women's Land Army during World War One.

While men in the forest may have felt threatened by Mary checking their work, in the more relaxed atmosphere of the school the rangers seemed to accept her as one of their own. *Te Karere o Tane* reported on their association football (soccer) game and noted, "At the interlude our Lady Ranger added to her popularity by distributing oranges to the somewhat distressed teams." It is clear Mary's status as temporary forest assistant was unknown by the rangers, and referring to her as "our Lady Ranger" suggests they readily accepted her.

Mary's influence and Ellis's support appears to have led to the employment of Maori women to plant trees in the Rotorua region. The member of parliament for Waimarino Frank Langstone stated in a parliamentary debate that he understood the women did the work well, but considered it not fit for them, and cheapness "was not a nice thing to encourage". The Commissioner of State Forests Sir Robert Heaton Rhodes agreed women should not be asked to plant large trees, but they were planting seedlings and picking out small plants: "Children could do the work."[35]

Creating a forest consciousness

Mary was anxious to leave Rotorua for Hanmer Springs, so departed for Christchurch where she stayed at the Federal Private Hotel. She later wrote to the State Forest Service chief clerk who was staying at the Geyser Hotel to ask him to collect the borrowed typewriter she had left there, and would he kindly tell forestry cadet Mr Gladden not to hurry to return the book she had loaned him.[36] Her arrival in Hanmer Springs was noted in the *Nelson Evening Mail*, which reported that Miss Sutherland was impressed with how New Zealand had tackled its forestry problem, and "if the work … gains public support in regards to the conservation of native bush and prevention of forest fires, New Zealand will begin to have a feeling of security in so far as the world threatened shortage of soft wood timbers is concerned, as the wonderful quick growth of exotic supplies will serve to conserve the use of the disappearing and slow-growing native trees".[37]

However, she was not welcome in the forest. Ranger Walter Morrison reported in *Te Karere o Tane*: "Miss Sutherland of Head Office is with us, busy arriving at the exact costs of the operations. The stopwatch is a source of trial and tribulation to the working crews, and the cause of not a little comment, adverse and otherwise. The advent of the lady forester caused no little stir in the camps."[38] But rather than dwell on the men's reaction, Mary did her job, and escorted schoolchildren through the plantations and forest nursery. She demonstrated how pine branches produced clouds of pollen when shaken, and explained how female larch cones released winged seeds, which were carried by wind to suitable growing spots. She sent the children's comments (including their spelling errors) to *Te Karere o Tane*,[39]

The 1924 Whakarewarewa rangers school. Back row: Rua Tawhai (behind Mary), Courtney Bigges, Robert Murray, Robert Collett, Henry Whitehorn, John Adams, Roderick Macrae, Jack Myles. Middle row: Herbert (Bert) Roche, Mary Sutherland, Fred Field, Rupert Uren, John Rodgerson, Joseph Johnston, Frank Grace, William Weir. Front row: Norman Dolamore, Frank Perham, Frank Hutchinson, William Montgomery, Halbert Goudie, Arnold Hansson, Robert Steele, Frank Foster. SCION

This Harrods advertisement for Women's Land Army outfits appeared in the *Daily Mail*, 1918. © EXCLUSIVEPIX.CO.UK

Far right: Mary kitted out in her 'reliable' land outfit. TE AMORANGI MUSEUM TRUST

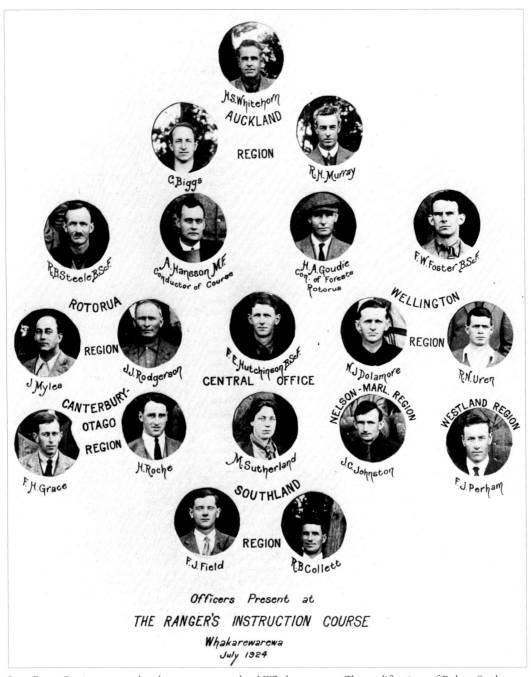

State Forest Service personnel at the 1924 rangers school, Whakarewarewa. The qualifications of Robert Steele, Arnold Hansson, Frank Foster and Frank Hutchinson are listed, but Mary's BSc F is unacknowledged. It seems her status as a temporary forest assistant was also unknown by school attendees as a report on their association football (soccer) game in *Te Karere o Tane* noted, "At the interlude our Lady Ranger added to her popularity by distributing oranges to the somewhat distressed teams." ARCHIVES NZ

and wrote a report on the walk for Ellis: "The small mites were eager to see baby trees in the nursery, and how scraped-away soil exposed recently planted pine seeds. Year-old seedlings were likened to carrots in father's garden. The children discussed fires when crossing an area of burnt timber. They voiced disapproval against dropping matches or cigarettes near growing trees." The older boys looked at crops that needed thinning, and Mary explained the growth habits of common timber species: "They took twig and cone specimens to school for future reference, extracted seed from cones, and were preparing a nursery bed in the school garden where a few young seedlings from the state nursery were already planted."[40]

When Mary finished the Hanmer Forest study, Ellis sent her to Tapanui for further co-ordination work. In response to her request for a few days off to tour the Catlins and view virgin bush being milled around Tahakopa, Ellis asked her for a report on the dedication and management of the Catlins Forest.[41] He also asked her to investigate cheaper, more efficient material to replace the scrim packing currently used in boxes of live tree consignments. Mary investigated English scrim, hessian and tarpaper packing, and cases that were lighter than petrol cans. In December 1924 she sent Ellis three reports: the one on replacing scrim packing, her Hanmer and Tapanui co-ordination work report, and a supplementary general report.[42] After Christmas she was back in Rotorua, and on 19 January travelled by train to Palmerston North and then on to the coast to conduct a co-ordination study at Tangimoana. The sand dune experimental station, which had relocated from Oroua Downs, had 10 acres (4 hectares) of nursery and was raising marram grass. Experiments were being conducted on marram and silvery sand grass (*Spinifex hirsutus*), and sand sedge (*Carix primula*) grown from seed. A forest tree nursery had been established and 69 acres (28 hectares) were planted with trees.[43]

Leon McIntosh Ellis believed the public needed to be involved in forestry to achieve a sufficient, sustainable timber supply, so making forestry popular became part of his national policy. He believed people needed a greater 'forest consciousness', and a culture of growing trees would foster a love for them and develop a wider appreciation and knowledge of their benefits. He approached the task through public lectures, free advice and demonstrations, films, publications, advertising, exhibiting at agricultural shows, producing and selling trees at low prices, and establishing a 'forestry in schools' programme. Mary contributed by speaking to several women's groups, including the Federation of University Women, the Pioneer and Lyceum clubs, and the Workers' Educational Association.[44] In its coverage of her talk to the Lyceum Club, the *Evening Post* described her as an entertaining and informative speaker. Mary observed that besides planting large exotic trees, which gave the quickest return, it was important to also plant slower growing species, such as those in the government plantation in Rotorua. Large areas of bush had already disappeared; all but one kauri forest

Packing methods for nursery stock: a consignment of plants in benzene cans and banana cases, and bare-rooted eucalypts packed into trays. SCION

Nursery stock ready for railway transportation. SCION

had gone, and white pine (kahikatea) forests were fast disappearing. Care was needed if the supply of white pine was to be maintained for future use. Planting quick-growing, introduced trees had created artificially formed forests that were larger than in any other colony and the forests required supervision to prevent destruction by fire.

Taking forestry into schools

During 1924 and 1925, the State Forest Service had nearly 3 million seed and tree sales. Nineteen local bodies were involved in planting projects amounting to over 92,000 acres (37,200 hectares), and thousands of farmers had planted trees. But planting needed to be ongoing, which meant connecting with the younger generation to foster an understanding of the value of forestry that in turn would make parents more aware of its importance. In Australia, Victoria's forestry in schools programme was progressing[45] and New Zealand's scheme, a joint venture between the State Forest Service and the Department of Education, aimed to stimulate children's interest in native and exotic trees. Mary loved working with children, and being a woman was considered ideal to co-ordinate the programme. After walking the school groups through the Hanmer Forest plantation and nursery, she wrote 'Forests and their protection', which was published in the *School Journal*.[46]

The initial focus of the forestry in schools programme was to establish school nurseries. The Forest Service provided free seed and the extension officers, Percy Page in the North and Frank Grace in the South, advised the Department of Education's agricultural instructors, who were directly involved with the teachers and classes, on raising and planting the trees. The instructors received their practical instruction at the Whakarewarewa and Hanmer State Forest nurseries.[47] Mary suggested to Ellis that the State Forest Service could establish school holiday camps for older boys and their schoolmasters. In Scotland, an Edinburgh school held Easter holiday camps at Murthly Estate where boys planted, carried out nursery work, felled small timber and thinned trees under the forester's instruction. Their work was paid at unskilled labour rates, which covered their travel and camp expenses: "The estate regularly uses this assistance in its annual forest programme, while the boys experience a healthy, instructive, profitable camp holiday, steeped in an atmosphere of forest growth and management."[48] An arrangement could be made between large town schools and the State Forest Service, and Scout troops might also be interested: "Boys would have the advantage of living and working in an atmosphere of forest production, conservation and management, while the service would get urgently needed work done at low cost." Ellis also received a letter from the Hawera Winter Show organiser Leonard Hooker, who was concerned that between seven hundred and eight hundred children in Hawera were not involved in the forestry in schools programme.[49]

Children preparing to plant trees in a forestry in schools allocated area of
Golden Downs Forest, Nelson Conservancy, 1920–30s. SUPPLIED BY P. BERG

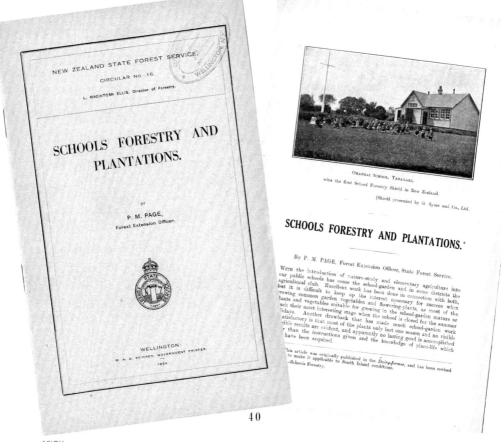

40

Mary, Percy Page and Frank Grace discussed their proposed policy before attending the Forestry in Schools Conference in Wellington early in 1925.[50] At the conference Mary talked about encouraging pupils at town schools to have an interest in forests, and about schools using municipal authority wasteland to grow seedlings if they lacked grounds to plant nurseries. She suggested introducing a short series of general forestry lessons into the syllabus. The lessons would be prepared by the Forest Service and information printed on cards or leaflets could be used for essay writing or nature study and would cover forest protection, formation, conservation, the national importance of forests, and forest nature. Nature study talks could include fire protection. A column in either the *Education Gazette* or *School Journal* could encourage schools to exchange seed, plants or herbarium specimens, and acquaint children with species growing outside their districts. The Forest Service could talk to teachers and facilitate visits to nurseries or nearby reserves. Perhaps forestry could be introduced as a teacher-training subject.

The conference was chaired by John Caughley, the director of education, who strongly encouraged the idea of schools forming nurseries, and supported co-operation between municipal and school authorities to give town schools the opportunity to plant city reserves. The *New Zealand Times* report on the conference covered the role that school nurseries could play to educate children about forests.[51] Conference discussions included a certificate of merit for schools, writing more material about forestry for the *School Journal*, having an Arbor Week rather than just an Arbor Day, and tree-focused schoolwork as well as tree planting. Forestry competitions were suggested, but not everyone favoured the idea as time to spend on school nurseries was scarce and preparation for shows had to be outside school hours.

Mary sent a report on the conference to Ellis.[52] She also wrote an article on how forests influenced stream flow, and stored and regulated water supply, which was published in the *School Journal*.[53] She asked Page and Grace to also write articles and to supply her with a list of schools so handsets of New Zealand timbers could be presented as prizes. She sent the conservators her proposals for forestry instruction in primary schools, asking them to note the recommendation that education boards needed encouragement to be supportive of schools establishing nurseries and obtaining access to local reserves, town belts or parks for afforestation.[54] She submitted her forestry in schools syllabus to Ellis.[55]

The first stage of the programme, establishing school nurseries, was successful. By the end of March 1925, over 760 school nurseries had been established, agricultural show committees were offering prize shields for school forestry exhibits, and other organisations, including the Forest Service, were contributing subsidiary prizes. A 'Schools, forestry and plantations' pamphlet on nursery procedure and planting school grounds was also available.[56] Every month Mary wrote the introduction to the *Education Gazette*'s exchange column where schools could list the seed, foliage, cuttings, and native or exotic trees and shrubs they wanted and what they had available to exchange in return, which could be anything connected with school nurseries or forestry activities, including specimens and photographs.[57] When Sir Robert Heaton Rhodes opened the State Forest Service's 4th Annual Conference in Whakarewarewa, he noted how the forestry in schools programme had given a fillip to forest culture and a deeper love of trees.[58] Mary later wrote his Arbor Day message to schoolchildren, which was published in the *Education Gazette*.[59, 60]

A suggestion had been made to the Australian Forestry Commission that the Victorian Minister of Forests should grant 20 acres (8 hectares) at Anglesea River to the Geelong Boy Scouts for a plantation.[61] Ellis suggested to Mary that she should also generate interest in forestry with the Boy Scouts while she was in Hanmer Springs, and investigate school plantation endowments.[62] Mary informed Ellis she would discuss the idea with Grace in Christchurch on her way to Tapanui. She would approach school authorities about plantation endowments and work co-operatively with the Forestry League in Canterbury. Local organisations could be interested in summer holiday camps at Hanmer Springs: "One such camp, with either Scouts or Christchurch schoolboys, would likely encourage the rest of the Dominion."[63] Mary sent Ellis a draft letter introducing the camp scheme,[64] which he passed on to the Christchurch conservator: "Miss Sutherland has brought the matter up and it has merit. If you [would] like to try it at Hanmer, cautiously and carefully, you have my support and full authority."[65]

The next stage of the forestry in schools programme — establishing and managing the plantations — was a different challenge. If schools lacked suitable land they would need to acquire it. Land had to be endowment areas, vested in the schools that would share proceeds. Mary was sure districts with educational reserves administered by the Department of Lands had suitable wasteland that could be let at a nominal rent, and local bodies might also hand over land for the purpose. She presented her ideas to Ellis,[66] noting that either the Department of Education, or school committees, local bodies or residents, perhaps helped by pupils, would need to fence the allocated areas. A definite amount of the stock raised in school nurseries had to be planted each year. Early stage tending would be required, but schools would ultimately benefit from harvesting and utilisation. Estimating yields would be difficult, due to the varying growth conditions and species, but a general estimate could be calculated. Other matters to consider were the plantation size, maintenance and fire protection. Forests took time to grow, so the best species should be used for planting. Mary recommended that the school or a separate committee should act as operational trustees.

The Department of Education had the final decision on whether the endowment scheme was adopted. It needed to finalise the technical points, define liabilities, fix the division of profits, and exercise general supervision over school committees by enforcing maintenance and continuity, and ensuring school labour would be available. This had to be done through head teachers and agricultural inspectors. The Forest Service would inspect and report on 'forest versus agricultural' use of proposed land, assist to prepare plans, provide seed and generally supervise the scheme. Mary recommended a slow start, and thought one or two successful schemes would lead to others. Several local bodies and education committees were already considering a school endowment plantation, and the Christchurch Education Board wanted the Bottle Lake reserve for three schools.

Forestry in schools was not Mary's sole occupation, she also undertook nursery and plantation experimental work. For the 1925 to 1926 season the proposals were to produce 10 million trees in the Rotorua region, plant 8.5 million existing trees on 12,500 new acres (5060 hectares) and sell 3 million trees. Two ranger stations were being built and 44,000 acres (17,800 hectares) of established plantations had to be maintained. Halbert Goudie informed Leon McIntosh Ellis in a note at the bottom of the proposals sheet that it was difficult to increase planting in the region due to a shortage of species other than pine (*Pinus radiata*).[67] Ellis replied that Mary would return to Rotorua in June to look into experimental work for the season and carry out nursery costings, and in July and August under Arnold Hansson's leadership she and fellow forest assistants Frank Foster and Robert Steele would instruct at the Hanmer Springs rangers school.[68] The course covered establishing sample plots, seed testing, growth studies, constructing yield and volume tables, and collecting and mounting herbarium specimens. Charles Foweraker, head of the newly established Canterbury College School of Forestry, lectured on Westland taxad forests.[69, 70]

New Zealand leads in afforestation

Mary was a gentle person who did not push herself forward,[71] but in August 1925 when she wrote to family in Britain, they passed her comments to the press. The *Evening Post* reported that her observations were published in the *Glasgow Herald* and the *Post*.[72] Though she was born in England, Mary regarded herself as Scottish, but New Zealanders did not believe her as she did not have a strong accent. It was no wonder they didn't, as many New Zealanders with Scots heritage had never left the country, but had broad Scottish accents. Mary believed New Zealand forestry had been influenced by Scottish methods, and the northern hemisphere trees around South Otago reminded her of Scotland.

New Zealand was leading the world in afforestation and Leon McIntosh Ellis recognised the potential for future exports. Softwoods had nearly vanished in

Australia where timber was being imported from North America.[73] The Forest Service was planting exotic trees to replace fast-depleting indigenous species, and Mary had gained considerable knowledge through her nursery and plantation research. By October 1925, over 60,000 acres (24,290 hectares) were planted, and more than 150 million trees propagated. Mary wrote 'Afforestation methods in New Zealand', which was published in the December edition of the *Empire Forestry Journal*.[74]

The first state forest scheme was started by the Department of Lands in 1896 in Naseby, Central Otago. State Forest Service planting began in 1921. The main plantation stations were in Rotorua, Hanmer Springs and Tapanui, each with one or two distributing nurseries. Smaller planting areas were increasing, some with nurseries, and planting was mainly on poor land in eroded areas where native bush had been cleared years before for pastoral settlement, or in high, treeless regions where timber supply was needed for settlement, or in sand dunes.

She likened Otago's tussock land to moor and hill planting in the Welsh hills, and Rotorua's pumice lands to Bagshot sand formation. Older plantations around Rotorua (with thermal activity) had been formed in two blocks of 7000 to 8000 acres (2830 to 3240 hectares): "It is possible to take two steps from a growing larch tree and land in an evil-looking black, boiling, sulphurous mud pool. One wonders how a vigorous, fresh-scented larch can bear to exist in such insalubrious surroundings." She described the operation site as a plateau of recent volcanic origin, about 1000 feet (305 metres) above the thermal region. The bare plain running 100 miles (160 km) north and south, was unsuited to farming as it caused bush-sickness in stock, yet it excelled in growing trees.

Maori worked the Kaingaroa Plains and Mary wrote: "These men show extraordinary agility and speed in notching in the trees. A gang of twenty or more men work across a 300-acre block (120 hectares), the planting line varying from ½ to 1 mile (0.8–2.4 kilometres). Planters show a wonderful sense of direction." In a lecture, Ellis extolled Maori for doing twice as much work as Europeans. He attributed this to an instinctive love of forestry, bred over generations: "Even the women enter into the work with a will."[75]

The Forest Service's success was recognised by private afforestation companies offering investment opportunities. H Landon Smith from Smith Wylie & Co lauded Kaingaroa, describing it as "a remarkable man-made forest over a vast tract of country" and "a sea of waving green",[76] but also commenting that the government's Waiotapu plantations of larch, and radiata (*Pinus radiata*), ponderosa (*Pinus ponderosa*), Eastern white (*Pinus strobus*), bishop (*Pinus muricata*) and Oregon pines badly needed thinning. He praised the forestry in schools programme, saying his firm also proposed to award annual bursaries for secondary school tuition. But Smith Wylie & Co's terms were unrealistic for secondary school students.

Examinations were to be conducted by committees elected by the headmasters of each state school, and marks awarded by a committee of Auckland University College professors. Terms of the bursary were, however, changed; the scholarships were made available for tuition at the Auckland University College Forestry School when it opened in 1926, but were not available for students at Canterbury.[77]

While the Auckland school would have been grateful for the scholarships, Ellis was wary of forest investment companies aligning with Forest Service activities. He advised the Auckland Chamber of Commerce that the twenty-five afforestation companies formed or in the process of formation, won support because of the 'forest sense' built by his department. State control was needed to protect people from unscrupulous or misguided promoters. Potential investors ought to question and to consult a solicitor before signing up for shares, and he recommended they visit the land.[78] A comment Mary made on another occasion indicates she too believed the public needed protection from unscrupulous afforestation companies.

Mary's co-ordination studies provided a baseline to improve nursery and plantation techniques and for the Forest Service to become more cost-effective. Her 1925–26 nursery and plantation experimental programme indicates she intended to conduct most of the research. Creating her own upcoming work and speaking to women's groups on State Forest Service activities probably helped secure her future employment, and in December 1925 her status as a forest assistant changed from temporary to permanent.[79]

In February 1926 she reported to Ellis on her Rotorua and Waipoua nursery visits.[80] Radiata, ponderosa and bishop pine had been sown in Rotorua using a Planet hand seeder; Pabco-Thermogen paper mulch was being trialled to reduce weeds; the 'season of sowing' trials of eleven conifer species were incomplete due to frost, mice and bird damage; and work pressure and weather had delayed chemical weed eradication, and shelter, line-growing and sowing density trials. The effects of phosphatic manures were being observed at Whakarewarewa and Waiotapu. At the Kaingaroa nursery, the tractor adapted for seed sowing with a grain drill and extra hoppers proved more satisfactory than the horsed drill, which had been "somewhat difficult to keep to the tracks". In the Waipoua nursery, 45,000 trees had been raised, consisting of radiata (*Pinus insignis/radiata*) and maritime (*Pinus pinaster*) pine, Douglas fir and redwood, and direct sowing and planting had been trialled on previous fern, manuka and gum land. Seed from radiata, maritime and redwood was collected locally and extracted by heating on a camp stove at the ranger headquarters.

In her 1926 in-house report Mary commented on the performance of various mechanical devices used at Hanmer Forest[81] including the Bolens tractor with cultivator attachments, the Planet 154 seeder (following an adaptation), the Onargo shrub digger, the Hauck burner, and the Primus hand burner. She reported that the Pacific fire pump's spray force was stronger than piped water and would quickly exhaust tank supply, so further trials would be arranged in planting areas during burning off. Prior to leaving Hanmer Springs, Mary inspected trees that had been planted at Balmoral in 1925. She visited the West Coast experimental station and the rimu nursery before going on to Tapanui for further co-ordination work.

Before returning to Wellington, Mary was delayed by Sir Frederic Truby King, the director of child welfare. He telegraphed the Forest Service head office from Dunedin, saying he was detaining Mary Sutherland for the weekend for her "on the spot advice regarding native bush conservation and eucalyptus afforestation of manuka clad hillsides".[82] Sir Frederic was a renowned tree expert, so it is interesting he sought Mary's recommendations. No doubt he was keen to hear her ideas, but he would also be seeking news of the Grays, as Mary's brother-in-law Dory was a previous protégé who had worked under him at Seacliff Lunatic Asylum. Delaying Mary may also have been to legitimise time off from her busy schedule.

In Wellington, her forestry in schools work continued. The programme required Ellis's financial authority[83] and it was decided some seed from eucalypt species and other exotics would be supplied free, depending on regional availability, but once a school had reached its limit, seed would be at cost price for either school or home planting. The scheme aimed to stimulate children's interest in growing trees, so plants were only to be supplied if it was impossible to establish a school nursery, or they were specifically for the school grounds. There was a limit of fifty to one hundred free trees for each school, which could be spread over several seasons, and a limited number of native plants available to establish specimen plots. As the programme would be sent to teachers, education boards and others, the conservators were consulted on modifications. Ellis had received a letter from Robert Somerville, secretary of the Te Kuiti Chamber of Commerce, with suggestions to stimulate schoolchildren's interest in forestry. Ellis sent him the forestry in schools programme details, and suggested he inform the Auckland area agricultural instructor, Mr Callaghan, that the Chamber of Commerce could offer assistance if his district considered a school plantation endowment.[84] In March 1926, the idea to involve Boy Scouts in forestry received a boost from Frank Hutchinson, who had joined the Canterbury School of Forestry as a lecturer, and was a scoutmaster for St Matthew's Lady Liverpool's Own Scout Troop.[85] He had previously organised popular Scout camps in North America, and his Boy Scout camps in New Zealand had a strong forestry emphasis.[86, 87]

The Planet seeder with a tractor, used to plant multiple rows. SCION

Mary wrote in her forestation manual that seed extraction would be more efficient if there was sufficient room left for ventilation, rather than piling cones to the top of a makeshift oven. It appears her suggestion might have been to place the cones in cans. SCION

Above: Mary investigated the use of the Hauck burner to burn off firebreaks at Hanmer. SCION

Right: The portable Pacific fire pump, which Mary also investigated for fire protection. The head harness supported a water tank. SCION

CHAPTER 3

THE CONSOLIDATION YEARS

Rio: Mercy mission or opportunity?

Leonard Cockayne, honorary botanist at the Forest Service, regarded beech (*Nothofagus*) as New Zealand's most valuable indigenous asset: the wood had excellent qualities and a variety of uses. Beech forests regenerated rapidly and he believed silvicultural methods could be used to speed up the process. His monograph on New Zealand beech forests had just been published,[1] so Mary would have sought his advice to write her Arbor Day article for the *School Journal*.[2]

She was on leave when it was published, having gone overseas at short notice. Her brother-in-law Howard Clark had moved his family to Brazil, having taken up an accounting position with an oil company, and Mary's sister Daisy was ill with puerperal fever following the birth of her second daughter, Frances.[3] A Rio de Janeiro doctor had sent an urgent cable to Truby King requesting a Karitane nurse, and as King's daughter Mary had just completed her training, in early July 1926 the two Marys boarded the SS *Mahana* in Wellington.[4]

They disembarked in Montevideo, Uruguay, and sailed across the Rio de la Plata to Buenos Aires, where they stayed a few days with relatives of Mary King. While there they visited the Botanic Gardens, where some students helped them explore. Mary Sutherland was impressed with the gardens, she later told Wellington's *Evening Post*: "Everything is splendidly arranged." The trees were grouped by their native country, but New Zealand was in the Australasia group and had only three "measly" species. In the interview Mary described the large number of trees lining the Buenos Aires streets — "Such a contrast to a Wellington." The report noted an attempt at beautification outside her window, where a little triangle opposite the Dominion Farmers' Institute was being dismantled and had an uprooted pohutukawa lying next to dust-covered seats.[5]

From Buenos Aires they sailed on the SS *Western World* to Rio de Janeiro where the harbour reminded Mary of Wellington's bush-covered hills. Daisy was recuperating under King's care, so Mary took time to explore the area and its forestry. The view from the Sugarloaf Mountain was wonderful, and looking down on green bush broken here and there with yellow flowers from the ipê (Brazilian walnut) reminded her of a giant parsley bed, but she was disappointed with Rio's Botanic Gardens.

Only three months earlier the Brazilian government had separated its forestry management from agriculture and was setting up afforestation centres, similar to those in New Zealand. A survey of Amazonian timbers was being conducted by a Forest Service expert. "Somehow, one thinks of the great Amazonian forests as inexhaustible, and therefore artificial forests unnecessary, but hardwoods form the commercial forests there, and they grow well inland in almost uninhabitable parts … so there might come a time when, for a while at least, no more timber can be extracted."[6] Paraná pine (*Araucaria angustifolia*), belonging to the same family as the monkey puzzle tree (*Araucaria*), was the country's general utility wood. Several paper mills were using it for pulp.

Dr André Navarro, Brazil's foremost forestry authority, was head of the forestry department of the San Paulista Railway that operated around Sao Paulo.[7] He told Mary he had worked in Europe and visited New Zealand and Australia, and that Uruguay was the most advanced South American country in forestry. Brazil's native guaranta tree, a high density wood resistant to rot used for external structures such as sleepers and transmission poles,[8] had become scarce except in isolated areas from where it was too costly to transport. Replanting was the only solution, but the trees took twenty-five years to grow.

The railway had a 100-acre (40.5-hectares) plantation outside Rio de Janeiro and had tried eucalypts to manufacture sleepers and poles, but the wood grew too rapidly and cracked at strain; toughness was essential for railway sleepers. To find another purpose for the eucalypt plantations, the department was experimenting with a chemical wood pulp process to produce newsprint.

Two weeks later in September when Daisy was sufficiently recovered, Mary accompanied her to their sisters' home in England, where King also arranged for Daisy to be seen at Plunket's London headquarters, Cromwell House in Highgate. Both Marys returned to New Zealand on the ss *Athenic* at the end of 1926. In an unfinished letter to Mrs Cole Hamilton, Mary wrote that she had met an acquaintance of hers on the ship, Mr Partridge, and was reminded of the Christmas she had spent with the Hamiltons and the good times they had shared.[9]

In England she had caught up with old forestry gang members: Joyce Young was now Mrs Guillebrand and had two lovely little girls; Helen Wedgewood, now Pease, had three; and Margaret Joseph's death had been a shock: "She'd been so full of life. I missed her when I went to Oxford." Mary described her forestry work in New Zealand: "It is interesting, and takes me around the country a lot to the different nurseries and plantations, but I am not such a [nomad] as I was in the old country. I am very fond of New Zealand now, and would not like to live anywhere else. It is a good country to folk who fit in."

A shift to Rotorua and 'manual' labour

When Mary returned to work for the State Forest Service in January 1927 she no doubt would have been disappointed to learn her proposal for a school plantation endowment scheme had been strongly criticised by education boards, school inspectors and agricultural instructors, who all felt it too comprehensive and laborious and required too much time. They thought the financial difficulties were formidable, so would not be supporting the scheme. However, they favoured proposals to encourage forestry ideas and plant small areas near school grounds. Mary bore the criticisms and carried on.[10]

The Hawera Winter Show organiser, Leonard Hooker, had asked the commissioner of State Forests, Oswald Hawken, for an article on school forestry to publish in *The Show*,[11] a task Hawken passed on to Mary. He asked her to model the article on his item about the dairy industry, which had been published in the *Taranaki Daily News*.[12] Mary wrote that it was in the interest of present and future citizens to awaken and develop concern for forests and reforestation, as destruction and poor utilisation of New Zealand's timber had reduced national reserves to a dangerous level. She made the point that any schoolchild with a properly developed forestry sense would automatically become a guardian of the nation's great heritage — its forest wealth. Owhango School had won the Symes Forestry Shield two years running, and Taranaki farmers were recognising the financial value of protecting stock with shelter trees.[13]

The Forestry League's magazine reported in 1927 that the Rotorua conservator, Halbert Goudie, had left the Forest Service and joined NZ Redwood Forests near Putaruru. Mary was the league's secretary–treasurer at the time. Redwood timber was generating higher prices than kauri and the company, which owned 6014 acres (2430 hectares) of freehold land near Putaruru with frontage to the Auckland–Rotorua railway, had contracts for half a million redwood seedlings and enough selected seed to plant the whole property.[14] Goudie had supervised planting the Whakarewarewa redwoods in 1904.[15] He would have chosen the best seed source, which was probably from a tree Mary later found at Taheke, Northland, and identified in her Rotorua and Waipoua nurseries report to Leon McIntosh Ellis as giving the best germination results in the country.

With the tension between Goudie and Mary eliminated, Ellis decided she should be based in Rotorua as most of her investigation work was there.[16] He expected afforestation and nursery techniques to be standardised, and the new practices to be incorporated for general use throughout the service. He asked Mary for a six-month plan of action: she was to concentrate on the investigational and co-ordinational side of afforestation, and while her headquarters would be at Whakarewarewa, her activities and interests would extend to all stations. The *New Zealand Gazette* reported Mary's move to Rotorua as a promotion, but her forest assistant status and salary remained the same.[17]

William (Bill) Morrison, who replaced Halbert Goudie, was the brother of Walter (Wattie), the conservator of forests in Canterbury. Morrison was unhappy about Mary's placement, but Ellis trusted and supported Mary, which possibly made her acceptance more difficult. Morrison asked Ellis for a copy of Miss Sutherland's specific instructions: "The fact any officer attached to the regional staff, although under control of head office, is working under what are virtually sealed orders, is not conducive to co-ordination of the work, nor is it complimentary to the conservator of the region, or the staff generally, to whom Miss Sutherland has to refer for information." He asked Ellis to consider his point of view and in future transmit instructions through him, so Ellis requested that Mary discuss her plans with Morrison as his full co-operation was desirable.

Mary first sought Ellis's approval for her work plan: she intended to observe the performance of the Rotorua experimental projects, and when possible do the same for other regions' trials. She would report progress and co-ordinate results from the various stations; co-ordination and investigation would be by periodic inspection, and standard information would be compiled into a manual of afforestation procedure. She expected to visit South Island stations in March, but first planned to complete a preliminary compilation of the manual.[18]

Nursery experiments would be concentrated in separate blocks dedicated to the purpose,[19] with labour borrowed from the nursery. Wages and payments would be charged to an investigational grant. She queried Ellis on the amount available for the 1927 fiscal year, and attached her list of proposed investigations, plus a draft letter explaining the benefits of making the information available to regional officers.

Ellis sent a directive to the conservators, asking them to submit nursery and plantation proposals, and for their suggestions for the coming year. They should indicate the investigations they proposed to conduct themselves and those they wanted carried out by the co-ordinating officer, Miss Sutherland.[20] In a memo to Bill Morrison, he regretted not informing him about Miss Sutherland, sent copies of all their communications after she had departed for Rotorua, and explained that her work would be similar to what she had been engaged in at head office in Wellington. He would be pleased if Morrison's officers would assist her to their utmost in the investigational work: "Miss Sutherland has in hand the compilation of a manual on nursery and plantation practice, and officers in your region will be able to afford her a great amount of assistance in this work."[21]

Morrison must have shown Ellis's letter and Mary's action plan to the chief inspector, for Arnold Hansson wrote to Ellis that Miss Sutherland's paper was

Lining out seedlings at Whakarewarewa nursery, 1924. SCION

California redwood (*Sequoia sempervirens*) a year after being lined out.
The stand of trees in the background is Torrey pine (*Pinus torreyana*). SCION

commendable for she had given the matter considerable thought, however, she had a tendency for too much brevity: "The various projects should be treated in detail, giving the amount of work contemplated for the year, the area, seed and labour needed, estimated time the project would consume, detailed and totalled anticipated cost, and the localities for specific projects. Investigations of soil conditions are not mentioned. I suggest the allocation to Miss Sutherland of the writing of a forestation manual without discussing the matter with Mr Morrison, who is now our senior afforestation officer, might cause some unnecessary feeling, setting theoretical training above practical experience."[22] Ellis was acknowledging Mary's accumulated knowledge on methods and experimentation throughout the country, whereas despite Morrison's afforestation experience, his overall picture was less expansive. Anxious to avoid upsetting either Hansson or Morrison, Ellis asked Mary to provide more details on her plan. She was to stay in close touch with head office regarding possible new developments or suggestions. He later asked for a monthly report on her activities, with a proposed outline of the following month's activities.[23]

Mary spent February 1927 at Whakarewarewa preparing five sections of the forestation manual, analysing labour returns, preparing the experimental programme, and photographing nursery work. She expected to be in Rotorua till mid-March doing office work, inspecting the Kaingaroa nursery, and collecting data from exotic sample plots in native bush in the Mamaku State Forest and from native bush sample plots at Kohuratahi. She would then visit the South Island stations for her co-ordination work in late March.[24]

Her workload was full, but was about to increase. While she was overseas supporting Daisy, ranger Robert Steele wrote a report on the 1926 forest extension work,[25] and Arnold Hansson selected projects from it for Mary. She was to investigate and prove the value of shelter belts on increasing agricultural production, and publish the findings as a circular or short bulletin, and in co-operation with the farm schools and colleges, she should aim to introduce forestry on the farm subjects to the syllabus, develop closer contact with local bodies to help them prepare planting plans, and develop co-operation between Central Otago irrigation boards and afforestation centres. Rather than producing the bulky manual she had under preparation, she should instead review the 1924 State Forest Service's *Tree-planters Guide*. Steele agreed the course for inspectors and instructors should continue, which would benefit the forestry in schools programme.[26]

Mary ignored Hansson's comment on the bulky forestation manual, and replied to him through Ellis[27] that forest extension officers had previously collected shelter belt information, but she would consider the matter with them, with the objective of farmers co-operating to collect facts and make definite observations. She cited the work of Carlos Bates of the United States Forest Service, who collected data on the mechanical influence of shelter belts, variations in wind velocity, air and soil temperatures, and increase in crop production. If New Zealand figures were desired, an investigation could be set up in shelter plantations at Kaingaroa. While the sand dune experimental station at Tangimoana already had instruments such as an anemometer, and maximum and minimum thermometers for soil and air, Tangimoana was not a typical environment for this type of investigation. "Perhaps shelter belts on neighbouring farms could be used?" She informed him that the North Island extension officer was already in touch with farm schools and high schools. A good proportion of farm forestry was included in the curriculum as a syllabus had been drawn up two years before at a North Island farm school's request; this was on file. She suggested that by co-operating with the South Island extension officer and farmers, trial plots of different species could be established on irrigation areas for a Canterbury–Otago project in the coming year.

After amending the 1927–28 programme, she sent it to Hansson via Ellis.[28] It included the labour requirements throughout the season for a one-acre (0.4 hectares) experimental block in Rotorua. Maintaining the experimental nursery crop would cost slightly more than usual, but general charges would cover usual plantation maintenance. Establishing regional trials would impact the investigational grant, whereas the only costs to carry out underplanting-in-bush trials lay in their establishment. The new ranger station at Tahakopa was suitable for Southland plots. She promised to discuss soil temperature investigations with the chief inspector and sent a requisition for materials and stores.

Forming a professional forestry institute

Arnold Hansson was unhappy that Mary was organising her own work, and he informed Leon McIntosh Ellis she was given too much leeway, with insufficient supervision. He also wrote to her, "… the Director has today expressed as his wish, that you carry out your work entirely under my control. This will of course, not affect the lines of work already laid down, nor your allocation to the Rotorua region." He would discuss this with her when she was in Wellington, but meanwhile she was to draw up her operational programme so a definite line of action could be approved.[29] Ellis, however, was not willing to relinquish support. He typed on Hansson's memo to Mary, "You will, as in other matters, keep in close touch with me in order that I may be able to follow progress, and from time to time instruct you in regard to the work." He sent all the conservators a memo saying it was time for a manual of New Zealand forestation practice, and forest assistant Sutherland had been instructed to collect and compile the necessary information. The methods and procedures evolved over 25 years were to be embodied, and variations in practice and new methods incorporated. "Every officer is asked to assist and co-operate by making available all data in the various conservation regions, so the manual is a complete representation of afforestation development."[30] The manual would put forestry practice on a more scientific footing.

Many employees, including some conservators, had no university qualifications; tertiary forestry studies were not available in New Zealand until 1925 when the Canterbury College School of Forestry began teaching, followed a year later in March 1926 when classes began at Auckland University College. Previously though, research, lectures and general forestry work had been carried out in the Canterbury University College Biology Department where Charles Foweraker was employed as a lecturer in Forestry in 1921, and three students enrolled in Forestry in 1924.[31] There had been much debate and political lobbying as both the Canterbury and Auckland colleges claimed a right to establish a school, and the government, unable to choose, split funding between them.

The proposed duplication of forestry schools had come under critical scrutiny with the 1925 Report of the Royal Commission on University Education in New Zealand conducted by Sir Harry Reichel, Mary's principal at the University College of North Wales, and Frank Tate, director of education in Victoria, who started the Australian forestry in schools programme. The commission observed that the State Forest Service was unable to absorb more than six graduates a year, and tempting young men and women to years of study to then not find profitable employment was unjust to students and uneconomical for the nation. It had recommended New Zealand have one school of forestry, located in Auckland, but from 1926 both colleges operated with inadequate financial support. After the 1928 British Empire Forestry Conference an inspection of the schools was instigated and it recommended Canterbury be chosen as the sole degree course.[32] The Auckland School of Forestry was closed at the end of 1930,[33] but the Canterbury school's monetary situation did not improve and the impact of the economic depression led the government to close the school at the end of 1934.

While the Forest Service endeavoured to incorporate science into its forestry management, and Mary's investigative work played a major role in this, the industry lacked a professional body. Forming a forestry association had been discussed for at least three years, but it was not till 1927 that formal steps were taken. In March, Owen Jones, administrator of the afforestation company New Zealand Perpetual Forests, wrote to Professor Hugh Corbin, head of the Auckland School of Forestry, arguing against restricting the proposed association membership to only those with formal qualifications. A low membership number would reduce the association's powers and arouse jealousy between professional and non-professional men, as had occurred in Australia: "To exclude men who acquired sound training in the hard school of practical experience, and who are capable exponents of their profession though they have not passed through a diploma or degree course, would create bad feeling."[34] In early April, a meeting held at the Auckland School of Forestry considered forming an association.[35] The attendees were Hugh Corbin, Halbert Goudie from NZ Redwood Forests, the Auckland conservator Roderick Campbell, forest assistant Frank Foster, and Frank Hutchinson, lecturer at the Canterbury School of Forestry. Wider approval was required to form an association, so Foster suggested a special meeting be held during the State Forest Service's 6th Annual Conference, to take place later that month.

Mary was in the South Island at the time, where she visited the Canterbury conservator and travelled to Tapanui, the Beaumont camp clearing and nursery, Crookston nursery, the Blue Mountains, Dunedin, and Naseby before going to Hokitika and the rimu experimental area where pine and Douglas fir were affected by fungal disease. After Easter in Christchurch, she visited the Hanmer nurseries, the Josephs area, and Balmoral. She discussed the proposed regional experiments, inspected nurseries, looked at seed extraction, examined experimental records and tallied plants in direct sowing experiments. In the plantations, she inspected previous underplanting, experimental pruning, thinning and the clearing of snow-damaged radiata pine. She photographed Douglas fir regeneration on a sluiced-over area, and plants in Hanmer's wrenching experiment, and gathered data for the forestation manual.[36] Mary was back in Wellington two days before the conference.

The meeting to form a professional foresters' organisation took place on the second evening of the conference. It was attended by Roderick Campbell and Frank Foster, who were at the Auckland meeting, as well as Leon McIntosh Ellis and Arnold Hansson, forest assistants Mary Sutherland and Alan Perham, conservators Cecil Smith, Bill Morrison, Walter Morrison, Duncan MacPherson, Samuel Darby and Alexander McGavock. Also attending were Charles Foweraker, lecturer at Canterbury College School of Forestry; Forest Service milling expert Camille Malfroy; forest rangers Norman Dolamore and William Montgomery; and the Forest Service accountant William (Bill) Taylor. Apologies were sent by Hugh Corbin and Frank Hutchinson. Ellis chaired the meeting: he had been part of a small band that formed a similar society in Toronto and the resulting Canadian Society of Forest Engineers had flourished.

The meaning of 'professional' forester was discussed, and whether forester or forest engineer was the better term. Mary had her say: "It is time to protect foresters and the public, especially with afforestation companies. Forester is the better term, meaning one who grows trees for timber purposes. The term forest engineer is narrower, covering the conversion aspect, while a forester is engaged in the more essential task of producing trees." The motion to form a New Zealand society of

Creating government timber reserves, 1925: reafforestation work at Whakarewarewa, Waiotapu and Kaingaroa. The plantations covered about 43,000 acres (17,401 hectares), of which 8000 acres (3237 hectares) were planted during 1924. Top left: 1. A planter at Kaingaroa. 2. A grove of 19-year-old Weymouth pine. 3. Waiotapu plantation established on land unfit for cultivation. 4. A woman ties seedlings into bundles. 5. The cookhouse at Kaingaroa camp. 6. The principal nursery at Whakarewarewa. 7. Boxes of young trees ready to send to farmers. 8. Experimental plot of Weymouth pine at Waiotapu. 9. Gardeners at Whakarewarewa nursery. 10. Wrenching and lifting seedlings. 11. Planting young trees. AUCKLAND LIBRARIES HERITAGE COLLECTIONS

foresters was moved, and the next day, a list of seventeen inaugural members was compiled, ten with professional qualifications.[37]

After the conference Mary stayed on at head office to arrange regional schedules for the experimental programme. In response to Ellis's letter asking which investigations the conservators wanted Mary to carry out, Bill Morrison sent a large list of trials he proposed to conduct. Ellis informed him that he must first discuss these with Miss Sutherland to prevent her investigations overlapping, and also talk to the chief inspector.[38] Ellis was in Rotorua and had sent a telegram to Arnold Hansson asking when the co-ordination officer would arrive to carry out the investigational work,[39] but Mary was in hospital. Her illness is uncertain, but those who remember her suggest it may have been asthma. She was expected to be absent for two weeks.

When eventually back at work, Mary spent another two days at head office writing the experimental schemes to send to the conservators, and when she returned to Rotorua, she weighed and counted seed for a seasonal sowing experiment in the new nursery, and worked on the forestation manual.[40] Ellis sent her a *New York Times* clipping on a fire-resistant acacia species that he wanted her to investigate.[41] To find out more about it she wrote to Arthur Hill, director of Kew Gardens. His reply indicated that the non-combustible acacia species used in France to protect coniferous forests from fire was unreliable. She took his advice to contact Monsieur Margin, inspecteur-adjoint des Eaux et Forêts de Chantilly (Oise), and also tried to procure green wattle seed (*Acacia decurrans var. normalis*) for experimentation.[42]

Mary's long-term plan covered eight years; in comparison, the national afforestation programme, started two years earlier, was expected to take ten years to plant 300,000 acres (121,400 hectares) of exotic forest.[43] As well as submitting reports on her experimental work and monthly reports on her activities, she was also required to produce a personal annual report. Arnold Hansson informed her the monthly reports were of no value. He suggested they should be two pages instead of one, and that stating 'at head office' or 'at Rotorua' was insufficient; she must write her chief purpose for remaining in a place and enumerate seed or plants for sowing or planting. Her monthly report was to be a progress report and she was also to submit a copy of proposals for the controlling officer's information.[44] But Mary already forwarded two copies of proposals and schemes to head office. Hansson then asked her to add two additional, permanent sample plots to the current year's radiata pine plantations; one to show the effects of lime and fungus on forest tree growth and the other for the control.[45]

In addition to Hansson's constant expectations, there was also tension between the Rotorua conservator and Mary. Following Leon McIntosh Ellis's instruction, Bill Morrison discussed his lengthy list of proposed investigations with Mary, and it was decided she would trial Morrison's patented transplanter board for small trees. It is not clear if he or his brother Walter, the Canterbury conservator, developed the board. The experiment occurred in October; one man with horses ploughed the ground, and two men either side cut a trench with a vertical face. Four women lifted the boards onto a table and filled them with small Douglas fir plants. Two women then carried the board to the trench and placed it in position. The ploughman pegged the board down and spaded earth against the plant roots. Empty boards were returned to the table and refilled. Mary photographed the horses, the table, the women filling the transplanting board and the planting lines. The method proved not to be cost-effective; to be equivalent to hand lining out, planting needed to increase from 1580 to 6000 plants per head, per eight-hour day.[46]

In November when Ellis asked Hansson for a progress report on Mary's work at Rotorua he also suggested a quarterly project review,[47] which Hansson asked Mary to write. Her interim report on investigation work to 30 October 1927 indicates she developed standard classification for all forestation experiments, detailed procedure plans for thirty-two projects, and obtained or had equipment constructed.[48] Seed studies investigated quality, germination, and storage; six species were pre-treated with gas fumigation, either mercury chloride or kerosene. Nursery techniques covered soil treatment, sowing methods, depth of covering, sowing density, season of sowing and shading. Wrenching experiments were conducted at the Westland experimental nursery and in Rotorua. She looked at weed and bird control, and growing untried species for sample plots. Trials to determine the optimum season for sowing took place in the Auckland, Rotorua and Southland regions, and different age and type plots were started in the Peke Peke block in Kaingaroa. Spot-sown plots were established in cutover bush in Southland where monthly sowings took place of radiata pine, macrocarpa (*Cupressus macrocarpa*) and Lawson's cypress (*Chamaecyparis lawsoniana*) at different depths under varying ground cover conditions. Soil conditions in plantations were also investigated.

Besides experimental work, Mary had the forestry in schools programme to consider. The North Island extension officer Percy Page suggested instigating a certificate of merit for teachers, so Mary sent Ellis her ideas on the expected standards for the award.[49] The Hawera Winter Show competitions needed to be reviewed, and she wanted value placed on specimen collections rather than on the mechanical recording of methods in a life history chart. Native wood specimen sets could be presented to manual training centres and technical schools, at the extension officer's discretion. She recommended that private schools should receive free seed, as state schools already did; nearly 850 schools had established forest nurseries. Although Mary's suggestion to establish school endowment plantations had been criticised, in 1925 during his visit for the Royal Commission on University Education, Frank Tate had advocated for endowment plantations to reduce educational expenditure, as was done in Victoria. The New Zealand Forestry League also supported endowment plantations and Leon McIntosh Ellis reported that ten schools had begun the process to establish them: some small school plantations had proved successful.[50] Thirty-seven Taranaki schools had plantations by the end of 1927, ranging from 1/8 to 3 acres, and the total area planted was just over 30 acres (12 hectares).[51]

The unwanted road

As well as the Northland afforestation projects, the State Forest Service managed Waipoua Forest, the last substantial remnant of kauri (one of the world's largest timber trees), which covered 29,000 acres (over 11,700 hectares).[52] Mary first visited Waipoua in 1925 to report on the nursery. She returned in March 1928, travelling to the Riverhead nursery and plantation and then across the Kaipara Harbour from Helensville to Dargaville.[53]

On her first visit, ranger Robert Murray had taken Mary and his niece on what was then a new track: "We were the first white women to get so far into Waipoua. I remember the wonderful scene of kauri rising out of the water, right in the heart of the forest." A road, opened in January, now ran through the forest to Waimamaku, and at a bridge where she had previously watched a bullock team take up timber there were motor wagons "careening about". "Why should everyone want to make all places the same and go rushing about the country without taking time to appreciate it." Ranger Murray and the forest guard she had stayed with on her last visit had since left, so she lodged at a farm that took in "stray people", and arrived there muddy and wet. There was plenty of hot water, but no locks on the bathroom doors, so she jammed shut the door between the bathroom and the kitchen with a broken chair, and listened for footsteps on the verandah. She had her meals in the kitchen with the family, farm workers and other folk staying there.

Mary borrowed a pair of men's boots and a horse from the ranger's wife to visit the nursery. The horse had previously been a racehorse, but was 'on strike' and was like a huge elephant on springs when trotting or cantering. Waipoua Forest was in a sad state: despite the Forest Service's objections to government plans to build the road,[54] it ran for 16 miles (26 kilometres) directly through the trees. The mess was not cleared and dead 'stuff' lay around with huge kauri fallen across gullies. "I am afraid it will all soon be spoilt, if not burnt," she wrote. There had been recent fires and she was concerned about cigarette butts thrown from car windows.

When her Northland work was complete instead of leaving by train the next day for Dargaville as planned, Mary rose early, borrowed a 'bronc' from the farm and rode 5 miles (8 kilometres) through the forest to the men's forestry camp.

Constructing the road through
Waipoua Forest c.1920s, When Mary
revisited in 1928, she despaired at the
'sad state' the forest had been left in
after the road construction.
ABOVE: ALEXANDER TURNBULL LIBRARY.
RIGHT: THE KAURI MUSEUM

She marvelled at how the horse threaded its way over fallen trunks, creepers and roots, and halted if led the wrong way: "It stopped briefly in the middle of the river, but then moved on. I was proud of myself, going on my own and fording the river, though the nag knew it by heart." As she passed ridge over ridge of green kauri forest, huge trees towered along the wayside. Below their crowns she noticed an under canopy of a different green — groves of nikau palms and ferns with the sun filtering through "like stained-glass windows". She rode past a stream, small waterfalls and whare, some built of large nikau fronds and thatched with what looked like bulrush. There were grinning Maori children, and mostly Dalmatian men living in scattered Public Works Department tents: "One old chap pulled up my [horse's] girth, and was quite guttural."

Mary watched men climbing the kauri trees for cones; a sight she had not seen on her previous visit. Wooden-soled boots with serrated iron edges and toe spikes, and handheld grappling irons helped them climb the trunks of 10–16 feet (3–5 metres) in diameter. About 50 feet (15 metres) up, the men rested on a platform of tree branches before continuing their climb, then out to the branch tips 100–150 feet (30–45 metres) above the ground. They used a swing seat attached to a rope wound around their waists to descend. Fixing the rope over a branch, they payed it out and near the bottom used their toe spikes on the trunk to stop themselves falling.

She subsequently departed for Dargaville in a 'sidecar'. In Auckland she visited the regional office to discuss the 1928 reports and proposals.[55] The weather was stuffy and thundery and although she had hoped to spend Easter with family the annual conference was on at Whakarewarewa. Leon McIntosh Ellis had unexpectedly announced his resignation. Only two months earlier his reappointment for another three years had been announced,[56] and he had not mentioned his impending departure when interviewed for a just-published issue of *New Zealand Life*.[57] Instead, he highlighted the Forest Service's achievements and talked of the "costs of establishing the Dominion's wasteland, estimated at 5 million acres (2 million hectares), into productive forests". Perfecting plantation practices would take two more years, but by applying them, commercial forests would be established within twenty-five rather than two hundred years. Sustained forest cropping would make New Zealand one of the first permanent exporters of wooden goods, and establish the Dominion as the Empire's timber farm.

The New Zealand Institute of Foresters (NZIF) held its inaugural annual general meeting on the first evening of the conference, and provisionally adopted the recommended constitution and by-laws.[58] Arnold Hansson was elected to the council, along with Edward Phillips Turner, Bill Morrison, Alexander McGavock and Cecil Smith. Later, in a letter to Frank Foster marked 'not official', Phillips Turner recommended that 'man' in words such as 'chairman' should be changed to 'person' because of the lady member.[59] The *New Zealand Herald* reported that

A kauri tree with a 48-foot
(14.6-metre) centre girth in
Waipoua forest. SCION

Climbing a kauri tree with handheld grappling irons,
wearing wooden-soled boots, 1935. THE KAURI MUSEUM

the forestry association aimed to further technical forestry and the profession's interests. Proper qualifications were needed: "The unqualified forester can be as much a power for harm as the unqualified engineer, and perhaps more so, seeing that he may be given control of property valued at tens of thousands of pounds."[60]

After the conference, Mary supervised the Rotorua experimental nursery investigations on wrenched crops and seed treated against bird attack with Semesan. Seed for Douglas fir, Japanese cedar (*Cryptomeria japonica*), Canary Island pine (*Pinus canariensis*) and western red cedar (*Thuja plicata*), which had been stored under varying conditions for six months, was sown in a nursery trial, and six different species were directly sown at the Peke Peke experimental block in the Kaingaroa Forest. While in the office Mary analysed results, worked on the Mamaku underplanting report and revised the nursery sections of the manual.[61]

Ellis left at the end of March 1928 and the *Auckland Star* reported that when he was appointed in 1920 fewer than 40,000 acres (16,000 hectares) had been planted since 1896. Under his leadership, plantations had increased by 60,000 acres (24,000 hectares) and almost 25,000 acres (8000 hectares) would be planted that year. Costs had reduced and the service was on track to achieve its planting objective of 300,000 acres (121,400 hectares) by 1935. The State Forest Service had an almost perfect record for fire prevention and a trading profit from timber sales, royalties and leases.[62] Why Ellis left is unclear; perhaps he was unhappy about his employment conditions,[63] and faced with reduced Forest Service funding, he would have been unhappy to cut his long-term plans short. He left, expecting to take advantage of the New South Wales afforestation boom, but opportunities to use his skills were never the same. He initially worked in Queensland and later joined the Australian Paper Manufacturers in Melbourne, organising technical aspects and procurement for their pulpwood operation.

Without Ellis's support Mary came under greater pressure from Arnold Hansson, who informed her that she was to show accomplishments and results in her annual report, and give a definite date to complete the forestation manual.[64] Hansson wanted the manual scrapped and the tree planting guide rewritten, but Mary pressed on. She did not want to waste the time and effort she had invested in it, and wanted to fulfil Ellis's expectations, but competing priorities took over.

Her monthly reports show the breadth of her work. In April 1928, Mary visited Karioi nursery and plantation. At Erua and Waimarino Plains she looked at experimental plots with forest ranger Norman Dolamore. In the South Island she inspected Tapanui and Crookston nurseries, then inspected direct sowing plots and spacing trials at Beaumont. From Hokitika, she visited the Woodstock nursery and the rimu experimental area to look at 1927 plantings and trials on goldmine dredge-tailing tips before visiting the Hanmer and Balmoral nurseries and plantations.[65]

The State Forest Service Conference, 1928. In front, Edward Phillips Turner (with beard); to the right, Mary walks between Leon MacIntosh Ellis and Arnold Hansson. SUTHERLAND/GRAY FAMILY

The first annual general meeting of the New Zealand Institute of Foresters, 1928.
Standing: Mary Sutherland, Courtney Bigges, Arnold Hansson, Camille (Cam) Malfroy, Bill Morrison, Edward Phillips Turner, the Minister of Lands and Forests Oswald Hawken, Leon MacIntosh Ellis (director), Alan Perham, Duncan MacPherson, Jack Myles, Cecil M. Smith, Walter (Wattie) Morrison. Front: Frank Foster, Fred Field, Sam Darby, Bill Taylor, Alex McGavock, and the minister's secretary, unnamed. SUTHERLAND/GRAY FAMILY

When she returned to Rotorua in early May, the prospect of completing the manual was again quashed. She had to supervise the experimental nursery, update records, sort seed requirements and write an Arbor Day article for the *School Journal*. The Rotorua conservator, Bill Morrison, sent her draft 'Bush, berries and birds'[66] to the new director, Edward Phillips Turner.[67] He noted on Morrison's letter that Mary's article would have been better if she had shown that most New Zealand birds were insectivorous and thus gave valuable aid to the forests.[68] Phillips Turner and Leonard Cockayne were working on *The Trees of New Zealand*, aiming to finish the book for the 1928 British Empire Forestry Conference, which was to be held for the first time in Australasia. The book was written for schoolchildren.[69]

Mary was also aiming to complete her forestation manual in time for the conference, but it required more amendments. She requested nursery stocktaking returns from conservators, and asked to borrow sand dune operation reports. Temperature, rainfall and sunshine hours needed to come from the Meteorological Office, and she required outline maps to show general topographical features and the position of plantations, nurseries and stations. She also wanted a copy of a topographical survey sheet to illustrate plantation formation. A typical nursery plan would demonstrate subdivision systems and shelter hedges, so she asked Hansson if he could arrange a reduced-size print of a nursery, either Woodstock or Riverhead.[70] As she was waiting for sand dune reports and nursery stocktaking returns, she planned and worked on experimental nursery trials, and marked off areas for the season's sowing.

Giant redwood (*Sequoia gigantean*) and white fir (*Abies concolor*) seed imported for storage trials had arrived from the Eddy Tree Breeding Station in California.[71] The Scots pine (*Pinus sylvestris*) seedlings from Britain needed planting on the Peke Peke experimental block.[72] She requested authority to purchase timber for forty-two shelter frames, and for lath shelter in the experimental nursery. The blue lupin crop sown in February needed ploughing in, ready for seed sowing, and she spent five and a half days supervising layout at a new experimental block next to the Wairapukao camp at Kaingaroa.[73]

Mary worked on the manual whenever possible and had just forwarded several more sections to head office when Phillips Turner sent her earlier sections to Bill Morrison with his comment: "It is an excellent compilation of data, but contains too much detail."[74] Phillips Turner thought individual nurseries should not be named, but the tractor type and plough size needed to be identified. He asked Morrison to revise the manual, or let one of his responsible officers do it under his supervision. Later, he questioned Morrison about letting Mary engage Miss Moore of Opunake to type the manual.[75] Morrison replied that he had suggested Miss Sutherland get typing done outside the service as clerical staff were too busy.

He accepted no responsibility for her not checking first with head office: "Miss Sutherland is not a regional officer and is not under my supervision."[76]

Previously, Hansson had described Mary's writing as too brief. He asked that her reports be constructive criticisms of operations. She must include the location of the various experiments and suggest improvements. He challenged her requisition for spending on forestation investigations and informed Phillips Turner, "the officer in charge of the work should be able to specify the actual items desired".[77]

The strain of finishing the manual under constant criticisms and her heavy workload could have affected Mary's health. She was off work sick for two weeks in August 1928. The workload did not ease when she returned: she had the experimental nursery ground disked, ready for seed sowing; extra lath shelter was constructed for a trial, and plants were lifted and prepared to transport to Kaingaroa; 129 lots of seed were weighed for sowing, and new trials were commencing at Peke Peke, Wairapukao and Waiotapu.[78] The Nelson conservator Cecil Smith complained when Mary mistakenly sent the wrong project scheme for larch trials of Western North American larch (*Larix occidentalis*) and Japanese larch (*Larix leptolepis*).[79] She apologised, for instead of Karioi's high tussock country the seed should have instead suited Golden Downs' heavy fern country.[80]

Preparing seedbeds at Whakarewarewa nursery, 1928. SCION

CHAPTER 4

A CHANGE OF DIRECTION

Rotorua research is cut

Mary's forestation manual was not ready when delegates arrived for the British Empire Forestry Conference in 1928 because Bill Morrison had held on to sections of it. He had asked Edward Phillips Turner for her co-ordination reports,[1] which would have updated him on afforestation in other regions and helped him to write his contribution for the service's annual report. The conference was a success according to Leonard Cockayne, whose comments were published in *New Zealand Life*. Experts from throughout the Empire toured New Zealand to witness the work being done to replace destroyed natural forests. Planting was greater than in Australia and South Africa combined, and the rapid growth of trees and apparent lack of disease was noted. While some delegates criticised un-thinned stands, others believed thinning was too expensive because it could not be sold. The experts approved of what New Zealand was doing, and Cockayne believed there would be little difficulty to persuade the State Forests commissioner, Oswald Hawken, that forestry needed to be pursued with greater vigour.

During Hawken's regime, methods had reduced planting costs to an absurdly low figure, and newly gained knowledge would enable New Zealand to meet its own needs and supply Australia and further afield. Cockayne concluded that although the delegates' tour was at considerable cost, the prominence it created by putting New Zealand forestry before the Empire and people of the Dominion meant it was money expended to the fullest advantage.[2]

Mary knew many of the delegates from her time in Britain, but although she had joined the Empire Forestry Association in 1924, she was not in the conference photograph published in the State Forest Service's annual report.[3] It is also unclear whether she was given the opportunity to share her knowledge at the conference, but she was elected a fellow of the Society of Foresters of Great Britain,[4] which had been set up in 1925, two years before the New Zealand Institute of Foresters.

After the conference Phillips Turner informed Morrison that the Public Service commissioner had approved payment for Miss Moore's typing bill. However, such expenditure was not to be incurred again without first referring to the commissioner.[5] Phillips Turner also advised Morrison that Miss Sutherland was to conclude her forestation investigations in Rotorua and present complete reports on all experiments, giving definite conclusions where possible, or at least result trends. He expected the reports by the end of the following month, December 1928. Where she would be relocated was uncertain: "She might work in an itinerant capacity." Phillips Turner also asked about the draft of Mary's forestation manual he had sent. Morrison replied he was unable to do anything with it, and the chief inspector, Arnold Hansson, had suggested he return it to head office.[6] When he received it back, Phillips Turner assigned it to the library as a permanent record. Thus the manual was never used for the purpose Ellis and Mary had intended. The unfinished draft, a unique record of 1920s forest nursery and plantation methods, is held at the National Forestry Library, Scion.[7]

Though Mary was undoubtedly unhappy the Rotorua experimentation programme was cancelled, she must also have been relieved. Her departure from the region would lessen tensions between her and Bill Morrison. He too would have been glad. However, shutting down the programme was not for personal reasons; the Forest Service was in financial trouble. Mary was meant to undertake silvicultural investigations at Waimarino, but the Palmerston North conservator had insufficient money. He asked Morrison to arrange a further sum from head office,[8] yet Mary was

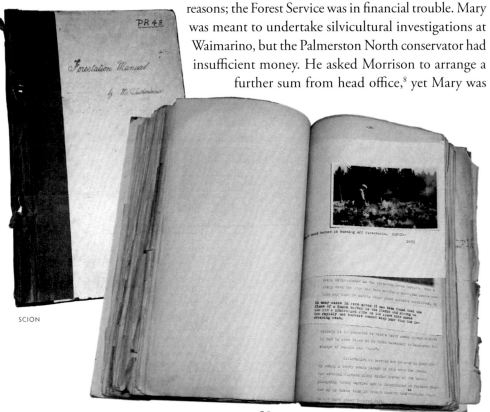

SCION

again in hospital,[9] possibly with recurring severe asthma, though reports are unclear. Her huge workload, negative reactions to her manual and insufficient time to report on the experimental programme had, no doubt, undermined her health.

On her return to work, Mary had to finalise the experimental programme and obtain trials data from the other regions to co-ordinate with the Rotorua results. The conservators were not immediately forthcoming. Some information that appears to have been for the manual arrived late, and data was occasionally sent to Phillips Turner rather than directly to her. Roderick Campbell sent spacing and direct seeding trial results for Riverhead and Waipoua, and a soil sample for the Riverhead nursery soil cropping trial. He presumed the co-ordination officer (Mary) would also include the experimental results in the annual report. Phillips Turner added a note to Campbell's memo, presumably for Mary to deal with, saying the data was "… too long and needs summarising".[10] Instead of presenting the forestation investigations report in December, as Phillips Turner requested, Mary completed it at the financial year's end.[11] She sent a separate report on the Mamaku underplanting project she was writing for publication, and a list of regional investigations co-ordinated to Rotorua trials and nursery stock numbers, which she also copied for Morrison.[12] In addition she was expected to write her personal annual report, summarising the operations under her charge.

There had been thirteen new projects and four continuing from the previous year in the Rotorua experimental nursery.[13] Her first draft, probably handwritten and waiting to be typed, was lost under papers on Morrison's desk, so her annual report was late.[14]

Although the Rotorua experimental programme had ceased, Phillips Turner decided not to reduce afforestation until 1934. He sent Morrison a 'tapering off' planting programme and asked for assurance on nursery capacity. He assumed afforestation in Rotorua would not exceed 4000 acres (1620 hectares) per annum from 1934, and asked Morrison for small lithos showing desirable lands to acquire.[15] But more trees had been planted than planned due to government unemployment schemes, and Morrison, who was worried about winding down the Forest Service's operation, informed Phillips Turner that his suggested programme fell considerably short of the Dominion's objective for planting.[16] Arnold Hansson was also concerned, not just about cutting back on afforestation, but also about reducing research. After Ellis resigned, Hansson was elected as the New Zealand Institute of Foresters president, and in his address to the second annual general meeting emphasised that demonstrating forestry's economic value would build public support. Progress in this could not be made without continual research, he said: "Where we can make the surest mark and lead the way in the advance of forestry, is in research work."[17]

Despite having made things difficult for Mary, Hansson helped set up a research project to suit her botanical skills and knowledge. Exotic conifers, introduced eighty years prior, provided excellent timber and were potentially a valuable source of paper pulp, turpentine and resin. But the trees often displayed variable growth patterns, and identifying the species was increasingly difficult. Frank Hutchinson had created a pine species identification guide for the 1924 rangers school.[18] It was useful, but macroscopic characteristics alone were unreliable. Hansson recommended that Mary analyse the microscopic features of pine leaves and create an identification key to use in conjunction with macroscopic features. Specimens were needed, and Mary suggested that as well as microscopic slides she could also create permanent specimens for reference. She proposed preserving small shoots with winter buds in methylated spirit, and requested the necessary materials.[19] Phillips Turner signed his approval in 1929 and regional conservators were asked to send needles from various species.[20] Specimens arrived from around the country, and Harry Kirk, emeritus professor of biology and honorary member of the New Zealand Institute of Foresters, made facilities available at Victoria University College.

To section the pine needles, Hansson set up a safety razor in a hand microtome, which was later replaced with a Bausch and Lomb swinging microtome. Stained cross sections were mounted on microscopic slides. Photomicrographs were taken using a Graphic camera with its lens removed. The camera was then superimposed on a microscope without its eyepiece. To keep out light, black velvet was wound around the connection between the camera and microscope. Both instruments were clamped to a wooden frame with an attached 75-watt frosted light bulb. Forest guard Arthur Forbes took most of the photographs using a green cloth during exposure. Mary investigated forty different pine species, probably using the photomicrographs rather than the microscope. She examined the shapes of cross sections, which varied with the number of leaves in the fascicle, the number and position of resin ducts and stomata, and the nature of hypodermal tissue. It is likely she sorted each species to indicate feature similarities and differences, and like previous investigators found it impossible to identify a species from one character. Both Mexican weeping pine (*Pinus patula*) and Canary Island pine (*Pinus canariensis*) were three-needle pines, but Canary Island species had marginal ducts whereas Mexican weeping species showed two median and two internal resin ducts. She found structural differences between big cone pine (*Pinus coulteri*) grown in Rotorua and the same species in the South Island. The study was revised in 1933 and published in the *Transactions and Proceedings of the Royal Society of New Zealand* the following year.[21] Although the article suggests nearly all species came from Rotorua, State Forest Service memos indicate they were collected around New Zealand.

Trans. N.Z. Inst., Vol. 63.

PLATE 53.

FIG. 1.—Swinging microtome fitted with special knife.

FIG. 2.—Photomicrographic apparatus.

Face p. 568

The equipment used in Mary's experiment to analyse the microscopic features of pine leaves for an identification key. TRANSACTIONS AND PROCEEDING OF THE ROYAL SOCIETY OF NEW ZEALAND

Mary's work on the microscopical features of pine needles did not go unnoticed. In 1966 Joyce Lanyon referenced Mary's findings when she produced a card key to *Pinus* based on needle anatomy for the New South Wales Forestry Commission.[22] Some later pine identification systems use information similar to Mary's key, such as the number and placement of resin canals.[23] Few people now have the patience or equipment to study needle cross sections, so her other findings are unlikely to be used, and the names and taxonomy have changed, for example, *Pinus laricio* and *Pinus austriaca* are now classed as subspecies of *Pinus nigra*, whereas in the 1930s they were considered separate species.[24] No slides, photographs or specimens from Mary's experiment survive, and as wet collections need regular alcohol replenishment, Mary's spirit specimens were unlikely to have kept in good condition outside of a well-maintained collection. Only two of Mary's botanical specimens are held in the Scion collection: pressed and dried mistletoe (*Ileostylus micranthus*) and matai (*Prumnopitys taxifolia*), which have no recorded collection dates or locations.

Mary's sample plot review

When the Rotorua experimental programme and the pine needle study finished, Mary was faced with the question of further work. She had extensive experience with experimental afforestation plots, but had recently worked less with sample plots for volume/growth studies as these were considered to be the regional officers' responsibility. Unfortunately, routine plantation work took precedence over treatments like pruning, or monitoring and remeasuring trees, and the government's use of unemployed labour often meant those who worked in the plots lacked experience. Their work methods varied and were frequently below standard; plots were neglected or not suitable for the prevailing winds and sometimes their locations were not even recorded. Whether Mary suggested she look into the issues is unknown, but Hansson and Phillips Turner wanted her kept occupied, so she was instructed to locate and inspect all sample plots in each region, and compile a schedule. Phillips Turner informed Bill Morrison that Mary would be returning to Rotorua for the sample plot review and asked him to assist her: she would be subject to the usual disciplinary control.[25]

Mary conducted her review from January to March 1930. By then she owned an Austin 10 she used to get around,[26] and as Phillips Turner was away the acting director Alexander McGavock approved her application for a travel allowance to use the car for the purpose.[27] Mary examined the Rotorua plots and then headed to Murupara, primarily to be out of Morrison's way. The ranger at Wairapukao, Sam Hunter, had kept Mary's afforestation experimental plots up to date, so she included them, the volume/growth plots and other studies in her review. Rotorua was the largest conservation area with seventy-three plots mainly in the Whakarewarewa, Waiotapu and Kaingaroa plantations. Mary discovered some of their previous data had been omitted, which made the research information useless. Seven plots at Waiotapu were given standard thinning treatment and their records brought up to date. In 1916 when forestry was under the Department of Lands, Halbert Goudie had established native forest sample plots at Mamaku to investigate the growth of indigenous species and the effect of combining exotics with natives. Mary recommended these plots be abandoned because the radiata pine and redwood trees no longer grew under typical bush underplanting conditions. Valuable data could, however, be gathered on exotic species growth as understorey in tawa-milled bush.[28] The Rotorua sample plot work was extensive and Mary recommended adjusting the remeasurement times to ensure the work was more likely to be done.

Hansson instructed Mary to go to Karioi and Whangamomona, and suggested forestry student Millicent Brooke could help her at Kohuratahi. As Brooke was expected to meet her own expenses,[29] Mary decided to pay her. She asked Hansson to send a camera stand, and suggested he come to inspect the underplanting bush plots he had established at Kohuratahi; he could travel from Wellington to Whangamomona in a day, either Monday or Saturday, and she would fetch him.[30] Mary and Brooke worked there for thirteen days. They repainted numbers and bands on timber trees, and manufactured and painted totara stakes to denote kahikatea seedlings in two plots, one of which contained regenerating kahikatea and rimu marked for periodic growth measurements. When it rained, they updated data and made tracings for ecological plans. When the Kohuratahi survey was completed, Mary proceeded to Palmerston North to review sample plot records before travelling to Ohakune. At Karioi she collected data from exotic species plots to study the effect of different elevations and spacing distances on growth.

Forest ranger Norman Dolamore had established plots in the Waimarino defence reserve (now the army base in Waiouru)[31] and Mary suggested he also include the small trial species groups planted in 1916 by the Department of Prisons and in 1924 by the Forest Service. The trees would provide growth data for high elevation forestation and were eight years ahead of recent plantings. She located nineteen sample plots and then returned to head office to learn her travel allowance had been extended to cover the South Island.[32, 33]

In the Nelson region, she visited Rough'ns Creek, Golden Downs, Rainy River Valley, Dumgree and Tasman West, locating fifteen plots. At Golden Downs, ranger Robert Pollock was selecting and demarcating plots for future growth studies. Mary helped him choose a sample plot area in a block of redwoods. She travelled to Greymouth then Hokitika, spending two days inspecting sample plots in the rimu experimental area and at Woodstock nursery. Westland had forty-two plots, some on dredge-tailings; she found the work was up to date with height,

Mary's Austin 10, loaded with debris after a working bee at her bach. According to her niece Helen Baxter, passengers had to get out of the car for it to be able to climb steep hills. SUTHERLAND/GRAY FAMILY

Millicent Brooke, the only female forestry student at Auckland University College, on a field trip to the Swanson experimental station, 1929. Although Millicent was in her final year of study, she did not complete her degree. AUCKLAND LIBRARIES HERITAGE COLLECTIONS

growth and strike recorded, but general plot features had not been recorded. Plantations established in 1922 on mental hospital lands showed less vigorous growth than in the previous year, and she wondered if the rimu experimental area, planted three years later, might also deteriorate.

Although Mary's Rotorua programme had been discontinued, research continued on the ponderosa pine specimens grown from seed collected in North America, so while she was in Canterbury she visited Mr J Dean's plantations at Darfield to collect material for further investigations. She then proceeded to Hanmer and Balmoral and located thirty-seven sample plots where past calculations were incorrect: some plots were unsuitable for representing growth data and others were established on unsuitable sites. Trees infested by woodwasp (*Sirex noctilio*) had been removed without recording stem measurements. It was clear a standard procedure was needed. Mary met ranger Robert Collett at Invercargill, and in Longwood Valley they inspected three regeneration plots of Southland silver beech (*Nothofagus menziesii*) grown from seed cast in 1928; the regeneration was sparse. Mary recommended establishing similar plots in an area of freer regeneration. Thirty-one Southland sample plots were located in the Dusky Hills and Conical Hills plantations, at Tapanui nursery, the Beaumont side of the Blue Mountains, Longwood, Tahakopa, and the Naseby plantation. The Dusky Hills records were uniform and complete, but lacked plot demarcation information.

Mary's report to the silviculture research officer suggested the multiplicity of routine sample plots to determine species mortality was impractical.[34] She recommended they cease as the universal practice now was to count surviving species on representative lines scattered over an entire planted area. Also, establishing and maintaining a sample plot was wasted effort if the plot's purpose was misunderstood, and site selection seemed influenced by ease of access rather than suiting the purpose. Plots were often too small for preliminary growth studies, though some could be enlarged.[35] She recommended that many sample plots be abandoned, and for closer co-ordination and technical supervision of others. Spasmodic remeasurements and thinning, and widely varying procedures made it difficult to check data and use the results. Long-term quantitative investigation results were lacking when growth data at different periods of a crop was necessary to define future treatments with certainty. A sustained, standardised mensuration process was required. Mary suggested a mobile staff of one or two be relegated to sample plot work to catch up with plot establishment arrears and gain urgently required information on growth conditions and thinning processes, and their effects. This was needed to determine future production economics for the different forest products from existing plantations. Besides standardising methods, establishing additional permanent growth study plots, revising data collection forms and compiling a register, Mary proposed that all reports from the regions with field data and rough workings used to measure and calculate yields should be stored in separate folders at head office. Regional offices could hold copies to refer to during remeasurement.

The NZIF official seal and the journal

Despite her difficulties in the organisational hierarchy, Mary had earned considerable respect from many colleagues. By 1930 the New Zealand Institute of Foresters was an incorporated society, and though she was nominated for the secretary–treasurer position, Frank Hutchinson was elected. The institute's forty-six members were asked to submit a native flora design for the official seal, and Frank Foster persuaded Mary to submit her sketch of a fruiting rimu sprig against a backdrop of mountains.[36] Hutchinson wrote to Mary saying her design struck the right note for him and Charles Foweraker.[37] Both men had studied rimu in Westland's taxad forests, Foweraker studying its ecology and regeneration[38] and Hutchinson its forest management.[39]

Hutchinson had submitted a design of a rimu seedling with a banner to include a motto and encircled by 'New Zealand Institute of Foresters'. He informed Mary the idea of rimu being New Zealand's future hope in forestry held a strong attraction for him, and he described his design as miserable compared to hers, which was easily the best. But Foweraker believed botanical adherence to the typical form required the spray to hang down in a weeping or dacrydic effect: "Such a form might not have the artistic form or balance your design has, but it would not be open to criticism. Would you consider doing a second design? If required we have fruiting sprays in the herbarium."

Mary tried, but her design did not tally with Foweraker's idea of correct botanical habit. She wrote to Hutchinson: "If you look at a rimu branch, the subsidiary stem comes off the main stem at an angle of about 45 degrees and then droops over, with the ultimate tips turned upwards vertically, so the position I gave it is not very far out, except for the exaggerated curl

Receipt for the rubber stamp of the NZIF official seal created from Mary Sutherland's design. The rimu sprig and mountain are used in the institute's current logo. NZIF RECORDS

around the whole branch. If you can improve it, just do it. I am rather keen on the species, as typical of the preponderating podocarps of the NZ bush."[40] Her design for the common seal was approved at the AGM in May 1931.

Members were asked whether the institute should publish transactions, form a library, give forestry student prizes, or build a cash reserve, and would they rebut a newspaper's suggestion that the State Forest Service merge with the Department of Lands as an economy measure?[41] The institute was also asked to consider jointly publishing *Te Kura Ngahere* with the Canterbury College School of Forestry for a two-year trial. Because of the economic depression, new subscribers were few and Forestry League members were not renewing their subscriptions. In the past the college met the shortfall between subscriptions and publishing costs, but their publication grant from the government was eight months in arrears and threatened with a heavy cut.[42] Institute members bravely accepted the proposal and Tom Birch was nominated as the institute's representative on the editorial committee.[43]

The publication of *Te Kura Ngahere* transferred wholly from Canterbury University College to NZIF in 1934; the final joint issue included the subtitle *The New Zealand Journal of Forestry*.[44] Perhaps it was a combination of the school's wish to expand the journal and form closer links with NZIF, as well the production costs, the economic depression and closure of the forestry school, that caused the change in publishers. Frank Hutchinson wrote in the editorial: "As most readers of *Te Kura Ngahere* are already aware, the School of Forestry at Canterbury College is to close its doors temporarily, due to financial stringency, at the end of the current year. Publication of the journal by Canterbury College will, therefore, cease with this issue." The journal's editorial committee were Hutchinson (editor 1928–34), Tom Birch (editor 1935–41) and Charles Foweraker from the School of Forestry.[45]

A return to the South Island

Arnold Hansson, who was responsible for staff training, was a stickler for doing things the right way. Many rangers, aside from Mary, found him challenging. Cecil Smith, previously the Nelson conservator, replaced Hansson as chief inspector in 1930.[46] In a 1977 NZIF newsletter article, Frederick Buckingham described him as "flamboyant, with an astounding memory". Smith knew about twelve languages, spoke with precise diction, and was generous and likeable.[47] He wrote to Edward Phillips Turner about Mary's recommendation for a mobile staff to maintain the sample plots.[48] For nearly ten years regional staff had been unable to catch up on measurement arrears and initiate new plots. Alternative suggestions to a mobile staff were to operate a special staff under the silvicultural research officer, Arnold Hansson, or send head office staff. But Hansson was conducting extensive research in Waipoua Forest with enough work for five years, so Smith recommended the latter and suggested purchasing and equipping a Ford utility van for the following year. In the meantime Miss Sutherland should be granted a travel allowance for her car in the North Island, and in the South Island she could use rail and a cycle. Student labour would need supervision, but the lady forestry student in her final year (presumably Millicent Brooke) could work with her. This "would overcome the past difficulty" — presumably Smith meant men supervising a woman student.

Edward Phillips Turner sent an unsigned note agreeing that sample plot work was important.[49] Head office staff could undertake present work, but in the future, they should use the silviculturalist. "An arrangement other than the lady student is to be made, and a car allowance is so liable to abuse that it is generally undesirable to grant. Accommodation with local rangers can be arranged, or failing that she can stay at the nearest hotel and use a cycle." Smith informed Mary that the director had decided there would be no extra labour for sample plot work during the fiscal year. A car-mileage allowance was not permitted, and to save money she must take only inevitable remeasurements; gaps in the data would not be her responsibility. She was to submit a summer work scheme that did not require a car, and used only regional labouring staff. He enclosed guidelines for keeping silvicultural operation records, which were "woefully scattered and soon irrecoverable". For the permanent sample plots established at each station the records could cover thinning and pruning response; the forest compartment, area, and species; original condition and treatment applied; and the date, costs and timber volume recovered. Information should be analysed, re-assembled by forests, kept with skeleton data for future working plans and filed regionally.[50]

Mary submitted her sample plot programme to Phillips Turner. She would do the recording herself and use regional labour. In January 1931 she intended to work on sample plots last measured in 1923: two at Conical Hill, eight at Dusky Hills and one at the Tapanui nursery. She would undertake measurement, classification and thinning on eight Hanmer growth study plots partly measured in 1929. During March and April, she would take standard measurements and classify two volume/growth study plots at Kaingaroa and one at Whakarewarewa. Her visits would be arranged and regional officers notified.[51]

In Southland she did extra calculations to ensure previously inconsistent data were comparable. In mid-February 1931, Mary left Dusky Plantation for the Tapanui nursery plantation at Glenkenich to measure a radiata pine sample plot established in 1915 by William Fraser. She recommended a light thinning, which required four hours labour. From Dunedin, she and the director of reserves went to inspect the Ross Creek plantation plots of Japanese larch and Sitka spruce. At Hanmer Forest, she worked with Maurice Skipworth to thin sections of a ponderosa pine plot. Large-diameter radiata trees on three plots had died, one infested with Sirex woodwasps. They laid out a plot to replace 15-year-old radiata

Mary Sutherland in compartment D7, Kaingaroa Forest, taking a measurement after light
thinning of *Pinus laricio* during sample plot maintenance, 1932. Her companion is probably
Maurice Skipworth, who is mentioned in the sample plot record. SCION

Mary Sutherland in nursery beds, c.1932. ARCHIVES NZ

pines and sub-plots of Corsican pines (*Pinus laricio*) originally planted in 1911. One sub-plot would be the control to show the effects of different grades of thinning. Mary inspected new species plots at Golden Downs and visited the Rough'ns Creek nursery. She believed the heavy losses of Scots pine, which had been grown from Spanish seed sown in 1929, resulted from the unsuitable site. At Meade's nursery in Motupiko she discussed regional plots with the conservator, and measurements and records with ranger Robert Pollock.[52]

The silvicultural management fund may have been depleted, for a year passed before Mary finished the sample plot work in Rotorua. Meanwhile, regional staff forwarded their treatment reports to her and she compiled the sample plot schedule. Her work was affected when rangers shifted to other plantations, or ran out of paint to mark trees for identification.

Into the Urewera Ranges

By the time Mary returned to Rotorua in February 1932, Edward Phillips Turner had retired and Alexander McGavock was the new director.[53] Her Wairapukao experimental plots were due for remeasurement, and yield and thinning studies waited in the Kaingaroa and Tarawera forests. Mary had her own horse in Rotorua and rode in jodhpurs.[54] When she was in the region the *Auckland Star* reported Miss Sutherland was undertaking a riding tour of the Urewera country with Sister K Smith from the Government Sanatorium and Miss Hinton of Ngongotaha.[55] Mary wrote about the experience in a letter to her sister Kate Gray. She called her horse "the nag" and referred to her companions as Smithy and Hinty "who rode thoroughbreds". They were headed for Waikaremoana and Waikareiti where the State Forest Service had reserves, and their trip was an "outing among friends".

Rain at Taneatua delayed the start of their trek, so on the first day they rode straight to the next intended stop where an old man offered shelter in his house, but they slept in his hut disturbed by "the inhabitants in the pillows", presumably fleas. As they made for the Maungapohatu track they met a young Maori who offered them plums and mushrooms. He was interested in their horses and Smithy bobbed her horse for him. Further on, a Maori family offered accommodation in their whare, but instead they pitched their tent, and it rained all night. It took ten hours to travel 19 miles (31 kilometres) the next day. The track became steep and winding with drops of 100 feet (30 metres), slips and fallen trees. Twice they had to remove the load from the packhorse so it could get up after it fell. In the mid-afternoon a Maori appeared: "Our nags were so heartened by the sight of a horse ahead they dashed on, then the track became not good and it was lucky we had no broken legs." Maungapohatu was only 3 or 4 miles away (5 or 6 kilometres), but it took over an hour to get there. The sleepers that paved the muddy track

This Urewera scene, 1927, is similar to country that Mary and her companions trekked over on horseback towards Maungapohatu and Lake Waikaremoana.
AUCKLAND LIBRARIES HERITAGE COLLECTIONS

and bridged the gullies were sometimes missing or sprang up under the horses' hooves. The track led through a lagoon and bog where horses had previously been lost: "The horses had a [mud] bath, us included. Our final descent was as steep as the side of a house." They arrived 'rather moist' at the Presbyterian mission house where they were given tea and a whare. The rain continued all night and the next day they attended a Ringatū service at the pa and then a missionary service that didn't much interest the Maori. Rua Kenana, the Tuhoe prophet who had set up the Maungapohatu community, was away. "We passed him and his retinue at Matahi. The remaining Maoris were having a good time [in his absence]."

The missionaries were Ann Henry (Sister Annie or Hihita) and the Reverend John Laughton (Hoani). Three mission teachers were present when Mary and her fellow travellers arrived; she thought they were inspired to stay.[56] They had holidays three times a year, but left only if the track was open. "[The] tracks are the worst any of us have seen. Everything is packed in. They occasionally get fresh meat, no fresh milk, little fruit and pay the Maoris £4 per cord for firewood, by Rua's order. They cook on an open fire in the sitting room and do everything — from nursing the sick, to preaching — when the Reverend is away." Mary described the settlement as rather dismal, and they decided to leave rather than risk being blocked in.

The track out of Maungapohatu was worse than coming in. It was steep, and runnels of rushing water had scoured beds over 4 feet deep and more than 2 feet wide: "We had our work cut out." Overhanging branches meant they had to take care their legs were not crushed, and bend their heads "so as not to get brained". They didn't have time to admire much scenery because they had to keep an eye on the track and where their nags were heading. An English boy hunting with Maori led them around a big slip, but then the bank gave way somersaulting the packhorse into a bog. The horse lay quietly while being unharnessed, then calmly stood up. They stayed overnight at Ruatahuna. The next day they had planned to ride half way to Waikaremoana, but there was no horse paddock *en route* so they continued on, managing to get through the worst slips before dark and arriving at Waikaremoana Lake House at 10:00 pm. The next day's weather was perfect for a launch trip across the lake to Waikareiti. They wore 'civilised' clothes and ate dainty sandwiches while the guide boiled the billy. The following day the launch took Mary to catch the service car to Murupara, from where a Forest Service lorry delivered her to Wairapukao camp where she lodged with Mrs Hunter. Smithy and Hinty returned with the horses, travelling on a new road up the coast through Te Teko.

Mary's subsequent sample plot review highlighted forest mensuration issues and the need to institute uniform procedures.[57] Cecil Smith chaired an informal meeting on sample plots management which Mary attended with Owen Jones from New Zealand Perpetual Forests (the largest afforestation company) and Charles Foweraker and Frank Hutchinson from the Canterbury University College School of Forestry.[58] Fifteen decisions were reached at the meeting, but the subsequent meetings, although planned, may not have occurred. The country was in a depression and by September 1931 New Zealand had over 51,000 unemployed men and more than 37,000 on relief work.[59] The State Forest Service was experiencing financial and labour problems.

In her autobiography, *A Fence Around the Cuckoo*, Ruth Parke wrote about the hard, physical work, coupled with frost, wind and cold, that her father suffered while planting Kaingaroa Forest during the Depression. Mary sympathised with the men's reluctance to work in such harsh conditions, and she wrote in a report "only good men should be employed". However, economic constraints impacted on employing sufficient labour, and having once before lost her position to an economic downturn while in Britain, Mary must have been wary of her own job security. With her previous investigations programme curtailed, her sample plot work had given only temporary reprieve.

In 1932 a National Expenditure Commission, appointed to determine how to cut government costs, presented its final report to Parliament. It recommended afforestation cease, the number of professional staff at the State Forest Service be reduced, and forest engineering and research be severely curtailed or eliminated.[60] The service's head office required an immediate overhaul and redundant officers retired. The staff list in the *New Zealand Gazette* was considerably depleted. Hansson was a casualty; he had spent most of his career at the top of the forestry hierarchy and was NZIF president from 1928 to 1930. He was demoted from chief inspector to silvicultural research officer, and when he left the Forest Service he worked as a forester for New Zealand Railways until his retirement.[61]

The work to complete the sample plot records gave Mary a few months grace before she too, again, lost her forestry position. She was 40 years old. Before leaving, she prepared the report 'Forest resources of New Zealand' to present at the Fifth Pacific Science Congress in Canada. Her paper describes New Zealand's

Unemployment relief work in the North Island, 1933. Men employed in State Forest Service camps in the Taupo district planted approximately 15,000,000 trees – Douglas fir, Oregon pine and three varieties of pinus — which came from the Rotorua nurseries. There were ten camps and the men, single and married, receive standard relief camp wages. Almost 500 unemployed relief workers were in the camps on the Kaingaroa Plains, Taupo district. Top left: 1. Preparing for planting. 2. The camp at Waipai. 3. The Waimahia camp about 16 miles (26 kilometres) from Taupo, accommodating 100 men, 4. Men at a camp. AUCKLAND LIBRARIES HERITAGE COLLECTIONS

indigenous forests, its tree planting history and afforestation; the draft holds a pressed ginkgo leaf.[62] We don't know whether Mary attended the congress after she left the Forest Service, though the abstract of her paper is published in its proceedings.[63] The day she departed is also unknown, but it was probably early in 1933. Her contributions of co-ordinating afforestation investigations, the forestry in schools programme and her sample plot work, helped build this country's knowledge of plantation forestry, yet she was never promoted above the role of forest assistant. Her final year's salary was less than her earnings in 1925 when her temporary position became permanent.[64]

Mary maintained her interest in forestry and continued her membership of NZIF and the Forestry League as both organisations aimed to sustain a forest consciousness in the population. The previous Forest Service director, Edward Phillips Turner, liked her suggestion that NZIF members, who were nearly all State Forest Service employees, should liaise with the league. He suggested to the NZIF secretary, Tom Birch, that members attend the Forestry League AGM: "Without public interest the Government will starve the Forest Service, restrict its activities, and quite likely amalgamate it with Lands or another department."[65]

Mary no doubt would have been saddened when the current Forest Service director Alexander McGavock informed the director of education that assistance for school forestry would no longer be forthcoming: it was not self-supporting and a drain on limited resources.[66] Reduced funding and a depleted workforce of knowledgeable people meant the Forest Service was no longer able to maintain its assets. People had been suffering through the economic depression for some time, and with few options to earn money, some saw timber as a way to improve their situation. However, they weren't familiar with the use of exotic wood, so the indigenous forests Ellis had aimed to protect were at risk. The biggest threat was to kauri, which provided timber for housing and boats and was used for carving. Economic events had set the scene for widespread forest devastation, and huge trees, hundreds of years old, were felled. Many kauri left standing were tapped for their resin, which was used for several purposes including fire starters and varnish.[67] The resin protected the trees by healing over cuts and if trees were damaged when tapped or bled too often, they died. With the forestry in schools programme cancelled, there seemed little hope the country would develop a forest consciousness in the future.

Change did come, but not for some time. Pat Entrican succeeded Alex McCavock as director of the Forest Service in 1939. He wanted to make people aware of this devastation, which worsened during World War Two and the post-war land clearance for agriculture. Entrican set in motion a national forest survey, from 1946–1955, to record the extent of timber and natural regeneration of native forests and create an afforestation plan.

CHAPTER 5

FROM FORESTRY to BOTANY

A new challenge

While Mary worked for the State Forest Service she contributed specimens to the Dominion Museum's herbarium in Wellington, and on one occasion accompanied the museum's botanist Ellen (Ellie) Heine on a collection trip to Kapiti Island. Mary joined the museum's staff when she left the Forest Service in 1933.[1] Sydney Markham recorded Mary's job as a librarian when he visited to gather information for the *Directory of Museums and Art Galleries in Australia and New Zealand*,[2] though the *New Zealand Gazette* classified her status as clerical and the museum's director, Walter Oliver, described her position as a librarian and part-time botanical assistant.[3,4] Early in her career Mary's responsibilities as a librarian would have left little time for herbarium work; each year through an international exchange the museum received around thirty cases of books from the Smithsonian and other institutes, which were recorded and distributed throughout the Dominion.[5]

When Oliver was appointed as director he went about purchasing new collections and undertook to mount and label the herbarium's badly neglected specimens and have them stored in insect- and dust-proof boxes. He had appointed Ellie Heine as a botanical assistant in 1929, and after training, put her in charge of the botanical department.[6] Oliver encouraged his staff to make regular field trips to build the museum's collections, and Mary, used to being outdoors, welcomed this. By April 1934, she was collecting botanical samples on Mt Tauhara's summit, at Ruapehu's base and the Silica Springs, in the upper Tawhia Stream, on the Waimarino Plains, at Waiouru, east of the Motu Range and at Morere.[7] She may also have accompanied Ellie Heine on a trip into the Canterbury high country in 1935, as the museum's records, now Te Papa's database, show she collected specimens in January and February that year around Cass, Castle Hill and the Torlesse Range.[8] It is thought Mary contributed nearly nine hundred plant specimens,[9] most of which came from her old haunts: the Mamaku Plateau, Atiamuri, Wairakei, Mt Egmont (Taranaki) and around Mt Ruapehu.[10]

Leonard Cockayne's collection was also being incorporated into the herbarium, and during the process Mary would meet with him at the Forest Service's head office on the corner of Ballance and Featherston streets in Wellington. Cockayne was nearly blind, and the surroundings would have been more familiar to him than the cramped museum building. Lindsay Poole, who first met Mary when he was a cadet working in the Whakarewarewa nursery, was also present when Cockayne dictated his last papers to Mary. At the conclusion of the visit he escorted Cockayne to the train station.[11]

Mary's tribute to Cockayne when he died in 1934 was published in the British journal *Forestry*. Delegates at the 1928 British Empire Forestry Conference would have remembered him: Mary described him as one of the few botanists who attempted to relate New Zealand forest ecology to the possibilities of silvicultural management. His southern beech (*Nothofagus*) studies were immensely valuable, and he guided and encouraged young workers: "His scathing indictment of the spoon-fed generation was a treat, which had to be heard to be appreciated" and "he was a stimulating, kindly friend, whose presence on a field trip contributed much to the wit and inspiration of the party".[12]

The old Dominion Museum behind Parliament, Wellington. Originally known as the Colonial Museum, it opened in 1865 when Wellington became the capital, and was renamed in 1907 when New Zealand became a Dominion. In 1936 the museum relocated to a purpose-built building in Buckle Street, now owned by Massey University on the site of today's Pukeahu National War Memorial. The museum was renamed the National Museum in 1972, and Te Papa Tongarewa in 1992. TE PAPA ARCHIVES

When Ellie Heine resigned in 1935 to take up a position as assistant to Charles Foweraker at Canterbury University College, Oliver recommended that Mary replace her as botanist. She was appointed, but her position remained classified as clerical. Oliver asked the Internal Affairs undersecretary to appoint someone to take over Mary's library work who could classify books and periodicals, make a card index of useful articles, and assist with general typing when required:[13] Josephine Benton was appointed to the position.

The old Dominion Museum behind Parliament was claustrophobic and infested with insects and mice — no doubt the cat in the staff photograph kept the vermin at bay. Rotten weatherboards let in rain, and pillars had given way, so the museum's best collections were stored at the Dominion Farmers' Institute[14] in the same building as the State Forest Service's head office.

The museum's previous directors, Augustus Hamilton and Dr Allan Thomson, had unsuccessfully tried to obtain a new building, but Oliver succeeded by agreeing to combine the museum with the National Art Gallery, which enabled access to the Society of Arts funding. By raising additional money and with a government subsidy, construction of the new museum commenced in 1933 on the previous site of the Mount Cook Gaol in Buckle Street.[15] Preparations to move into the new museum included labelling the specimens and organising educational exhibits to illustrate the Dominion's forestry, agriculture and fisheries industries.

A kauri exhibit was proposed for the opening, so Mary had arranged a trip to Waipoua Forest and Whangarei for December 1935. The museum had purchased Frank Peat's kauri gum collection and she intended to visit his Titirangi private museum.[16] Heine, on leave from Canterbury University College, had agreed to accompany her, but Internal Affairs did not approve the trip and the arrangements were cancelled.[17] Two weeks later, Mary organised an expedition to collect a 'vegetable sheep' (*Raoulia eximia*)[18] and other alpine specimens from Mt Torlesse.[19] Walter Oliver was keen to obtain a sheep as botanist Lucy Cranwell[20] had collected a fine specimen for Auckland Museum. The trip was approved with the travel costs capped. A Public Service vehicle was ordered and the Wellington postmaster relayed details to Christchurch for a five-seater Ford or Austin without a driver. A carrier was to be added and the back seat removed to store specimens. Heine arranged accommodation at the university's Cass Biological Station and at Enys Hut, and the party also included students Betty Flint, who became a specialist in desmid (green) algae,[21] and Don Brooker, later a school teacher. They were accompanied by the Dominion Museum photographer John Salmon, an entomologist trained by Eileen Plank. Salmon recollected Mary was a "thrifty Scotch lady", a good botanist and a pleasant, conscientious person with an even temper and fine sense of humour.[22]

The interior of the Colonial Museum, Wellington c.1910. ALEXANDER TURNBULL LIBRARY

Dominion Museum staff, 1932. Standing: William McKay (custodian), William Phillips (ethnologist), Charles Lindsay (photographer), Tom Heberley (carver). Seated: Eileen Plank (entomologist), Miss Ida Gray (office worker, holding cat), Walter Oliver (director), Ellen Heine (botanist) and Mary Sutherland. Ursula Tewsley (librarian) is absent. TE PAPA ARCHIVES

During the trip, Mary collected specimens at Arthur's Pass, Lake Sarah, Ribbonwood Valley, Castle Hill, Porters Pass, and the Thomas and Porter rivers junction. Salmon collected high-montane butterfly species, cicadas, wetas and grasshoppers. On the day they had planned to collect the vegetable sheep they were snowbound, so Mary telegraphed Oliver: "No possibility sheep before Wednesday. Barometer falling. Instruct whether remain." Expecting Oliver to order their immediate return to Wellington, they broke camp and fed their left-over bread to the Castle Hill Station chickens, but Oliver replied they were to stay, collect a vegetable sheep and wire the result. It was too late to rescue the bread, so they made do with baked beans. When the snow melted, they climbed Mt Torlesse in glorious weather and found a 4 x 2 foot (1.2 x 0.6 metre) vegetable sheep specimen. After it was dislodged with a pickaxe, it took four people to stretcher it down the mountain. It weighed 128 pounds (58 kilograms) on the woolshed scales. The sheep was cased and consigned to Wellington, but Oliver telegraphed that it had not arrived. Mary replied he should enquire at the Union Steam Ship Company, the Harbour Board sheds, and the Public Works Department, which responded that unless cartage was arranged the case would still be at the wharf shed.

The sheep was eventually located and stayed at the Dominion Museum for many years, other than during the war when Defence took over the building and the sheep went to stay in Kate and Dory Gray's living room in Wellington.[23] It was eventually returned, but because its condition deteriorated the sheep was deaccessioned in the 1980s.[24] Te Papa has another on display, and also holds other specimens from the expedition, including the bloodstain lichen (*Haematomma alpinum*) collected at Dry Creek Ridge.[25] Mary wrote letters of thanks to those who had helped, including the students Don Brooker and Betty Flint, Professor Edward Percival at Canterbury University College for use of the biological station, and James Poulton for use of the Enys Hut, which Mary described as a lovely spot for mustering a vegetable sheep, fossicking botanically, entomologically and geologically. She regretted she could not obtain more seed for Mrs Poulton, but Miss Heine had a little, and seeing the larch set against a background of beech had warmed her heart.[26]

The field trips and preparing exhibits for the new museum's opening interfered with other work Mary now had responsibility for, including the herbarium's international exchange programme. After packages arrived from the University of California Department of Botany, Mary wrote back apologising that her exchange lagged due to lack of herbarium staff and the time required to prepare exhibits, but she would reciprocate with material as soon as possible. She noted from previous correspondence that the university offered an exchange collection of fungi, which would be acceptable.[27]

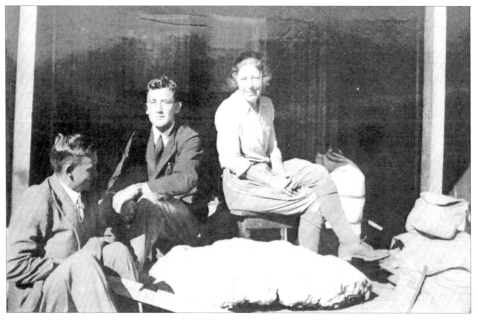

Mary with Don Brooker, John Salmon and the 'vegetable sheep'. TE PAPA ARCHIVES

A trip in the Fox Glacier region when Mary (right) was working at the Dominion Museum. SUTHERLAND/GRAY FAMILY

The new Dominion Museum

For the forthcoming official opening, Mary wanted her botanical examples displayed in the best possible way with accompanying details concise and clear. Not yet satisfied with some exhibits, she wrote to people around the world seeking information, botanical specimens, photographs and product samples. For her morphological exhibit, Ross Bean, assistant professor of botany at the University of Hawaii sent a 12–15 pound (5–7 kg) fruit from the specimen sausage tree (*Kigelia africana*) growing on the Honolulu campus.[28] To demonstrate rubber she obtained material of various species; the India rubber bush (*Ficus elastica*); Castilla rubber tree (*Castilla elastica*); the Guayule desert rubber shrub (*Parthenium argentatum*), and Para rubber tree (*Hevea brasiliensis*).[29]

She asked the Samoan Agriculture Department for 'anything botanical' to show plant uses in the Pacific islands.[30] A marijuana (*Cannabis indica*) specimen for the medicinal plant section came from the Le Zecuelpa Rubber Laboratory in Mexico; and a cotton plant (*Gossypium hirsutum*) arrived from the Brisbane Botanic Gardens. Leaf, flower and fruit specimens from the silk rubber tree (*Funtumia elastica*) came from Lagos, along with crude rubber samples and a description of the production process. Until 1928, European firms bought this crude product in considerable quantities to manufacture tyres. Firestone sent their pamphlet 'From crude rubber to motor tyre'.[31]

Bill Morrison, the Rotorua conservator, provided exotic species in the cotyledon stage and planting-out condition, which Mary had requested from Forest Service director Alexander McGavock.[32] George Fowlie, the gardener at Kingseat Mental Hospital, sent a peanut plant with attached fruit on the instructions of the medical superintendent at Avondale (probably Mary's brother-in-law Dory). Fowlie included a note which said: "The few hazelnut trees grown from seed are not yet bearing fruit, but a reliable Porirua patient, now resident at Kingseat, informed me there are good-sized trees growing in the Porirua orchard near a row of pines."[33]

After receiving sixty-eight fungi specimens under the museum exchange scheme, followed by seventy specimens, including twenty-seven buckwheat (*Eriogonum*), Mary replied to the sender, Herbert Mason, associate curator at the University of California herbarium, that she was unable to reciprocate due to work pressure and lack of staff. She asked about the preservation methods, for the thick-stemmed specimens retained good green colour and the leaves of the hawthorn (*Crataegus*) specimen were not shrivelled or crushed.[34] However, not all the specimens she received from other sources arrived in good condition, for example, the cacao pods from Western Samoa for the chocolate exhibit were mouldy.[35]

Mary wrote to the American Museum of Natural History about methods to make accessories for the exhibitions and received a pamphlet, 'Building the museum group', from the associate chief, Albert Butler, who promised Mary a copy of his planned article on making foliage from crepe paper.[36]

The accumulating exhibits added to the museum's usual clutter, so Andrew Fletcher, managing director of Fletcher Construction, made storage available in the new premises. In March 1936, a few months before the official opening, the shift into the new museum began,[37] and Mary continued writing letters, dealing with specimens and creating her displays. In the month before the museum opened, she worked sixty-four hours overtime.[38]

The official opening of the National Group—Art Gallery, Dominion Museum, and War Memorial Carillon—took place on 1 August 1936. Despite the bad weather, about 4000 people attended and Governor General Viscount Galway opened the building with a golden key.[39] The *Evening Post* reported that the old, white-painted, two-storeyed museum was pitiful, pretentious, and without dimensions sufficient to attract visitors. For seventy years it had squatted behind Parliament Buildings, housing Maori relics and items, without the space they merited for display. The new museum was a modern institution, rivalling those in other countries and with ample display room. Maori arts were the museum's main feature, including several large canoes, the most notable being the war canoe *Teremoe* from Whanganui, which had been restored by staff member Tom Heberley. The sixteen hundred pieces of kauri gum from Frank Peat's collection were displayed in sixteen cases. They had been gathered over thirty years and were the largest, most valuable gum collection in the world.[40]

The botanical department was in the southwest corner of the new building, next to the entomology department. Compared to the old museum, Mary would have found the new facility spacious. The herbarium was a room of about 16 x 33 feet (5 x 10 metres) with benches around two walls for study and several rows of shelving for boxes and specimens. It was adjacent to the curator's office and across the corridor from an annexe.[41]

A steady stream of people visited the newly opened museum, while Mary continued adding to her exhibits. To demonstrate 'sugar', the Colonial Sugar Refining Company sent her six specimen canes each of dark green Malabar, dark brown Badila and light green Pompey, and photographs of cane cultivation in Fiji, and mills and refineries in Australia. She was promised flowering heads in May, and photos showing the stages from cane to refined products would be forwarded with small samples and descriptions of the manufacturing and refining processes. The Hawaiian Sugar Planters' Association also promised photographs.[42]

Seeking material to illustrate 'tea', her letters resulted in the Ceylon Tea Propaganda Board sending her publications featuring China's commercial tea industry, several models and herbarium sheets, Ceylon tea, industry photographs and a map of Ceylon.[43]

The National War Memorial, Dominion Museum and National Art Gallery ALEXANDER TURNBULL LIBRARY

Display cases of Frank Peat's kauri gum collection at the Dominion Museum, Wellington. ALEXANDER TURNBULL LIBRARY

Maori artefacts on display at the Dominion Museum, Wellington, c.1936. ALEXANDER TURNBULL LIBRARY

Mary's letter writing continued; for the mustard exhibit she wrote to J & J Colman, London, seeking specimens of black (*Brassica nigra*) and white mustard (*Brassica alba*). Colman replied that their Norwich works would prepare plants, seed, mustard flour and photos showing the manufacturing stages, and Mr Galvin from Colman-Keen in Wellington would personally deliver the material. For the 'cereals' exhibit, Mary asked the Lincoln Agricultural College Department of Cropping for either bearded and beardless wheat or Tartarian and common oat. The assistant director, John (Jack) Calder, replied that they would collect specimens at harvest time.[44]

In September 1936, the Dominion Museum was featured in four broadcasts to schools on the 2YA radio station in Wellington and 4YA in Dunedin.[45] Walter Oliver gave the introductory broadcast, the museum's assistant director William Phillips discussed the Maori exhibits, Mary talked about botany and John Salmon covered entomology. A pamphlet on the broadcasts was produced. In his broadcast Oliver described the museum: offices and workrooms were on the ground floor; the lecture hall seated over 350 people and had a film projector; exhibits were on the first floor; and the Maori hall contained waka taua (war canoes), pātaka (storehouses) and a large, carved wharenui (meeting house). Other halls held exhibits of china, glassware, foreign ethnological items, mammals, birds, fishes, insects, shells, kauri gum, and the botanical and geological collections. Mary's broadcast, aired in September, covered the meaning and uses of botany, indoor and outdoor botanical museums, and how plants in the museum were illustrated. The exhibits explained systematic botany (naming and describing plants), economic botany (plants for food, textiles and products) and ecology (the living conditions and habitat adaptation of plants).

Community and family

Mary was extensively involved in community activities that widened her social network and strengthened her work practice. She was a member of the botanical section of the Wellington Philosophical Society, which later became a branch of the Royal Society of New Zealand.[46] She was elected to the New Zealand Institute of Foresters Council for 1935–36,[47] and in 1936 served on the Forestry League Council with Edward Phillips Turner.[48]

Mary was proud of her university training, and advocated for women's rights to tertiary education. She joined the Wellington branch of the New Zealand Federation of University Women in 1932, was elected to its committee in 1933 and served on the hospitality subcommittee.[49] Wellington federation members extended their hospitality by welcoming emigrating and visiting women graduates at the wharf. Mary suggested possible speakers for meetings, helped arrange the

Left.—Cutting the sugar-cane crop.

(Photograph by Colonial Sugar Refining Co.)

Above.—A wooden bowl or kumete used for domestic purposes.

Right.—Natives of Ruatahuna using ko or digging implements.

Right.—Transporting cane to factory.

(Photograph by Colonial Sugar Refining Co.)

Miss M. Sutherland.

3. September 24th—2.43 p.m.

BOTANY AT THE DOMINION MUSEUM.

Miss M. Sutherland, B.Sc. (For.),
Botanist, Dominion Museum.

The Meaning and Use of Botany: Indoor and Out-of-Door Botanical Museums. — Plants are illustrated in the Dominion Museum by exhibits showing:—
(a) Systematic botany (the naming and description of plants)—
    e.g., seaweeds and fungus;
(b) Economic botany (the uses of plants)—
    (i) Food from plants—*e.g.*, sugar, tea, cocoa, coffee, rice;
    (ii) Textiles from plants—*e.g.*, rope, &c., from flax, cotton;
    (iii) Plant products—*e.g.*, timber, bark, resin;
(c) Ecology (the living conditions of plants), the adaptation of plants to their habitat—*e.g.*, vegetable sheep.

Case of fungi.   *Products of N.Z. Flax.—Phormium tenax.*

Left.—Exotic timbers grown in New Zealand, and wood products made from them.

Below :
Left.—The puriri moth.
Right.—Portion of honey-bee exhibit.

The New Zealand National Broadcasting Service

EDUCATIONAL BROADCASTS
to SCHOOLS

September - December 1936

2YA, WELLINGTON
4YA, DUNEDIN

Pages in the promotional pamphlet for the educational broadcasts to schools featured Mary's work on the botanical displays at the Dominion Museum: a case of fungi, New Zealand flax (*Phormium tenax*) products, exotic timbers in New Zealand and their products, and photos from the Colonial Sugar Refining Company showing cane being cut and transported to the factory by locomotive.
NATIONAL LIBRARY OF NZ

'welcome to new graduates' evening, entertained delegations of university women at the Dominion Museum, and assisted with an afternoon tea for Dr Agnes Bennett, who was due to represent New Zealand at the 1936 international conference in Kraków, Poland.[50] Bennett was a previous federation president, a champion of higher education for women and among the first women to practise medicine in New Zealand. The International Federation of University Women was formed after World War One, and by 1936 had thirty-nine member countries. It aimed to create world peace and promote friendship and understanding by bringing together graduates from around the world. Dr Winifred Cullis, professor of physiology at the University of London, founder and past president, travelled the world promoting higher education for women and spoke to local members when she visited New Zealand.[51]

At the New Zealand federation's 1936 conference the Wellington branch conducted an open meeting on exploring women's status. Discussions covered the fellowship fund, the exchange of secondary school teachers with Britain, and a memorial to the British Empire's first woman university graduate, Kate Edger (née Evans) of Auckland.[52] The memorial was to be a parquet floor in the minstrel's gallery at Crosby Hall in Bishopsgate, London, which the British Federation of University Women had purchased as an international hall of residence for graduate women.[53] Mary was secretary of the Wellington branch and assisted the president Violet Greig, principal of Wellington Girls' College,[54] to present the annual report. Her secretarial work was considerable: during the year she attended seven general and ten committee meetings, received eighty letters, wrote seventy letters and dispatched one thousand notices. The annual report noted the federation was authoritative on educational matters pertaining to women's work, and urged that a dean of women be appointed at Victoria University College to ensure the welfare and interests of women students. It also sought representation on the university's Council.[55] Mary made many friends with like-minded women through the federation and through contacts at work.

In January 1937 she took leave from the museum to attend the 23rd Meeting of the Australian and New Zealand Association for the Advancement of Science (ANZAAS) in Auckland. She drove to the meeting with an unnamed Dunedin lecturer and her nephew Bill Gray, going by way of Tauranga where she left Bill at Marion (Marie) Stewart's chicken farm, Cheriton.[56] Marie had trained at the Massey Agricultural College poultry unit under John Kissling, and knew both Mary and the Gray family; Mary's sister Kate had taught at the same school in Birmingham as Marie's sister Kathrine (Rena), who was also a farmer and political organiser.[57]

There were four other Bangor graduates at the conference and three of the five presented papers, which Mary thought wasn't bad for the University College of North Wales.[58] Her paper was on sustained yield forestry in New Zealand, and supported

Leonard Cockayne's views that managing indigenous forests in an economic and sustainable way would lead to less destructive exploitation. Her topic was well timed; it seemed to interest those present as a good discussion followed. The lecturer who accompanied her to the meeting returned by train, so the Cunninghams were her companions on the return trip. Because of her botany connections, it is likely they were Gordon Cunningham and his wife. Cunningham established the New Zealand fungal herbarium, which was transferred to the Department of Scientific and Industrial Research (DSIR) in 1936. They must have made a stop *en route,* as the current national museum's (Te Papa) plant collection database indicates Mary collected specimens at Rainbow Mountain, Erua and Horopito on 21 January.

Mary periodically stayed with the Grays in Khandallah, being part of their close family, but she also had a bach at Raumati Beach overlooking Kapiti Island, only accessible by driving along the sand. It was built by Dory Gray, had a verandah, a big living room, a "wee" kitchen and two bedrooms. There was a long-drop toilet and visitors always had to be frugal with water use. Mary entertained family and friends there, and Nettie Spencer, who lived in Jubilee Road and painted watercolours, was a frequent visitor.[59] The Grays' children—Ted, Dave, Helen, Barbara, Bill and Nancy—were grown and largely independent when she, Dory and Dave would go to stay at her bach, sometimes managing without Kate and the rest of the family.

In a family letter Mary expressed her dream to spend springtime in Europe and go on a Swedish tramp steamer, but there would be no pay for a year: "The museum cannot cough up any help. We are bankrupt since opening. It is only because the staff remain under the government that we get salaries."[60] But work took up much of her time. The importers L Yen & Co loaned the museum an old Japanese five-needle pine (*Pinus pentaphylla*), which would have been a bonsai specimen.[61] Mary contacted Harvard University about making tree models and the assistant director, A C Clive, sent a pamphlet on construction methods[62] and suggested she write to Theodore Pitman of Guernsey & Pitman, Massachusetts, who made museum models.[63] In May 1937 Roger Walpole, an assistant at the museum, informed Walter Oliver that Miss Sutherland was present when he cracked a rib while attending to the tuatara: no other details were provided.[64] Keeping a live tuatara seemed to have been a highlight and a long-standing tradition of the museum:[65] a previous director, Augustus Hamilton, once wrote in his desk diary, "the old lizard died".[66]

A staffing crisis

Although Frank Hutchinson's tribute to Mary in the 1976 NZIF newsletter says she re-joined the Forest Service as botanist in 1937,[67] no evidence was found to support this. In a letter to family, Mary mentioned her attendance and presentation at the 1937 ANZAAS meeting,[68] and its report published an abstract of her paper that said she was working at the Dominion Museum.[69] Te Papa's database indicates she was collecting specimens in early 1937, and Dominion Museum archives confirm she was on sick leave from August 1937 until 1940.[70] Soon after she collected specimens at Mt Holdsworth for the native plant exhibition, Mary became ill and was unable to finish the pre-exhibition planning. The records make no mention of the cause of her illness. Four months later, Walter Oliver sent her a form to sign for further sick leave.[71] He hoped she could soon return to duty and informed her Charles Lindsay and John Salmon had filled a postal van with living plants from Akatarawa Saddle for the exhibition. They proposed to make two more trips as at least one hundred living specimens were wanted. John Scott Thomson, honorary botanist to the Otago Museum,[72] had promised to supply forty enlarged photographs.

When it became clear Mary's absence would be prolonged, the museum's botanical assistant, Valerie Norman, took on Mary's role to deal with correspondence, answer enquiries, arrange the native plant exhibition and construct the new Carnegie exchange exhibit. Oliver recommended an allowance

The Raumati bach and Mary in the garden.
SUTHERLAND/GRAY FAMILY

for her during Mary's absence.[73] He was overseas studying museums[74] when the acting director, William Phillips, requested a temporary assistant for the botanical department: "Miss Sutherland's prolonged absence through sickness has made the situation urgent. Miss Norman can no longer cope and specimens are being attacked by fungi and other organisms."[75] Amy Donne was appointed as temporary office assistant. In October 1938 Valerie Norman resigned.[76] Two months, later when another native plant exhibition was planned, no botanical assistant had been employed. When Oliver returned from overseas, Lucy Cranwell at Auckland Museum recommended he employ Katie Pickmere, who had assisted Cranwell with native plant exhibitions and managed one herself while Cranwell was in Hawaii.[77]

Mary was receiving care at Te Karaka Rest Home in Waikanae. She was encased in plaster because of a back ailment, possibly from an injury,[78] and was totally incapacitated. Being dependent on others would have been difficult for her when she was used to an outdoors working life. Oliver sent Mary a gift from the staff for Christmas, a book about birds, which was probably his *New Zealand Birds*.[79] Her letter of thanks states she spent a quiet Christmas Day, which was a great improvement on the previous year. Everyone had been good to her and made things festive. She was grateful for her care. The Federation of University Women sent flowers and expressed their appreciation for her work. Mary had been on subcommittees for an educational conference and the fellowship fund, as well as the hospitality committee, and served as secretary of the Wellington branch.[80] That financial year, in her absence, it was suggested two secretaries be appointed in her place: one to handle correspondence and the other to record meetings. Mary resigned as a trustee of the federation's savings account, and though "flat on her back" was elected an honorary vice president along with Agnes Bennett and Mary Clachan.[81]

Katie Pickmere's temporary appointment at the museum was approved and the office assistant Amy Donne applied to be transferred to the Department of Agriculture, so Oliver recommended employing Primrose Self as a part-time botanical assistant. Self was studying at Victoria University College, but could work at the museum three days a week.[82] In August 1940, Pickmere resigned and Self was either on leave or sick, for Oliver wrote to the Art Gallery and Museum Board of Trustees that both Miss Sutherland and Miss Self would probably return to duty within two months. He no longer felt it necessary to provide relief in the botanical department.

When Mary was discharged from the rest home, she spent time recovering at an address in Kelburn, Wellington, and also time at her bach. During her convalescence she wrote to her niece Frances (Frankie), the baby born in Brazil now grown and living in Canada. War had intervened while Mary was ill and she had been about to send the stamps she had saved for her niece and her friends, when a notice was sent out stating no-one was allowed to send used paper out of the country.[83] Mary informed her niece she must wait till "Hitler was finished" and she would send the Health Camp stamps. She expected to like her new car, a Hillman Minx, but there was a restricted petrol allowance and having not driven for more than two years she needed to resit her driving test. She commented that her belongings at the bach had become muddled since she had been ill. Her nephew Bill had maintained the property: slashing creepers, cutting the grass, mending the wire mosquito door, chopping wood and burning green hedge cuttings in the living room fireplace as outside was too dry. She hoped to bathe in the sea next day for the first time. Bill had won a high jump competition and his mother, Mary's sister Kate, had attended three school break ups: one of her daughters, Helen, was in a play and another, Nancy, was top equal in her music exam.

After three years' absence Mary returned to work in October 1940. She responded to Owen Fletcher's request for flowering native plants for the Otago Museum's Centennial Native Flower Show in November.[84] Kohekohe flowering was over and the fruits not yet formed, so she sent foliage and suggested he open the titoki berries to show the inside colour. She had found no rata in flower, but sent around fifty plants, most from Bernard Aston's garden. Owen Fletcher wrote back thanking her: "Your flowers were very much admired and made a valuable addition to the extensive collection. The show will continue till the flowers die."[85]

Mary replied to Herbert Mason at the University of California herbarium about his last exchange parcel received in June 1936.[86] Walter Oliver had worked on coprosmas for years and published a monograph; a near-complete set of species was being consigned. In her exchange there were sets of *Taxaceae* minus Kirk's pine (*Dacrydium kirkii*), and *NZ Pinaceae*,[87] plus a selection from various families. Owing to a paper shortage they were not mounted. She would try to supply the special families he wished for in future consignments.

Though pleased to be working again, Mary was unhappy her position remained classified as clerical. Oliver supported her application to transfer to professional status,[88] but as with Ellie Heine, his pleas to the National Art Gallery and Dominion Museum trustees were unsuccessful.[89] Mary could take no holidays, but was to spend Christmas 1940 at Torphins with the Grays in Khandallah: all the family were expected. Her sister Nancy was over from Britain and some of Mary's friends were coming to spend a week with her at the Raumati bach.

CHAPTER 6

WAR WORK and AGRICULTURE

Collections, exhibits and helping botanists

Mary returned to her community activities in 1941 and was re-elected to the Wellington branch committee of the Federation of University Women. As vice president of the New Zealand Institute of Foresters she chaired the annual general meeting, where methods to speed up the institute's business were discussed. Executive members were scattered throughout the North and South islands, which made communication difficult and slow. The minutes were recorded on the back of used paper as being wartime there was a paper shortage, but perhaps true to her Scottish heritage this was also because Mary did not like waste.[1] In October, while possibly on institute business in Rotorua, she collected lichen (*Parmelia*) from miro trees and other specimens in the Kaimai Mamaku Forest.[2]

Mary wanted to upgrade the museum's sugar exhibit, and as she had heard sugar cane was grown and given to children to suck in the Bay of Plenty she wrote to Norman Potts, a lawyer and botanist in Opotiki, asking if he could procure a plant specimen and a piece of ripe cane.[3] She wondered if her informant had mistaken sorghum for sugar cane? Potts told her sugar cane was grown in the district, mainly by "natives", and was eaten mostly by children. He grew some the previous year and did not find it exciting, though it was pleasant on a hot day. He had no idea of the strain, or if there were more varieties. It grew 9 feet tall (3 metres), but he could send seed for her to study the growing stages, or small plants later. If she did not want to grow the cane he could send specimens in summer or late autumn. Sorghum was grown locally for fodder, but only occasionally due to the labour involved. Mary asked for full-grown specimens in the season as cane seedlings would not grow well around Wellington. They could be cut to a convenient length as she could mend and camouflage the repair. Specimens from Fiji had been varnished and were keeping well.

The Banks and Solander collection that had arrived several years earlier was at last mounted and classified,[4] and as well as sugar, other exhibits were being revised. A table of live plants was set up and the potted plant collection was labelled. The museum grounds had been planted and native plant specimens dispatched to the Auckland and Invercargill museums.[5] Mary prepared a temporary exhibit on ergot, a fungal disease mostly affecting rye, and wrote to the Lincoln Agricultural College director, Professor Eric Hudson, asking for samples of healthy and ergot-affected rye, plus other cereal specimens for the economic grasses exhibit: "Half a dozen plants each of barley and wheat grown in the South Island would do." Hudson told her the risk of introducing a new and virulent strain of ergot into the country's cereal crops was too great, so the rye crop had been ploughed in. Her request for the other cereals had been referred to Professor John (Jack) Calder, who queried whether she wanted the ripe or green stage. She requested two whole plants of barley and wheat, and half a dozen heads of each specimen in the green stage. Later, she asked if both Tartarian and common oat could be included, as well as bearded, beardless, red and white wheat, or any other cereal. Calder had been mobilised to war service so Dr Ian Blair, a lecturer in field husbandry, sent her several varieties of wheat, barley and oats.[6]

Mary received correspondence from the assistant curator at the University of California herbarium, Lincoln Constance, who wrote that he was unaware of the specimen exchange scheme, even though it had operated since 1932. Mary suggested the material she had posted in November 1940 may have been lost in transit, and with uncertain mail conditions due to the war it seemed unwise to attempt further exchanges at present, but if Constance wanted specimens, she would forward a consignment. The November dispatch had arrived, but while Constance was in Philadelphia at the Christmas meeting of the American Association for the Advancement of Science. The university wanted the exchange revitalised so it could fully represent New Zealand plants in its collections. Despite sufficient cultivated material, it possessed few native New Zealand and Australian flora, and though it was not feasible to send specimens until the war ended, they would lay aside items from Ira Clokey's Charleston Mountains collection to send to the museum.[7] Constance assured Mary this was exceptionally desirable material: "If you have any particular preferences we should be glad to honor your desiderata. We look forward to a resumption of exchange with you when the victory is won."[8]

The Dominion Museum had a collection of algal material from the 1800s, and later acquired the collections and research of Victor Lindauer and Wallace Scarfe.[9, 10] Mary and her assistant Primrose Self were collecting marine algae specimens from bays around Wellington for an exhibit on seaweed utilisation. Their work would have been of interest to Lucy Moore, the botanist at DSIR who was charting the location of seaweeds to assess local agar resources.[11] Agar, extracted from seaweed, was used for laboratory culture, and the country's main supply was cut off when Japan invaded the Pacific. Agar was not the country's only war shortage, and the DSIR's plant research bureau was growing medicinal and fibre plants at its Waiwhetu experimental station in the Hutt Valley.[12] Mary took a keen interest in this work.

Lucy Moore was a friend and collaborator of the Auckland Museum botanist Lucy Cranwell, who became renowned for her work on ancient pollens taken from bogs. Leonard Cockayne called them the 'two Lucys' and the nickname stuck. In June 1942, the month of the 7.2 magnitude Masterton earthquake, Cranwell wrote to Mary to thank her for her kindness when she visited Wellington. She knew Mary had been ill, but thought she looked well. Cranwell wrote that she had almost given up trying to find Logania pollen, and was looking for pollen from *C. mariscus*, *Lemna*, and *Lepidosperma*.[13]

The museum's 1942 annual report[14] recorded that the collector William Martin had donated ninety-one plant specimens from Marlborough, and Victor Zotov, assistant to Harry Allen, the DSIR botany division director, had identified and categorised specimens in the Colenso collection.[15, 16] Reference works on algae, lichens and exotic plant collections were available, and exchange material had

Eric Godley's article on the DSIR's first 50 years included this 1942 photograph of Mary and the DSIR botany division staff at Waiwhetu examining a *linum* (linseed/flaxseed) crop: Ruth Mason, Dr Harry Allan, David Cairns, Lai-Yung Li, Lucy Moore, Dr Hamilton, Mary, Arthur Healy and George Briggs. REPRINTED FROM ERIC J GODLEY (1980)

been sent to the Melbourne National Herbarium, Pomona College in California, and Victoria College.[17] Large exhibits on plant nutrition and sugar production were complete.

Most of Frank Peat's kauri gum collection was removed from showcases for safe storage during the war, which proved fortuitous as in June 1942 a major part of the building was taken over at short notice for defence purposes.[18] The art gallery was vacated and the museum's collections, library, office and personnel records were dumped on the display floor, suffering major damage, and some specimens were irretrievable. The building was closed to the public for several years. The library was re-housed in temporary quarters and staff re-arranged the collections and created makeshift working spaces among the cases.

Despite the disruption, work continued: Mary responded to Miss Perry's 2YC radio quiz question about the introduction of blackberry to New Zealand:[19] "Where and how blackberry was first introduced was not definite. Seed may have arrived with imported plants and soil, or early colonists might have brought in plants. Spread was rapid, both through seed dispersal and by vegetative means with runners from root stock." The earliest record of *Rubus discolor* was its discovery by Thomas Kirk near Auckland in 1867.[20] Harry Allan and Kirk disagreed whether it was in 1867 or 1877 that blackberry was first found at Ohariu and Happy Valley, Wellington. The most common blackberry in 1942 was *Rubus fruticosus*, but Allan listed nine other species in *A Handbook of the Naturalized Flora of New Zealand*.[21] Some species differed little botanically, so species numbers would probably be reduced after further critical examination.

A large part of Mary's role was to assist botanists in their work. When George Simpson[22] was undertaking the last revision of his monograph on New Zealand broom (*Carmichaelia*) and foxglove (*Ourisia*), he wrote "It will be generally a headache to others after mine has subsided, and its length an obstacle to publication." He hesitated to ask for further packages in case Mary was too busy, but foxgloves and leatherwood (*Olearia colensoi*) were welcome: "Just one box at a time; its safe arrival indicating I am ready for the next."[23] Mary returned his notes on New Zealand brooms and sent several species of foxgloves. One box of mountain foxglove was still to be sent, but when Simpson wrote requesting it, Mary had left to undertake national service at the Woburn YWCA hostel supervising women directed to war work.[24] Some thought her talents wasted on such a task. Her niece Helen Baxter described her aunt as a gentle person, caring and community-minded.[25] She had been tapping a book in Braille for the Foundation for the Blind, and was also contributing to the war effort in voluntary ways, including knitting socks for the soldiers.

At Torphins, Jubilee Road, Khandallah, Christmas 1942. SUTHERLAND/GRAY FAMILY

Deployed to Woburn

It became difficult for New Zealand's essential industries to keep running when workers left businesses and industries to join the defence forces during World War Two, so in 1942 the government passed emergency industrial manpower regulations to control how and where labour was used. Legal restrictions were lifted to allow women to work shifts, and if aged between 18 and 30 and without children, they were directed into work.[26] As the industries of national importance were located around the cities, women's organisations and Maori were concerned that staff in manpower offices would send young women from the provinces to 'wrongly conducted' guesthouses. By December 1942, between 800 to 900 women were needed for a fuse-filling munitions contract at the Ford factory in Petone. Appropriate accommodation was especially scarce in the Hutt Valley, so the National Service Department worked with the State Advances Corporation to build a hostel opposite Woburn railway station, and the YWCA was asked to administer it.[27]

The hostel had eight two-storeyed wooden houses for residents. A ninth building housed the dining room, kitchen and recreational lounge. Staff selection criteria included Christian conviction, adaptability, maturity and commitment. Violet Macmillan, a dietitian from the University of Otago Home Science Department, was appointed as supervisor. She was also a YWCA board member and chairperson of the cafeteria committee. Greta Wright and Mary were appointed as assistant supervisors at a salary of £200 per annum with free board and lodgings.[28] Mary's experience during World War One of managing the forest nursery workers' hostel at Bangor and supervising female gangs in the Forestry Corps, as well as her involvement in the Wellington Federation of University Women and her personal contacts, may have influenced her appointment. She knew Macmillan, who was from Tauranga where Marie Stewart also lived.[29]

The Woburn hostel was officially opened in April 1943 by the YWCA patron, American-born Lady Olive Newall, wife of Sir Cyril, governor general of New Zealand, 1941–46.[30] She spoke on the need for patriotic women to have "good meals, good sleep and good air in a friendly, pleasant atmosphere".[31] The hostel was governed by the Hutt Valley YWCA hostels advisory committee; Jessie Ewen was chair, Marjorie Welton-Hogg was secretary and Mrs Wilkinson the treasurer. Staff members had specific responsibilities and all served as house matrons.[32]

The first residents, mostly from North Island provincial towns and rural areas, were directed to work at the Ford munitions factory. They signed a boarder's agreement. There was one bathroom and lavatory among seven women, and each house had a hot water tank heated by a coal-fired boiler. No pantries, ironing rooms or hot water cupboards had been installed, and complaints led to a parliamentary

The **YWCA** hostel provided 'appropriate' accommodation for women deployed to the cities to work in essential industries during World War Two. HUTT CITY LIBRARIES, PETONE

Mary, in her early 50s, wearing the YWCA hostel uniform.
SUTHERLAND/GRAY FAMILY

debate on the conditions in July 1943.[33] Edward Gordon, member of parliament for Rangitikei, asked for immediate steps to investigate and remedy the unsatisfactory accommodation and catering. The hostel was draughty and leaking, when it rained, beds had to be moved to avoid the leaks. Food was improperly cooked, and women who missed the first meal sitting had to eat half-cooked food, which caused ptomaine poisoning. There were no drying facilities, and women were boarded three to a room and charged £1 7s 6d a week for bed, breakfast and dinner (annually, over half of Mary's salary). They had to pay bus fares to the Ford factory and buy their own lunch. The prime minister, Peter Fraser, expressed concern for the hostel staff, who were doing their best, especially the supervisor Violet Macmillan, who had qualified at the Otago University Domestic School of Science. He did not think it fair such charges should be brought against her. The controversy over conditions must have been an unpleasant experience for all the staff, and Mary as an assistant supervisor would have felt a level of responsibility. However, the parliamentary debate and investigation helped to bring about change, so two instead of three women shared a room, and rooms were altered to create pantries, ironing rooms and hot water cupboards. Wash houses were also added. The catering problems were solved when appropriate cooking equipment was obtained; the hostel had initially not been provided with large cooking pots.

Two months after the hostel was opened, when she was barely settled into her new role, Mary received news that her sister Daisy had died from cancer. Howard and Daisy Clark were living in Ottawa, Canada, at the time. It is unknown whether Mary knew about her sister's illness, and no record was located indicating whether she attended her funeral, but with the war affecting the Pacific, travel was not a wise option. Mary was also committed to the national service she had signed up for. Looking after the women who were keeping the essential industries running was an important role.

There was a steady flux of residents, so the full quota of 330 women and domestic staff was seldom maintained in the first year: most residents were between twenty and thirty years old, and around twenty percent were Maori. There were a few younger women and a small group aged 50 to 60. They were previously shop assistants, domestic workers, hairdressers, office workers, theatre attendants, or had home duties. Dinner was provided for those working late and thirty residents were employed as cooks, housemaid–waitresses or kitchen hands. More women arrived when the W D & H O Wills and Godfrey Phillips cigarette factories increased production, needing one hundred and fifty extra staff. With longer working hours, and some women unwilling to be regimented, organised recreational activities lapsed, such as gymnastic classes, reading circles, and table tennis. Two basketball (netball) teams continued and gardening remained popular, as did needlecraft and

Eleanor Roosevelt (centre) visits a Woburn hostel built for women munitions workers, 1943.
With her are Joseph Heenan, undersecretary of Internal Affairs, and the hostel supervisor Violet Macmillan.
ALEXANDER TURNBULL LIBRARY

Workers in a Wellington munitions factory, 1943. During World War Two women throughout New
Zealand were directed to the main cities to work in these factories. ALEXANDER TURNBULL LIBRARY

the resulting handcraft exhibitions. The lounge stayed open until 11:00 pm for residents and their men friends, who were often United States servicemen, and the different houses sponsored dances.[34]

The hostel hosted many distinguished visitors, including Eleanor Roosevelt, wife of the United States president, who was in Wellington in August 1943. She also spoke to women at the Ford munitions factory, watched women's precision work at the DSIR laboratory, and visited military personnel at Silverstream Hospital where the marines called her 'Eleanor'. The *Auckland Star* reported on her interest in the hostel, noting it had 320 residents and also provided breakfast and dinner for fifty women in the Women's Auxiliary Army Corps.[35] The marines would also often eat there, and payment for their food was used to buy teacups, one of which Mrs Roosevelt drank her tea from.

Lady Newall, who had officially opened the hostel, returned in 1944 to dine with residents. Other visitors included: Lady Zara Hore-Ruthven the Countess of Gowrie; the Hon Hilda Grenfell, vice president of Great Britain's YWCA; Dr Walter Riddell, Canadian high commissioner; Alice Patton, wife of the United States ambassador; Veronica Forde, wife of Australia's acting prime minister; Lady Margaret Duff, wife of the British high commissioner;[36] Dr Edith Summerskill, British politician and physician; Sir Alfred and Lady Dorothea Davidson from Sydney; Lottie Nash, wife of the minister of finance; and the ministers of Manpower (Angus McLagan), Education (Henry Mason) and Supply and Munitions (Daniel Sullivan).

Violet Macmillan resigned in January 1944, and at her farewell the chairperson of the Hutt Valley YWCA hostels advisory committee, Jessie Ewen, spoke about Macmillan's administrative and organisational skills. She also expressed the committee's good wishes to Mary Sutherland, who succeeded as superintendent.[37] Not long after, in February 1944, the kitchen block with the cafeteria, lounges and offices, was gutted by fire in the early morning hours;[38] the three hundred residents evacuated the hostel in their night attire. When the building's roof fell in, the fire fighters concentrated on saving the kitchen and protecting the nearby dormitory. The cause of the fire was unclear, but it was thought to have started in the cafeteria. There was no injury or loss of life, but alternative facilities were required, so the army made a cafeteria available at a hostel commandeered from the National Service Department for its own use in nearby Richmond Road. The Woburn hostel was rebuilt and reopened in May. The fire had highlighted safety issues, so heaters were banned in bedrooms and fewer residents were accepted till more fire escapes were provided. A month later the army returned the Richmond Road hostel, which accommodated 276 residents, to the National Service, and Mary supervised both.

Mary kept a record of residents' health issues, which included appendicitis, scarlet fever, tuberculosis, measles, mumps, chicken pox, scabies, influenza, and colds. The women who worked in munitions often complained of powder rash and cigarette factory workers suffered from tobacco rash. A severe bout of bacillary food poisoning was thought to have been caused by infected eggs. Twenty babies were born, but only one birth occurred at the hostel. Thirty women left to start training for work in mental hospitals in June 1945.[39] It is likely Mary encouraged these women as her brother-in-law Dory Gray was responsible for mental health services.

After VJ Day (victory over Japan) on 15 August 1945, the munitions workers were transferred to other industries, and those who were married or older were released from manpower controls. Other residents were employed in industrial work, shops or private firms. Workers did not always return from leave, but following Christmas 1945 some came back to Wellington, no doubt finding provincial life dull and missing the pace of city life and company of other women. But with resident numbers diminishing, other organisations used the hostel including Methodist Church youth groups, returned servicemen attending rehabilitation courses, dental students and their matron, secondary school teachers attending a vacation school, the New Zealand Dietetic Association, the Federation of University Women, and hostel supervisors from the YWCA. Ten boys from the Pahiatua Polish camp stayed six days while touring Wellington factories.

In February 1946, manpower controls were completely lifted and the hostel became the Hutt Valley YWCA centre. One of the houses was allocated to students, mostly for the teachers training college, with the remaining beds occupied by university, library school and free kindergarten union students. Accommodation was also provided for shorthand typists, office assistants and home aides, by arrangement with the public service commissioner.

When Mary left the Woburn hostel in 1946 perhaps her farewell tea was served in cups bought with money paid by the marines for their meals. SUTHERLAND/GRAY FAMILY

Mary left the Woburn hostel in September 1946. During her three and a half years there over fourteen hundred residents and domestic staff passed through. In her 1946 report she acknowledged the women who had left their homes and jobs to work in munitions and other essential industries, and the loyal staff who cared for them.[40]

Mary was remembered as a slightly built, quiet, gentle and softly spoken woman.[41] Ethel Law's history of the YWCA says she had the ability to objectively review all manner of difficult situations without letting personalities obscure her judgement. "Mary's reports to the YWCA and Department of Labour had been 'admirably succinct' and dealt with matters such as housing Maori girls in the hostel and entertaining men from the American forces and neighbouring Public Works camps."[42]

During the war years, Mary had maintained contact with the Dominion Museum and collected specimens from Homer Saddle, Fiordland in December 1944.[43] Walter Oliver also often took field trips into this area.[44] Her absence continued to cause him difficulties, and the museum remained closed to the public for some time. The botanical department had no staff, and the plant collections needed regular disinfection, and more than two thousand boxes required examination and treatment.[45] But instead of returning to the museum, Mary accepted a position with the Department of Agriculture.

Agriculture, beer and cement

While men and women were absent serving their country, many rural properties became less productive, so after the war the Department of Agriculture created farm advisory positions to increase efficiency.[46] The department recognised the importance of shelter trees for agricultural production, and appointed Mary as its first farm forestry adviser. She started work in the rural development division where Percy Smallfield was the director. Her initial salary was more than she had received from either the State Forest Service or the Dominion Museum, and steadily increased.[47] Her job was to initiate an extension service for farm shelter, tree plantations and wood lots, and to write for the *New Zealand Journal of Agriculture*.[48] Improving aesthetics at the front gate of run-down farms would no doubt have improved farmers' morale, and in 1947 Mary wrote a series of articles for the journal: 'Planting round the homestead', followed by 'A working plan for homestead shelter', 'The planting of homestead shelter' and 'Rapid shelter from minor species of trees'.[49] No departmental records relating to her work were located, but correspondence, articles and the annual reports shed light on this period.

In June 1947 she started a letter to her niece Frances in Canada saying she was scouting the central North Island for farm plantations.[50] After a two-day NZIF conference in Rotorua, she arrived in Palmerston North cold and wet from travelling through hours of rain. The gas fire gave no heat: a gale had delayed coal supplies from the South Island, so the gas company had to borrow coal from the freezing works, and a gas workers' go-slow meant there was only six hours' supply a day. Mary tried warming her feet with cushions. She had visited a large property on the coast where six good dairy farms were established after fixing and planting the sand dunes. Her fieldwork was interesting and she enjoyed meeting the farmers and their wives more than writing articles in head office.

Frances's father, Howard Clark, had remarried, and in her letter Mary asked about Frances's baby brother Michael. She also asked about her occupational therapy studies: did she work with ex-servicemen, and had her mother, Daisy, ever mentioned her experiences when she nursed soldiers in World War One? Mary told Frances that Daisy was a favourite with them, and aided and abetted their pranks. She suggested Frances come to New Zealand; no doubt her uncle Dory mentioned the occupational therapy possibilities in mental health services. She finished her letter in Auckland two months later where because of the school holidays and two of His Majesty's ships being in port it was difficult to find good accommodation. After a night in an uncomfortable hotel, Mary went to stay with friends. She thanked Frances for the moccasins, which were "useful for travelling, as they go flat", and wrote about the family. Betty was back in England and the aunts enjoyed having her (probably Betty Flint, who was on the vegetable sheep expedition). Kate and Dory would be alone at Torphins as Dave was working his passage as a steward to England, and Nancy had come with her to Tauranga to stay with friends before starting nurse training in Christchurch.

In 1948, the Department of Agriculture amalgamated the fields division and the rural development division into the extensions division.[51] Local instructors were expected to bring farmers and advisers together, and arrange lectures, farm visits and field days. The farm schools and radio programmes on farming that had ceased during the war were revived.[52] When the department employed Hilda Stevens as an assistant farm forestry officer, Mary's position was reclassified as professional.

Mary's two-part series, 'Growing tree stocks for shelter planting', was published in the *New Zealand Journal of Agriculture* in February and March, followed by 'Multi-purpose trees for planting on farms' in July.[53] But whenever she was on leave, Mary found herself looking and thinking about shelter belts, so to get away from her preoccupation with work she decided to take a trip aboard a lighthouse-servicing vessel to the New Hebrides (now Vanuatu). The SS *Matai* had a three-week voyage chartered to the Pacific, so she booked passages for herself and her niece Barbara (Barbie), who was to start a herd testing job the following month, and they sailed from Auckland in October 1948.

The New Hebrides getaway

The 1000-ton ship carried a cargo of beer and cement and was headed for Port Vila. Captain Holm was in charge and fourteen passengers were aboard: his wife's brother, three Kellihers (father, mother and son), a sister of an acquaintance Mary knew at the Department of Health, two men from the firm that chartered the boat, and other oddments. In a family letter, Mary wrote "one woman is the *bête noir* of both Barbie and myself. We mutually disapprove of each other."[54] The seas were choppy and Mary was "glad to find her good sea tummy, after years of non-use". It was too cold for summer clothes, but when conditions improved they entertained themselves by playing shovelboard and quoits. Mary described Port Vila as a "lovely harbour with several green-clad islands. The town runs up the hill behind the waterfront. Hills are jungle-clad, with large patches of coconut plantations and isolated plantation houses."

The New Hebrides was under British–French condominium rule and passengers were travelling on French visas. No one knew what currency to bring: some had francs or dollars, and Mary obtained Australian money through Ted Fussell (presumably the Reserve Bank governor Edward Fussell).[55] But they were not given an opportunity to spend: the Customs men arrived by launch, but did not board, and passengers were told they could not disembark because of New Zealand's poliomyelitis epidemic. Later, a doctor came and peered down everyone's throats, and only those with legitimate business were allowed ashore. Mary wanted to look at trees, yet also felt concerned for the locals: "They are right to be sticky. If we did bring a germ, it would make a mess of the natives as it did in Samoa. They have no resistance."

The weather was cooler than expected. Unlike her 1925 trip to Brazil with Truby King's daughter Mary when the ship lay off the coast of Pernambuco: "This time one doesn't ooze when one moves." She wrote that the launch boys were short statured with curly hair, and wore US marine occupation remnants — old military mackintoshes with plastic belts. Only three people on 'legitimate' business were allowed ashore and just for a short time. The doctor, whose wife had studied agriculture in Melbourne, agreed to take Mary to see tree specimens at his home, but he was delayed at the hospital.

They picnicked ashore on a nearby point, but the Australian chief of police and a police posse kept everyone under surveillance. Two barefoot boys walked Mary and Barbie a long way "amid broad grins and chuckles" to see a particular tree and learn the names of other trees. The boys wore khaki shorts, puttees, and blue Scottish tammies, and both carried a sheath knife and a knobbed cane. Mary and Barbie were taken on a launch trip around the harbour and they bathed in a coral-bottomed sea. For a week the passengers did almost nothing except watch beer being unloaded. Mary wrote in her diary that the British police "ran the natives in" for drinking, whereas the French joined in the drinking. "France and Great Britain are both represented in the five courts of justice, so the law is somewhat Gilbertian."

They sailed overnight to the island of Espiritu Santo, which Mary described as "chiefly French, with a few broken-down British ..." There were few houses or stores, and a "double residency", presumably a duplex, was 5 miles (8 kilometres) away. She had brought two written accounts of the region on the trip; the one about the military occupation and its "... fifty thousand men and miles of air strips" was from a 1944 *National Geographic*. "The place must have buzzed," she wrote, but since then the unused wharves had rotted, the piles were gone and there were huge holes in the decking.

The ship had to be moved. "We have been lying off wharves all week, still in quarantine, with the usual wrangling and intrigue about business ashore." When on guard, the French police carried large knives and unloaded rifles they later replaced with knob-headed canes. When the British took over the guard they had no rifles. It rained almost continuously for three days while the cement was unloaded. When the sun did appear, a wharf-load of old iron, machinery, Nissen huts and junk was loaded on board. "The place is littered with war material: abandoned huts and buildings, machinery, car and lorry remains and old noticeboards. Airstrips are overgrown, and roads go into morasses. Scrub beneath the palms is 20 feet [6 metres] high. It is depressing."

The passengers were allowed to visit an island where the marines had cleared bush for a recreation area with tennis and squash courts. Wide tracks had been cut through the jungle to the beaches, but the problem of sharks meant when they bathed, they stayed near the shore. The land crabs were a bit fearsome; some measured a foot across, but "they were marvellous when they danced on their hind legs". Mary described the trees as legion with wonderful fruits and flowers: "I came here to get away from trees, but I can't help being intrigued by the different kinds." Knowing scarcely any plant names, she collected specimens, which are now held at the Auckland Museum herbarium.[56]

The trip was expected to take two more weeks because of the delays, which Mary attributed to "... ship-loading mess ups, waiting for health clearances because of polio, and beer negotiations. A lot of big business and funny business. No one knows where we are going, not even the captain." A planned landing at Walpole

Island did not eventuate. At Nouméa the price of copra was high and the natives bought tinned foods. Mary intended to shop, but thought the goods, some from Australia, were inferior. There were, however, lots of French wines and liqueurs.

Barbie had not been impressed with the constant washing and ironing required in the tropics, and Mary noted she had the ship's officers in tow. When Barbie wanted to go to a dance club, Mary foresaw a late night ahead to keep a tag on her niece. With the ship's delay, she hoped Barbie's new job would be kept open,[57] and having missed several farm shows, she was concerned her own work was a month behind.

When Mary was back at work, her two-part series 'Trees and hedges for the approach to the farm' was published in November and December.[58] The first article covered the need for farmers to adapt the methods and lessons of predecessors, but on a smaller scale. It was a comprehensive article with details under the headings 'The approach to the farm', 'Position of the homestead site', 'The types of approach in relation to access of the house and farm', 'The use of unfenced areas', 'Dealing with enclosed areas', 'Hedge-lined, tree-lined and shelter driveways', 'Evergreen and deciduous avenues', and 'Graded planting and providing ample space'. The article included eight photographs, diagrams showing various homestead and farm approaches, and one on the importance of providing ample space for growth using Lawson's cypress as an example. Her second article dealt with planning to scale and access details, such as combining a planting layout with a traffic turning loop, choosing species and using temporary varieties to protect those suitable for permanent planting, for which she provided a list.

CHAPTER 7

FARM SCHOOLS and BOATS

Farm schools in the North

In the 1950s, soil erosion was becoming a major issue for hill country farms, so the Department of Agriculture began to research land conservation measures. Part of Mary's research was a survey of Arnold Williams' Puketiti Station, a hill country farm near Te Puia, on the North Island's East Cape. Over a forty-year period, Williams had been planting shelter for stock and to prevent erosion on vulnerable land.[1] Mary surveyed the different tree species the farm had tried and in an article for the *NZ Journal of Agriculture* discussed aspects of the formation and growth of the plantations in terms of silvicultural development.[2] She also prepared plans for shelter trees at the Invermay agricultural and Winchmore irrigation research stations,[3] and with her colleague Hilda Stevens travelled with other staff to Northland to run the department's farm schools. In a letter to family, Mary wrote that on the way they visited a Dargaville farm where they collected eucalypt specimens and ate lunch in the barn. The next day, after visiting the Waipoua Forest headquarters, they lunched by Tāne Mahuta, the largest kauri in the forest first encountered by Europeans in 1924 while surveying the road through the forest.[4] The women arrived in Kaitaia "in time to dine like ladies" and the following day set up the marquee and exhibits before inspecting the trees of an old, local farmer who was the son of a missionary pioneer. The farm school was well attended, but the tent was very hot.[5]

Mary and Stevens spent a night at the Awanui pub, which was well-known for its food. When they arrived they were "met by a dame who had long ago lost the battle of the bulge". Their meals were huge with lashings of cream; they were told to finish up and then pressed to have seconds. Most people in the settlement were Dalmatian; they watched a man, his dog and nags wander by, and were amused by two ex-gumdiggers with magnificent moustaches dressed in their Sunday best. The following day the farm school, or 'circus' as they called it, headed south through Kaitaia and Pukepoto past the gumfields. The lorry driver took them along the south end of Ninety Mile Beach at Ahipara to visit plantations along the sand dunes. They then travelled through Herekino to Broadwood, which was the next stop on their tour. Broadwood had two stores, a smithy-cum-garage, a post office and church. Mary and others from the party were hosted by the president of the local Federated Farmers: "We were well looked after and our hostess was most entertaining. She knew everything about everybody." The people who attended the farm school the next day said they were lucky to have it come to such a small place. The North was in drought and Mary and her colleagues were only allowed a cupful of water to clean up in, so they washed their clothes and bathed in the river running alongside the main road: "You can bathe and wave to your friends." The Herekino pub, west of Broadwood, had no water and was shut. "The cows are going dry and milk is scarce. There are scrub fires somewhere every day, and the countryside is terribly burnt." A farmer's wife walked 5 miles (8 kilometres) each day to carry water home.

Their next farm school was at Waimate North, about 9 miles (14 kilometres) from Kaikohe, "an ordinary township with a comfortable hotel". Mary described Waimate North as "a very English district, with an old church, a store and houses dating from the 1850s".[6] They visited one house where a missionary surveyor's plan was found in the attic. From Kaikohe they headed to Paihia in the Bay of Islands where they had rented a beach cottage with an electric range and light. Hot water was pumped from an outside boiler and their food included pears and peaches from the 'long orchard'.[7] They took a cruise on the Cream Trip,[8] which included lunch on Urupukapuka Island at Zane Gray's fishing lodge "with all mod cons".[9] The launch called in at farms and Maori settlements, and in one bay waited for a Maori lad rowing against the wind in a dinghy so over-loaded with cement bags it sank to the gunwales. In another bay, two small Maori boys arrived in a whaleboat to collect their father.

At Paihia, Mary and Stevens called on Vernon Reed, the secretary of the Waitangi Trust,[10] who escorted them around the plantations and Treaty House: "Restoration of the old Busby house is quite good, but they need period furniture. The house is beautiful and you feel how gracious and peaceful they managed to make life in those early days when it could have been so rough. We were impressed you can wander by yourself and look where you want. There is a written guide." They went to see the Church of St Paul, built in memory of missionary Henry Williams, but it was closed so instead they explored the churchyard by torch light.[11] In a cold wind they attended an open-air picture theatre, which Mary believed was the only one in New Zealand. The next morning they wandered around the Forest Service plantations, enjoying the "gorgeous viewpoints of the Bay of Islands over the planted hills", and then drove to Kaeo for the next farm school. The weather was extremely hot and the roads dusty. Kaeo, which is inland from the Whangaroa

Harbour, was the site of the first Methodist mission in 1832, and "the place has been asleep since". Mary described it as a small hamlet tucked into the hills with lots of original houses and shops with Victorian fronts and windows. The hotel was old, but well run and comfortable, and had water piped down from the hill. The farm school was affected by the deaths of a mother and baby. "As the mother was related to everyone, the whole community was in mourning. We hung about chatting to anyone who wanted to know about the exhibits." Mary spent Sunday writing, and listening to the stories about various Kaeo inhabitants told by the lady who drove them to see the Whangaroa Harbour. The men from the Department of Agriculture had been on a fishing trip and returned with a swordfish. There was a good turnout for the school on Monday, after which they packed and drove to Kerikeri where they stayed at a 90-year-old homestead with a wide verandah and French doors. It had originally been a charming residence, but was now dilapidated.

The women were scheduled to visit a remote holding and were to meet up with the farmer who would walk with them there as the tide would be too low for a launch. They drove down a headland through poor clay and gumdigging country. At first the road was good, but then for 18 miles (29 kilometres) fine white dust billowed through the car's floor. After stopping briefly to talk with a couple of men in a lorry they carried on to the station only to be told, "Mr H had gone in a lorry with the owner to meet the man from the Government … The owner's wife was tickled [to learn] we were the 'Government men'." They backtracked to find the men, and then set off with the farmer: "He lived in primitive fashion with his partner, a rather charming young widow, in two huts amid fruit trees in a very pretty bay reached either by a bulldozed track or by sea." The farmer's wife fed them a "compost" salad, fish soufflé and bread baked in an outside clay oven.

Before leaving for Whangarei, they called on Miss Kemp in Kerikeri, who lived in Kemp House, New Zealand's first wooden house built in 1822. The house and Stone Store were the heart of the early Kerikeri Mission Station.[12] Mary regretted not having her sister Nancy with her: "She would have enjoyed all the queer folk and funny stories, as well as being interested in the countryside, which is different to the rest of New Zealand."

Mary found the trip strenuous, with having to set up the tent, model farm and exhibits for just two days of lectures at each place: "Mine [her lecture] comes the morning of the second day and each time I have to think it out because different things grow. Then at the end we wreck the tent and pack everything." Whenever there were two or three days between schools, the women scouted the countryside looking at trees and old houses. Prior to the trip Mary suffered an injury or infection in her hand and also had dental problems. When the infection and swelling cleared she could again drive "… terribly rough roads without a twinge. My mouth parts have settled. I feel heaps better and am full of beans. Everyone says I have a good

A model farm and exhibits of farm management by the Department of Agriculture at a 1930 trade fair. The Northland farm school would have set up similar models at each location. ALEXANDER TURNBULL LIBRARY

The Sutherland sisters, Kate, Nancy and Mary, at Torphins, Khandallah c.1950. Mary was 57 years old. SUTHERLAND/GRAY FAMILY

colour again. The rural sociologists have undertaken to put half a stone on me this trip, and so far I've put on two pounds." Her car also needed to be fixed: "I am off a Hillman of the new kind, and feel I'd rather have an Austin 40."

After packing the tent and exhibits for the last time, the travelling farm school for small Northland communities returned to Wellington and was deemed highly successful.[13] Lectures were provided for country women as well as farmers and there had been good attendances. The rural sociologists had looked at population trends and standards of living and culture, and articles for women as well as men were published in the *New Zealand Journal of Agriculture*. As well as participating in the Northland farm schools, Mary had written the chapter 'Native vegetation' for the Department of Agriculture's book *Farming in New Zealand*,[14] supervised tree and shelter planting on seven of the department's farms, and also continued a regional study of farm plantations in Canterbury and Central Otago.

On the *Alert*

Marie Stewart's poultry farm, Cheriton, was a large business. She supplied Rotorua and Taupo hotels with eggs and dressed chickens, and helped to establish the Tauranga Egg Marketing Co-operative, which supplied American forces in the Pacific during World War Two.[15] Marie wrote a number of papers on poultry and regularly contributed articles to the *NZ Farmer*. She was also a member of the Tauranga Hospital Board. She and Mary Sutherland were friends, and Mary had advised her family on planting eucalypts.[16]

Given how hectic the year had been, it is little wonder that at the end of 1950 Mary was exhausted. Though a good portion of her work was outdoors, she still yearned to get away to somewhere with stunning scenery and a strong sense of history where interesting and different trees and plants grew, and what could be better than to share the experience with a like-minded friend. So in November, Mary and Marie travelled together through Fiordland: Marie kept a diary of their trip,[17] but Mary lost her writing pad overboard, so her letter to family was written on "borrowed" paper.[18]

Mary was in Dunedin working on the Canterbury and Central Otago farm plantations study when Marie flew down from Tauranga on a flight that made twenty-minute stops at Gisborne, Palmerston North, Paraparaumu and Christchurch. The next morning a service car took them to Bluff where they found a tiny, grubby vessel below the wharf at low tide and climbed down a long ladder with their suitcases. The MV *Alert* was a former World War Two harbour defence launch deployed around Fiordland and in waters off the South Island coast. It had just returned from the Antipodes and Bounty islands expedition led by Robert Falla, who had succeeded Walter Oliver as director of the Dominion Museum.

Aboard the *Alert*. Marie Stewart (second left) with Mary (far right) and fellow passengers.
M. MACKERSEY

The ship's captain and owner Alec Black, who was the Dominion commissioner of Sea Scouts,[19] had gone home after the long journey. He left the vessel in the command of the ship's master Alistair Thomson, who was the nephew of Bill Thomson, captain of the *Ranui* on which Marie Stewart had explored Paterson Inlet in 1939. Alistair Thomson was completing a BSc in mining and "knew every inch of the coast". The passengers who embarked were Mr Bee (a sergeant major) and his "gallant" lady; septuagenarians and retired farmers Mr C H Wilson from Invercargill and Tom MacKay from Balclutha; a Lancashire nurse, Matron Jackson; a Dunedin business woman, Noreen Olsen; and one "absurdly handsome and spoilt nurseryman", Mr R Willcox. The cook–steward was Neil, and Ted was the engineer. The master's unnamed brother-in-law was "neither passenger, nor crew".

The vessel set off into rough seas and a south-westerly gale and everyone became sick except the skipper Thomson and one woman. They sheltered overnight at Port William and the following day sailed for seven hours across Foveaux Strait. Marie went below while Mary and Mrs Bee clung on in the saloon. The roll of the ship caused canned goods to shower out of a cupboard, and an oil drum lashed

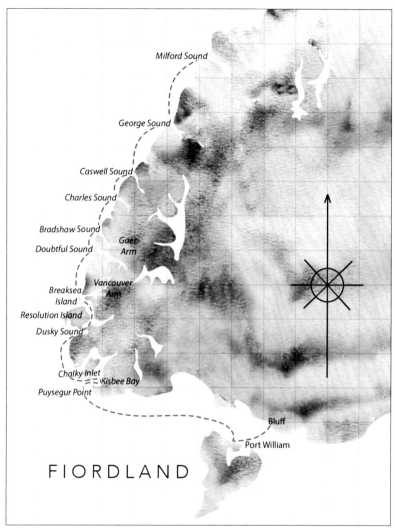

Two years before Mary and Marie Stewart explored Fiordland, takahe (*Porphyrio hochstetteri*) were rediscovered after being thought extinct for forty years. The region is also the kakapo's (*Strigops habroptilus*) final refuge. Due to its relative isolation, Fiordland's flora and fauna is mostly endemic, and some is unique. Early Maori hunted and fished in the region, and collected pounamu from the rivers. When European sealers arrived, they set up small settlements in the fjords, and later species such as moose, red deer and thar were introduced for hunting. In 1952, over 3.2 million acres (1.2 million hectares) of mountains, lakes, fjords and rainforest were designated as Fiordland National Park. It is the largest park in New Zealand, and is managed by the Department of Conservation, which has programmes to increase the numbers of takahe and kakapo. MAP: EMMA MUIRHEAD: CAPTION WWW.FIORDLAND.ORG.NZ

to the side came adrift. The vessel had to heave to while the skipper and Neil, helped by Willcox, dealt with a damaged dinghy as Ted was unwell. The Puysegur Point lighthouse keeper, Douglas Bawden,[20] saw the *Alert's* mast disappear into the wave troughs and concerned for his mailbag, which contained his daughter's correspondence course material, made radio contact with the boat. When the *Alert* anchored at Kisbee Bay in Preservation Inlet opposite two deerstalkers' tents, Thomson radioed Alec Black to say all was well, except they had witnessed three bush fires on the coast. The next day they were entertained with beetroot wine made by Jules Berg, an elderly Swedish hermit with a fishing boat who lived in a tin shanty by a stream. His garden was deer fenced and surrounded by dense bush. He cooked in a camp oven, marked the days off on a calendar, and so as not to miss Christmas confirmed the date with his visitors. Later, Berg and the deerstalkers came alongside the *Alert* in a boat that had a large outboard motor and was towing a barge. They wanted to exchange venison and paua for bread and cigarettes.

The ship's passengers were taken by tractor and trailer on a metal road to the Puysegur Point lighthouse where they all sent telegrams. There were two households; one for the keeper and the other for the assistant. Their gardens were sheltered by deer fences, and they kept cows, sheep and white leghorn chickens, which Marie noted looked remarkably well in such exposure: "When it blows hard, they pick the birds off the wire netting and pop them into their shed." Alistair Thomson later told them a hermit living on Coal Island had at one time burnt down the Puysegur Point lighthouse.[21] The fire was thought to be deliberate as the hermit often complained of the light flickering. A police party from Bluff, equipped for deerstalking to gain the man's confidence, took him away.

As the weather became colder, snow fell to a low altitude and the crew secured everything moveable on board before sailing into the open seas. They lunched at Chalky Inlet and then left for Dusky Sound where they entered narrow, winding straits where tree branches and kelp brushed the vessel. Marie wrote that the sealers' cove — Luncheon Cove on Anchor Island where HMS *Britannia* dropped off twelve sealers in 1792[22] — was "practically landlocked with perfect virgin bush mirrored in such tranquil water, it was difficult to believe it was salt". The next day in brilliant sunshine they followed Captain Cook's exploration route to Facile Harbour on Resolution Island where they replenished the vessel's water tank from a cascade, drank 'Adam's champagne' and filled jugs for the refrigerator.

Resolution Island was New Zealand's first bird sanctuary. Richard Henry, the curator–caretaker from 1894 to 1908, had lived just off its south coast on Pigeon Island. He moved more than seven hundred kakapo and kiwi there from the mainland to protect them from stoats and weasels.[23] At Astronomer's Point the bush had swallowed the tree stumps left by Cook's men. On his second voyage

The Puysegur Point lighthouse, Fiordland, c.1940. ALEXANDER TURNBULL LIBRARY

in 1773 the HMS *Resolution* anchored in Pickersgill Harbour for repairs, and during the five weeks there, land was cleared for William Wales to set up a temporary observatory to fix the position of New Zealand; the tree stumps were the only remainder of their presence.[24]

From Cascade Cove they sailed to Fanny Bay, then Supper Cove at the head of Dusky Sound, but being more than twenty-four hours behind schedule they did not go ashore, so Marie rowed Mary ashore to botanise, avoiding rocks, boulders, logs, deer antlers, swamps and midges. Overnight the 'boys' tried shooting unwary deer at a waterhole, but returned the next morning, muddy, tired and empty handed.

The cruise continued around wooded islands inhabited by penguins and seals. It was raining at Wet Jacket Arm, and Vancouver Arm was shrouded in mist. The men fished with a shark line, and Mary caught blue cod with bait kippered for days on the gunwale. Neil cooked Mary's cod in batter and served it with fried chips. In the evening, over the two-way radio Alec Black informed the skipper they were wanted by the police and he was to stand by for another call. The passengers were "unashamedly listening while playing canasta" when the police asked about the fires, as three in a row could indicate violence. A murderer had escaped from hospital and a search was underway. Thomson was reluctant to return to Bluff to give evidence, and after two more radio calls the matter was shelved.

Their next anchorage at the head of Broughton Arm was "a green amphitheatre surrounded by high stony peaks, some with snow". The bush was full of kaka, pigeons, tui, bellbirds, paradise ducks and grey ducklings. This was the only anchorage where there was considerable bird life; at night they heard kiwi and other unrecognised birdcalls. The next day Mary thought the seals were "like in Antarctic expedition movies, with the fat old bull rolling about the rocks, his ladies bowing and scraping". They left Dusky Sound in calm seas, sailing past mutton birds, mollymawks, porpoises, penguins and seals. Breaksea Island's huge, round boulders were covered in flowering daisies, angelica, raupo, and ferns.[25] Half-grown, grey, fluffy crested penguins were hopping up a small waterfall in the dappled sunlight, but were difficult to photograph.

At Doubtful Sound they anchored at the head of Hall Arm in an inlet, named by Marie as 'Smith's', which was near twin cascades almost hidden by dense bush.[26] Mary and Marie rowed ashore to discover the light green foliage they saw from the ship was young fuchsia, five finger, lacebark, and wineberry. Away from the open coast they found miro and southern beech. Snow fell overnight and later when they were in Deep Cove it rained as they rowed ashore. The wide, shallow Lyvia River, which flows into Deep Cove, was grassed on one side and had southern beech on the other: "Fit for an Arcadian theatrical scene," Marie wrote. They 'dimped'[27] the sandflies and tried to photograph weka and a waterfall too tall for the camera lens.

Alistair Thomson showed them Morrell's hut, which could accommodate twenty trampers. Sides of bacon were hanging in the hut and a washbowl of preserved eggs was on the table ready for the coming season. The *Alert* looked small against the backdrop of high mountains and waterfalls as they rowed back to the ship in an overloaded dinghy with a cold wind whipping the water.

They motored past Elizabeth Island, through Smith Sound to Bradshaw Sound and Gaer Arm for a 'late again' lunch. "Whenever we approach the head of a sound or arm, where precipitous mountain sides give way to flat swamp, where deer graze or game birds nest, out comes what Mary calls the artillery, with the idea of augmenting canned meals": Ted, the engineer, had shot a black swan. At the entrance to Charles Sound they caught red cod, a gurnard and twenty-six crayfish in open baskets. They enjoyed a meal of crayfish and fresh buns and spent an hour and a half taking water from a cascade. The previous season the crew of the *Alert* exported crayfish tails to the United States, throwing the animals' bodies overboard. Mary, with her interest in the environment and the wise use of resources, would have felt this an awful waste.

The Fiordland trip provided spectacular scenery and indulged Mary in her love of native trees and plants, and Marie who had similar interests was an ideal companion. While ashore they meandered among Southland beech "with trunks so black and foliage so picturesque", and discovered white unscented violets, daisies, southern rata, and several species of *Ourisia*. The sun emerged as they sailed out of Charles Sound past "beautiful bush to the water's edge, fairy islands and trees so close that the whole looked like fine stitched tapestry", and in Caswell Sound the mountains were higher and the peaks more picturesque. They walked 3 miles (5 kilometres) to Lake Marchant along the Stillwater River, "inaptly named, as it meets the lake in a series of rapids", and Mary and Marie gathered specimens, including a violet-purple toadstool. A United States scientific group had left a track of debris all along the way.[28] "The bush would soon swallow the mess they'd left behind, though the bottles would not perish." A wide road started by Public Works had also markedly diminished. Their fellow traveller Tom MacKay was on his way back to the *Alert* when he passed Noreen Olsen in high heels still walking to the lake: Matron Jackson had given up when the sandflies descended and returned to the boat.

While at anchorage in George Sound their planned 6:00 am walk to Lake Alice had to be cancelled after all-night rain, so they set sail in a stormy sea for Milford Sound. They tried to play cards, but Marie took to her bunk for the sailing north. They entered the Sound in rain, fog and heavy mist, but finally the sun appeared. Six large blue cod had been caught off Brig Rock, an island between Yates Point and Stripe Point, and Mary was indignant at the crew for shooting sharks. Marie was less impressed with Mitre Peak than she expected. She thought the scenery was 'giant', and cascades fell thousands of feet from every cliff, but it needed the glacier on Mt Pembroke and its majestic peak seen from the head of the sound to complete the picture.

An Automobile Association camp was being built at Milford, and the wharf and existing hostel looked little and drab. After mooring, neither Mary nor Marie were pleased to be back on land, but some passengers, lured by the thought of a hotel bed, left for Te Anau immediately after lunch, which was "later than ever" at 5:00 pm. Mary and Marie crossed the sand at low tide to photograph Bowen Falls, and found themselves botanising among a different range of endemic and exotic plants.

Alec Black met the boat at Milford and brought fresh lettuces and tomatoes, and photos from the Antipodes and Bounty islands trip. Marie was amazed the birds had been so tame there had been no need for a telephoto lens. A commercial traveller arrived in darkness, too late to stay at the hostel, so Black gave him a bunk on the *Alert* for the night and told him he'd broken the law by driving through Homer Tunnel, which was not yet opened (although locals unofficially used it).[29]

The next morning Mary wandered to the accommodation house and photographed the graves of Donald and Elizabeth Sutherland for the forebears;[30] it is uncertain whether they were ancestors, or if Mary was referring to unrelated Sutherland descendants. Scottish-born Sutherland was a sailor, prospector and wanderer who jumped ship in New Zealand from the *Prince Alfred* and landed in Milford in 1877 to stay for forty years. When the Milford track opened, he and his wife Elizabeth built an accommodation house, the Chalet, near Bowen Falls for the tourists.

Alistair Thomson drove Mary and Marie back to Dunedin, starting the journey in Black's 1934 Austin 10, but the car boiled amid the boulders and hairpin bends on the climb to Homer Tunnel. Mary described the tunnel entrance as a tube station with the inside densely black. Water dripped through the rock, making the roadway wet and slippery. They enjoyed the forest and lakes of Eglinton Valley and changed cars at Te Anau. After an overnight stay in Dunedin, both pleased to have a bath, Marie flew home to Tauranga and Mary coached to St Andrews, South Canterbury, where she was met by Dr Philip Randal Woodhouse. He had been medical superintendent at Wellington Hospital, but having seen too much death and suffering in military hospitals during World War One, gave up medicine to became station manager of Blue Cliffs when his wife Airini inherited the sheep station. Mary described it as an early settled sheep run in a beautiful spot in the foothills, with old trees and gardens. Woodhouse also took Mary to inspect two neighbouring sheep stations where the farmers were keen on trees. She stayed three days, and then caught the Friday night boat from Lyttelton to Wellington.[31]

Mary described Homer Tunnel as 'a tube station' with the inside densely black. ALEXANDER TURNBULL LIBRARY

Donald and Elizabeth Sutherland, proprietors of The Chalet, with their maid and a guide at Milford, c.1900. ALEXANDER TURNBULL LIBRARY

CHAPTER 8

EUROPE and CANADA 1952

A journey to Britain

After her sister Nancy returned to England, no doubt Mary longed for the home country, so at the age of 58 she sold her Raumati bach and arranged unpaid leave to visit family and friends and study forestry and farms overseas. She also planned to visit her niece Frances in Canada, so arranged an introductory letter from the New Zealand Institute of Foresters to the Canadian Institute of Forestry.[1] Mary's previous assistant, Hilda Stevens, had resigned, so the new farm forestry officer, Juliet Burrell, would take on Mary's role while she was away.[2] Her final jobs before departing were to produce a booklet on homestead shelter planting,[3] based on her earlier work, and to write two articles for the *New Zealand Journal of Agriculture*: 'Farm tree planting' and 'Forest taxation in Europe and New Zealand'.[4]

Mary sailed to Sydney in January 1952 on-board the MS *Wanganella*. Her cousin Fraser Bremner lived not far away from the wharf at Potts Point, so they spent time together walking through the nearby Botanic Gardens and National Herbarium, where she talked with Lawrie Johnson who was in charge of eucalypts, and a botanist from Kew Gardens, Joyce Vickery, who was researching grasses. Mary boarded the SS *Orontes* for the onward journey, sailing to Melbourne where she was welcomed at the dock by women from the Federation of University Women (FUW) and visited the Springdale nursery with Forests Commission staff. When the *Orontes* docked in Adelaide and Perth, Mary was again welcomed by members of FUW. In Perth she toured the Collier Pine Plantation with Mr Burrill from the Agricultural Department and Mr O'Grady from the Forest Service. The maritime pines had been planted twenty-five years earlier to meet the anticipated need for soft wood in the 1960s. Mary also went to the Somerville Forest headquarters and the Gnangara Forest mill and plantation where women, working in scrub-roofed shelters, were employed to watch for fires.

Mary's articles from the *New Zealand Journal of Agriculture* were collated into a booklet on homestead shelter planting. SUTHERLAND/GRAY FAMILY

HOMESTEAD SHELTER PLANTING

By
M. SUTHERLAND,
Formerly Farm Forestry Officer,
Department of Agriculture,
Wellington.

Bulletin No. 346   N.Z. Department of Agriculture

Price: 2s.

The *Orontes* set sail across the Indian Ocean for Ceylon (now Sri Lanka), and as it was "crossing the [equator] line" the entertainment halted to announce the death of King George VI. At Colombo, Agnes Jackson, wife of the British Methodist missionary Basil Jackson, took Mary to visit a Buddhist temple that had a sacred bodhi tree (*Ficus religiosa*). The sight of people sleeping on pavements disturbed Mary.

A stop at Aden gave time to visit the Tawila Tanks — an ancient rainwater system hewn out of volcanic rock. Mary wrote that they were rediscovered in 1854, her guide said they dated back to the Queen of Sheba, but nothing is accurately known of their origins.[5] From the top of the crater, she walked down to a museum built in 1930, past flame trees, cassia, acacia and jasmine, and through a tunnel where camels brought foodstuffs from Saudi Arabia into the town.

At the entrance to the Suez Canal, Mary noted eucalypts and casuarinas, and irrigation ditches fed from the Nile. The trains were not running because an explosion had caused a derailment. The *Orontes* spent two hours in the Great Bitter Lake while the southbound convoy passed, and then moved through the canal in a seven-ship convoy: "Land here is high and where Moses is supposed to have crossed the Red Sea." A case of chickenpox on board caused a three-hour delay to disembark at Port Said, so she missed the souvenir sellers and getting to see the gully-gully man perform his tricks.[6,7]

In the Mediterranean near Naples, Mt Etna and Mt Stromboli rose out of the sea and Vesuvius emerged from mist. Marseilles was rebuilding after severe wartime bombing and Mary thought one new residential block looked ugly; it was built to house two thousand people and had different coloured verandahs. She climbed the steep steps to the Basilique Notre-Dame de la Garde: "It is a type of Lourdes, and has been credited with cures. The steps would either kill or cure."[8] The basilica had been damaged in the war, and the old fort by the entrance had "vanished, removed stone by stone" to build a tearoom to pay for renovations. The antechapel had crutches and plaster casts from soldiers of the two world wars, and plaques in the church expressed gratitude for Edward VII's recovery from illness at Hyères in 1871, including one Queen Alexandra gifted years later in 1901.

Mary took a bus into the mountains through barren limestone with sparse gorse, broom, rosemary, small olive trees, bog myrtle and poorly regenerating maritime pine. Houses hid among the pines, Peruvian pepper trees, oleander, bougainvillea and green wattles or mimosas — she wasn't sure which. When she asked for a maritime pine cone to check the seed type, an alarmed woman shouted in French that it had a hairy brown caterpillar, which would irritate her skin.

During a stop at Gibraltar, Mary visited the restored King's Chapel. It had been damaged the previous year when the RFA *Bedenham* exploded in dock; depth charges were being unloaded into a lighter when they ignited and sank the ship, killing thirteen people, injuring hundreds, and damaging the nearby chapel, two cathedrals and the convent where the governor resided.

When Mary arrived in England her travels were filled with family and friends, old haunts and colleagues, and connecting with women's groups and forestry and botany professionals. She stayed with her sisters Nancy and Nell at Anerley, south London, and with Betty Flint attended the da Vinci quincentenary exhibition, which had a scientific display of photographs and da Vinci models.[9] Mary also visited the British Federation of University Women at Crosby Hall, Bishopsgate,[10] attended the Royal Academy of Arts exhibition *The Last Hundred Years of Pictures*, and went to the Ideal Homes exhibition. She attended a council meeting of the Society for the Oversea Settlement of British Women chaired by the Countess Bessborough. At the meeting, Mr Bierman from the South African High Commission spoke on immigration opportunities for women in South Africa, and two Australian women were also present. Mary later interviewed four women for the society, who presumably intended to settle in New Zealand.

On her way to Bangor she stopped at Snowdonia for a guided tour through Gwydyr Forest led by the head forester Mr Harrison, and at Bangor visited people from her university days, including 'Thomas the school', most probably her tutor Thomas Thomson, who she noted was growing New Zealand shrubs at Llanrug. Her trip to the university farm at Abergwyngenyth (Aber Farm) where she had raised forest tree seedlings in 1916, would have been nostalgic. At Oxford, she met with Professor Harry Champion, Robert Troup's successor at the School of Forestry; she was impressed with the panelling of exhibition woods in the faculty's rooms.

Mary's interest in agriculture was at the fore when at Stratford-upon-Avon she showed particular interest in the farming implements at Shakespeare's mother's house. She attended the Nottingham Show[11] where she talked with dignitaries and experts, and at the Royal Reception she met their Royal Highnesses the Duke and Duchess of Gloucester. Mary appreciated genuine people, and wrote in her diary that the duchess was a "very nice and natural" person. Among the other people she met were Lord Charles Bledisloe[12] and his wife Elaine. Lord Bledisloe, a former New Zealand governor general, had a lifelong interest in agriculture. Mary also talked with the Duke of Westminster's head forester, and Colonel Floyd, who was previously a commanding officer of the Timber Corps and knew Lindsay Poole of the New Zealand Forest Service. She was impressed with a forestry exhibit that included wood impregnated with creosote in 1893, and after seeing a display with a revolving light to simulate fire, she wrote in her diary "apply to wind"; perhaps she meant a fan could demonstrate the effect of wind on trees.

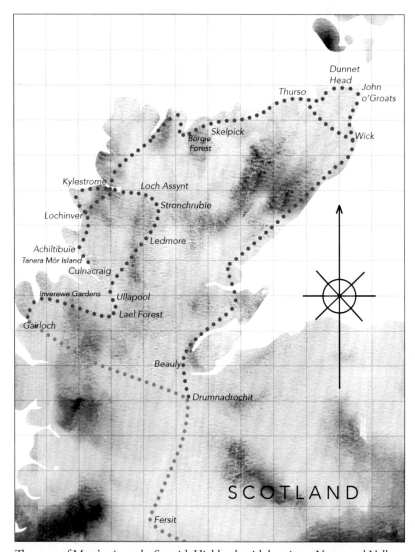

The route of Mary's trip to the Scottish Highlands with her sisters Nancy and Nell, and niece Helen. Mary separately returned to Corrour Estate, catching a train at Tulloch south to Loch Ossian. Scotland occupies one-third of Great Britain and contains most of the island's mountainous terrain. Its border with England runs for 60 miles (97 kilometres) from Solway Firth to the North Sea. The rugged, mountainous Highlands are separated from the Lowlands by the Highland Boundary Fault. Most of the population, 5095,969 around the time Mary visited, live in the Lowlands. In 1952, reindeer were introduced to the Cairngorms, BBC television launched in Scotland, Queen Elizabeth made her first visit to Balmoral Castle as monarch, and John Cobb died on Loch Ness while attempting to break the world water speed record in his jet-propelled speedboat 'Crusader'. MAP: EMMA MUIRHEAD. CAPTION: WIKIPEDIA

In early summer the Sutherland family took an eagerly anticipated trip to Scotland. Mary, Nancy and Nell, their niece Helen (Frances's sister) and Rata the dog met at Drumnadrochit to begin the journey to John o'Groats at the north-eastern tip of Scotland, and then along the west coast and through the Scottish Highlands. Their first stop was at Glen Urquhart plantation where Mary noted Sitka spruce, Japanese larch, and 30-year-old noble fir. The journey to Wick passed Lord Lovat's experimental cattle ranch near Beauly; Lovat had chaired the Acland Committee after the first world war.

At Wick they visited the Bruce family, but while there Nell fell over Rata and hurt herself, possibly tangled in the dog's lead, so she stayed behind while the others, including Maysie Bruce, made a trip to John o'Groats. It was cold, rainy, and the town was "just a big hotel and a cottage or two, a newly planted shelter belt of what looked like privet, and fuchsia in a corner". Proud of her Scottish heritage, and in the right part of Scotland, Mary wanted to see the country's rarest flower, *Primula scotica* (Scottish primrose), which is endemic to the coast of northern Scotland. At Dunnet Head, she asked the lighthouse keeper's wife about it and was directed to a nearby golf course. The man she spoke to there knew of the plant, but had not seen it.

On the journey from Thurso to Scourie Mary made note of heather and small larch trees; at Skelpick there were silver birches and conifers; and in Borgie Forest they drove through old Scots pine and trees that were either mountain pine or shore pine, but mostly Sitka spruce. They took the ferry from Kylestrome to Kylesku where the car had to be reversed onto the wharf. At Lochinver they

The car ferry at Kylestrome, mid 1950s. CREATIVE COMMONS

stayed at Miss McKenzie's on the shore. The next morning they travelled around Loch Inver and Inverkirkaid through pretty valleys out to the coastal road and south though magnificent scenery on the way to Culnacraig. Along the coast near Achiltibuie Mary noticed crofts separated by dry, mortar-less stone walls (dykes) growing potatoes, grass and oats on strips of land down to the sea. Tanera Mòr Island, where the naturalist Fraser Darling lived from 1939 to 1943, was just off the coast. Darling wrote extensively about his wildlife research and life on Tanera Mòr, including his book *Island Years*.

They backtracked to visit Ardvreck Castle on Loch Assynt, the site of the Marquis of Montrose James Graham's betrayal in 1650.[13] Mary noted a nearby Stronchrubie[14] cattle farm had good pasture, but the adjacent land near Drumrunie was open peat and stony, thin soil. On a road near Lael Forest they happened upon Mr McRae, who was thinning trees. McRae was a forester with a small sawmill that sold fence posts; he talked with Mary about the Corsican pine at Glen Brittle Forest, Skye, and the Japanese Sitka, noble fir and European larch in Lael Forest. A dose of history was included in the visit to Gairloch to see a statue of a poet, most likely the Gaelic poet Uilleam Ros. They also went to the new Cemetery of Remembrance where sailors from World War Two are buried, and a private cemetery on Osgood MacKenzie's land. Mary would certainly have been interested in MacKenzie's garden at Inverewe and its collection of temperate plants from the northern and southern hemispheres his daughter gave to the Scottish National Trust in 1952.

Two weeks later Mary parted with her family. She had a trip planned to Fersit and Corrour where in 1917 she worked for Sir John Stirling-Maxwell. She left her car at Tulloch Station where she discovered that Mr Dorward, the old stationmaster, had recently died, and caught the train to Corrour. A shepherd forester on Sir John's staff was also on the train taking his dogs to Corrour to help Andrew Tait muster sheep. From Tulloch station Mary could see the Fersit plantation; the larch and Scots pine were now grown, and there was still a burnt gap about the middle at the spot where fires always started, just beyond the bridge. The pathway through the plantation along the railway tracks was still there, though Fersit Halt was "done away with" and a low dam at the north end of Loch Treig made it less pretty: "Our boat cove is no longer there", and two of the plantations she helped to establish beside the lake were "given away during this war".

Tait met Mary at the station, and Mr Willcox, a forester who had been there five years, accompanied her to the burnt-out lodge and garden. The nursery was where she remembered it, but with lined-out plants only, and the north of the roadway was now pasture. The old stone was still by the lodge doorway, but the rowan tree had gone. Willcox told her a water ouzel still nested in the north end under the bridge. The old trees at the western end of the southern shore plantations,

Foresters at Corrour, 1932/1933. Sir John Stirling-Maxwell (forestry commissioner) is seated in the middle behind Rust the Labrador, and Simon Cameron, head forester at Corrour, is seated to his left. © CROWN COPYRIGHT FORESTRY COMMISSION

Right: a 1982 photo of Scotland's Corrour Station, the highest main line station in the UK; below, the Caledonian Sleeper at the station in 2015. CREATIVE COMMONS

noble fir, Oregon pine and Sitka spruce, were all now marvellous in size. They walked through her previous plantings to the arboretum and noble fir regeneration plot, passing Japanese larch and laburnum.

Her return trip south to London passed through "Midlothian country; first dairy, then sheep". She picnicked in a pine plantation with good mixed belts on the hills opposite, and as she crossed the England–Scotland border, further commented on the Sitka and Norway spruce in Wauchope Forest, and the rolling green or peaty hills and plantations. When she asked a forester at Kielder Castle about how shore pine grew on peat, he pointed to a block of 15-year-old trees in an experimental plot: "They are going branchy as usual".

Onward through windbreaks of Scots pine, ash, sycamore, beech, Scots elm, elder, crab apple and hawthorn, she later passed heavily wooded valleys of beech and oak and a young plantation of Japanese and European larch, then into the industrial towns. From the top of the moor south of Halifax, Mary looked down on the cobbled streets and washing hanging in the breeze. Nest Jones, who she may have worked with during World War One, was waiting for her at Woodstock. Mary observed that she was an "enlarged edition of herself thirty years ago, but very downright." When she arrived back at Anerley, a message was waiting for her that New Zealand House had arranged a visit to the House of Commons, so she saw the Speaker's procession and had a good view of Churchill from the Strangers' Gallery.

Britain has a plethora of forests and arboreta, and Mary was in her element visiting them. She spent a weekend at Abinger Hammer with Dame Frances Farrer, general secretary of the National Federation of Women's Institutes and the National Union of Societies for Equal Citizenship. No doubt they had much to discuss about women in society, but they also visited a nearby arboretum, probably the renowned Winkworth created by horticulturalist Wilfred Fox in the 1930s. Mary noted that young trees were planted above the ponds and a river, and similar species were grouped together. In the older part, specimens grew near a summer lodge and by the lake. They also visited Polesden Lacey, a grand edifice once the home of Edwardian socialite Margaret Greville, where King George V and Queen Mary planted trees. The grounds, including a dog cemetery, were open to the public. Later, on a visit to Tilgate Forest near Crawley with Margaret Mackay, Mary noted old sample plots, probably remnants of the 1932 horticultural research station run by F W Burke & Co. The Forestry Commission bought the forest in 1950 and the felled woodlots were being replanted with conifers, beech and American oak. Tulip trees grew near the abandoned French-style Tilgate House and a large, old western hemlock grew in the avenue.

Mary was only briefly back in Anerley before her sisters delivered her to Kings Cross Station; her destination is unclear, but her diary mentions a conference held in July, possibly the 1952 Danish–Orcadian Agricultural Conference in Orkney.[15] She shared a sleeper with Mrs Young, an Aberdonian whose parents, the Allens, opened their garden at Bieldside for charity; the two women had mutual friends, the McHardys.[16]

Post-war Norway

Mary, now 59 years old, never realised her dream of a Swedish tramp steamer trip, but while in Britain, the Northern Lights were calling, so she and her sister Nell, now retired from teaching, set sail for Norway in July 1952.[17] They left Tyneside for Bergen on the SS *Venus*, where they joined a bus tour to Hardangerfjord. The tour included a visit to composer Edvard Grieg and his wife Nina's summer house, Troldhaugen, overlooking Lake Nordås. The estate is exactly as it was when Grieg died in 1907: house, contents, garden and composing hut in the garden with a table, piano, scoreboard and metronome. The caretaker recalled Grieg had two mascots: "a sort of ape doll dressed in red, about five inches long, and a small, black and white pig with a shamrock that he said goodnight to every evening". He showed Mary a picture of kiwi and asked her about the bird.

As the bus drove to Mundheim, and on to Norheimsund, Mary took note of silver birch, alder, Scots pine and spruce, and they passed a forest nursery which exported trees to Iceland; schoolboys planted the remnants in municipal forests.

Their tour was to be a mixture of a Baltic cruise aboard the SS *Ragnvald Jarl* and bus trips between towns along the west coast of Norway. Mary extolled the magnificent fiords, islands, mountains, glaciers, farms, people and the trees.[18] Much of Norway was severely damaged in World War Two, and the towns were gradually rebuilding.

The first leg of their journey north was by sea from Bergen to Molde where they took a short bus tour to Kristiansund. The drive through Molde alongside the fiord passed new houses and gardens. The town had almost been destroyed in the war, but rebuilding was nearly complete. On the road through to Kristiansund, Mary recorded broadleaved trees, ash, horse chestnut, lime and maple, and after crossing a fiord by ferry the bus stopped on a rocky moor where they walked through silver birch, blueberries, bog myrtle, cranberries and an *Alnus* species.[19] Steep and winding roads descended to the town, which was across a fiord and surrounded by rocky hills. Germans, presumably prisoners of war, had stayed to rebuild the houses and bridges of the damaged town.

Their cruise continued from Molde to Trondheim where Mary and Nell disembarked to visit Stiftsgården, possibly the largest wooden building in Europe used by royalty since 1800. They proceeded on to Stoksund, where the ship sounded a warning as it rounded a narrow passage. It stopped for fifteen minutes

In 1952, when Mary and Nell cruised the west coast of Norway, Haakon VII was king and Oscar Torp the country's prime minister. The Olympic Winter Games were held in Oslo in February. It was the first time the Olympic torch was brought to the winter games by runner relay. Norway won seven gold medals. For two years prior there was considerable debate between Norway, Germany and the International Olympic Committee over whether German athletes should be allowed to compete (Germany occupied Norway during World War Two, 1940–45). The IOC ruled they could, but a month before the games Norwegian speed skater Finn Hodt and other athletes imprisoned for Nazi collaboration were banned. MAP: EMMA MUIRHEAD; SOURCE: WIKIPEDIA

at Rørvik, a port on the island of Inner Vikna where fish were drying on high racks. The next morning, patches of snow and a glacier were visible in the east and they were about to breakfast when the ship crossed into the Arctic Circle. They passed small flat islands, rugged mountains, valleys with green patches and farm buildings, low lighthouses with dwellings at their side, and every so often fishers, some using rods, in high-prow Viking boats.

At Bodø they hired a taxi to a nearby mountain lookout to see the views of islands, mountains and jagged peaks. The snow-covered Lofoten archipelago could be seen in the north-west, and they walked through silver birch trees, a pointed leaved alder and white spruce, gentian, and cranberry, blackberry and crowberry, and what Mary thought might be chervil. In town by an old, grassed-roof house she spied a sawmill with cut lengths of spruce. "All Bodø," she wrote, "from the school eastwards, was destroyed by the Germans, but it has been rebuilt: it is modern with wide streets on the squared system." But there were still visible bombed spaces.

With the sun shining brightly at 9:00 pm they sailed to the Lofoten archipelago, and an hour later docked at Svolvaer on Austvågøya Island. Mary described it as a town built on various bits of projecting land and an island joined by a bridge. It was still light at 11:30 pm when the ship set sail to Harstad.

A visit to the Trondenes Kirke was a must. The stone church is the world's northern-most medieval building, made of six-foot thick stone walls and dating from around AD 1100. The Germans used it to stable their horses during the occupation. Inside were 300-year-old embroidered brown velvet vestments, and a wooden cage in a side chapel used to punish backsliders, who were spat on by the congregation. Their guide, carrying an electric lead, led them into the crypt to view the ancient coffins.

As well as scheduled stops, the ship called briefly at other ports for passengers and goods, and during a short stop at Finnsnes, a washing line stretched from a window caught Mary's curiosity, so she quickly went ashore to check out how it worked. A keen botanist on the cruise suggested Mary visit the Tromsø Musée; it turned out to be 'kaput' because of the war. There was a new one, but the botany department was not yet open. The museum had a nomad tent display where she saw a reindeer stomach, traditionally used by Sámi to hold blood for dog food. The exhibit included everything from reindeer bells to slaughter knives and castrators, which were modern implements instead of those she had previously seen made of teeth. Mary didn't elaborate on the workings of these implements, but it is likely they were elastration pliers used to apply rings to cut off the blood supply of livestock testicles, which eventually dropped off.

Mary's visit to Bodø included a trip to this scenic lookout, pictured four years after her visit in 1956. Bodø is above the Arctic Circle and beneath the Auroral Oval. Because of its situation, Bodø has spectacular views of the Northern Lights and midnight sun. Nearby Saltstraumen has the world's strongest tidal current, with epic whirlpools. NATIONAL LIBRARY OF NORWAY

Bergen in 1950, population 162,381. The Hanseatic League opened an office at Bryggen in 1350 and influenced the city's architecture for nearly 400 years. In 1754 the league ceased operations and properties were transferred to Norwegian citizens. Some wooden buildings were rebuilt after fires, but the Hanseatic architecture was retained. NATIONAL LIBRARY OF NORWAY

The porters on the quay at Hammerfest wore brown corduroy trousers, lumber coats, and bright scarlet and yellow caps, and Mary photographed a woman dressed in a blue, full skirt with a red edge, a blue bodice, red-winged cap, long black stockings and turned-up reindeer hide shoes. Adrian, a Norwegian on the ship, told Mary the Sámi used reindeer to travel, but owned few, whereas 'whites' used Caterpillar vehicles. Frost and snow made it hard for the Sámi to scrape together enough food; they soured their milk, cut it into lumps and put it in coffee with salt.

During the war the Germans based their U-boats in Hammerfest harbour, and twice in 1944 the town was bombed by Russian air forces. Two transport ships were sunk in the harbour and everything was destroyed except the Hauen Chapel. Mary was interested in the structure of buildings and how the town was being redeveloped. She noticed concrete buildings were replacing those destroyed, and electricity was being laid. The temporary wooden camp dwellings were painted and insulated, but there were no trees or gardens, except a pansy bed by a statue, and grass with sphagnum in the hollows. Snow fences ran along the ridges of the hills.

Mary met the Norwegian director of education and a party of teachers travelling on the ship to Kirkenes for a library opening. Teachers across Norway had paid for the library to thank the locals for helping colleagues from Oslo who were transported by the Germans in 1942–43. Mary thought their leader was likely to be a botanist as he was "very good with information and knew the names of flowers".

Sámi people in traditional winter clothing, 1962.
THE NATIONAL ARCHIVES, NORWAY

Kirkenes was so close to Russia that Mary and Nell shared a taxi with fellow tourists to the Norway–Russia border about 9 miles (14 kilometres) out of the town. Their taxi took them through silver birch trees, rocky areas of blackberry, lichen and moss and past an occasional house and ski-slides on the skyline. At one stage a horse with a bell trotted in front of them. They passed reminders of the war including a rusty German helmet on a roadside stone by a lake, and a sign announcing 'Jarfjord'.

The ship had been two hours late in docking at Kirkenes and their taxi had a puncture on the way, so by the time they arrived at the crossing the Russian sentries had closed the border into the Soviet Union and left. A woman who had made the trip earlier told Mary the sentries had forbidden her taking a photograph.

After the treeless, flat-topped, sloping hills along the coast, Mary found Kirkenes pleasant, with new houses and gardens growing white spruce, rowan and silver birch trees. A fisherman took Mary and Nell to his shrimp factory and gave them a tin of shrimps. On the wharf, Mary watched as the ship unloaded creosoted poles and sleepers. She was told they came from the Trondheim Impregnation Plant.

On the return voyage to Bergen the ship called at Vadsø and as they were sailing into the mouth of the Varanger Fjord what looked like thick hedges turned out to be fish racks. The German Wehrmacht had occupied the town during World War Two and it too was heavily bombed by Allied forces. Mary found little of interest except for two old houses with grass roofs and the Vardøhus fortress.[20] At its museum she looked through displays of Vardø's past, ancient and modern war implements, including gas masks, the cord from Roald Amundsen's boat used in the 1903 survey of the magnetic North Pole, and harpoons and whale guns.

As the ship was going into Kjøllefjord it passed the Finnkirka sea cliffs, a place of worship for the Sámi people. The captain told Mary the ladders on the roofs of houses at Kjøllefjord were to clean the chimneys: men either climbed down into them or lowered ropes with stones and birch branches attached to them. Mary was disappointed on leaving Honningsvåg that she had been too slow to photograph a pretty, white house with a driveway of trees, a potato plot and hayfield, right on the Arctic Circle. At Hammerfest they watched wooden pails of cloudberries being loaded on the ship. Mary had hoped to experience the midnight sun, but it shone brightly until 9:40 pm, then disappeared. The hills turned pink-purple and the greens in the sky were like emeralds in the shade. After coffee and marzipan cream cake they were presented with Arctic Circle certificates and stayed up till 12:30 am; others waited till 3:00 am to watch the sunrise over the mountains.

The ship made a quick stop at Sandnessjøen where crowds embarked but passengers were not allowed ashore. A small boy who missed the ship earlier was brought alongside in a rowing boat. On another brief stop Mary watched a man disembark with a large frame holding pressed plants. She was dismayed to have missed the opportunity to see the plants and talk to a fellow botanist. Proceeding onwards they passed a state-owned sheep-breeding farm on a flat coastal island, a church and monument to the Lutheran priest and poet Petter Dass, and a memorial cemetery of one thousand Russian prisoners killed when a Norwegian steamer, commandeered by the Germans, was bombed.

The cruise ended in Bergen, and Mary and Nell accompanied a Russian–French woman, Rita Makarova, to the railway station to catch the train to Oslo. Rita travelled third-class, which was "like New Zealand's first class on the open coach system". Mary and Nell were in second class in a carpeted compartment with a table. The train passed through Hop, Bergen, followed the road to Trengereid and then travelled alongside the 68-mile-long Sørfjorden (110 kilometres) with its "lovely reflections and silver birch". It climbed moor and rock country growing spruce, and through tunnels — the longest of which took six and a half minutes to get through. The railway curved upwards through snow patches and high hills to Voss, a "pretty village with hotels". Mjølfjell, on upland moor, had a large youth hostel but fewer trees, and then they passed towering mountains and waterfalls. It was cold at Hallingskeid station, which was built under a snow shield. Mary noted conifer forests in Torpo, sawmilling and timber work in Nesbyen, and rafts of spruce and stacked thinnings at Keodargen Lake. She and Nell shared an empty compartment with Rita and ate strawberries they had bought while on the ship.

In Oslo they walked a lot, including along the cobbled main street Karl Johann's Gate. They visited friends and went to the museum where the wooden sailing ship *Fram* was housed.[21] Mary went on board: the cabins were filled with clothing, books and instruments from Fridtjof Nansen's 1893–96 Arctic expedition, and items from Roald Amundsen's 1910–12 South Pole expedition were below deck. The clothes were made from various animal skins including bison and polar bear. The museum also had the Kon Tiki which was built for Thor Heyerdahl's 1947 voyage from Peru to French Polynesia. When they left Oslo, Mary and Nell travelled south to Copenhagen, and at Helsingborg their train was put onto a ferry to cross to Helsingør, famous for its Castle Kronborg. At Copenhagen there were letters waiting for them at their hotel; one from the Danish Forest Association invited Mary to visit Viborg to see shelter planting, but the prospect of an all-night journey there and the return journey dissuaded her: she was tired so decided not to go.

They did, however, visit the Rådhus where a floor was set out as a historical street with old-time shop signs and doors of apothecaries and bootmakers (which had a long-top boot), and watchmakers showing huge clockworks. On one side were cases of china, and another room had huge bowls and jugs of Royal Copenhagen china, old treasure chests with brass-studded leather, and silverware. They also visited the Christiansborg Palace, now a government building, situated on Slotsholmen Island where they were fitted with felt overshoes to protect the parquet floors and marble steps, and taken around the King's reception rooms: "The rooms were magnificent, with lovely furnishings and lots of crystal chandeliers."[22]

Across Canada by train

Mary's planned visit to her niece Frances in Canada provided an opportunity to look at Canadian forestry and agriculture, and pass on information about work in New Zealand. In 1950, Canada dissolved its Department of Mines and Resources and transferred its functions to the Department of Resources and Development. Its forestry branch was responsible for developing forestry research, management and products.[23] Mary was interested in how its developments were progressing, and to benefit her work at the New Zealand Department of Agriculture wanted to learn as much as she could about Canadian farm forestry.

Before leaving Britain, she discussed her itinerary with the agricultural commissioner, J G Robertson, at the Canadian High Commission, London. She recorded in her diary that Robertson would contact the chief at Indian Head where the Prairie Farm Rehabilitation Administration (PFRA) was situated. Canada depended on its Great Plains and prairie provinces for crops, and in 1935 PFRA was established to address the effects of the widespread drought and wind that drifted soil across the prairies and left the land degraded and farms abandoned. The tree nursery at Indian Head, set up in 1901 by Norman Ross, promoted shelterbelt planting and provided free tree seedlings to prairie farmers.[24]

Late in 1952 Mary left England for Montreal, sailing through the St Lawrence Seaway aboard the Canadian steamship RMS *Empress of Scotland*. She spent a few days visiting her niece Frances, who was now an occupational therapist at the Veterans' Hospital, Sainte-Anne-de-Bellevue. Her stay included a visit to McGill University's Morgan Arboretum, a forest conservation and research reserve managed by Bob Watson,[25] who asked her to send seed from kowhai and other New Zealand native trees.[26]

Ottawa was her next destination, and she recorded in her diary that the train journeyed through Holstein dairy farms with long, narrow fields, which drained on one side, and shelter belts of birch, ash and sumach (a *Rhus* species). It passed through black spruce hedges, eastern arborvitae, and small woodlots of maple, birch, poplar and aspen. Mary had a full schedule of forestry and farm visits, including to the Department of Agriculture's central experimental farm established in 1886 for scientific research into improving Canada's agricultural methods and crops.[27] The farm's original homestead had an elm avenue, an old arboretum, hedge specimens and experimental crops, including tobacco. She met entomologist

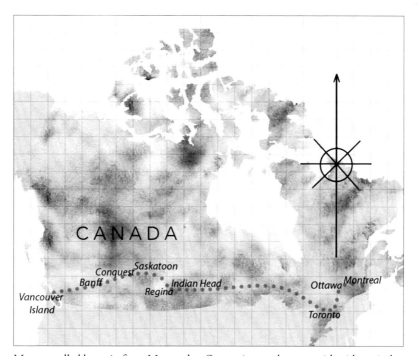

Mary travelled by train from Montreal to Ottawa in a parlour car with wide, swivel seats along each side. For the journey from Toronto to Indian Head, her sleeper was equipped with a wardrobe, fold-away bed and *en suite* facilities. The Canadian Pacific Railway was built to connect east with west — from Montreal to Port Moody. The first service ran in 1886. During the 1960s, air travel and an expanding road network made passenger services less profitable; today's passengers are primarily tourists.
MAP: EMMA MUIRHEAD. SOURCE: WWW.CPR; WIKIPEDIA

Dr Levonné there at an afternoon tea, who asked to be remembered to fellow entomologist Dr David Miller, head of the Cawthron Institute's Department of Biology.[28] The next day at the Foreign Trade Service she met Mr Dunn, who specialised in wood and wood products. He introduced her to Mr Rochester. Mary wrote that he knew 'Enty'— the NZFS director Pat Entrican. Rochester suggested Mary should meet Frank Harrison at the Forest Service where she later discussed farm forestry with the staff silviculturist, Arthur (Art) Bickerstaff.

Colonel John Jenkins, chief executive officer of the Forest Products Laboratories of Canada, introduced Mary to Mr Andrews at the Ottawa laboratory. Andrews was the author of a paper on the taxation of farm woodlots in Ontario. Mary had done considerable research and writing on taxation in New Zealand and Europe, so he outlined the Canadian taxes for her and supplied her with his notes; he then introduced her to Dr Greive, who discussed trials with Osmose, a preservative for green wood products. Greive told her of good results using the timber treatments Tanalith under high pressure to permeate the wood, and Wohlmer salts, which worked by diffusion, but trials had only been going for five years. Other tests showed poplar could make good plywood.

On her last day in Ottawa, Mary visited Parliament Buildings and walked from there to the river, noting that Lone Pine Island now had no tree.[29] She was in her sleeper carriage an hour before departure, and eight hours later arrived in Toronto where she telephoned the Department of Lands and Forests to arrange a visit. Mr Bishop from the department accompanied Mary to a research station at Maple where Dr Carl Heimburger was grafting quaking aspen (*Populus tremuloides*) and big tooth aspen (*Populus grandidentata*) onto silver poplars (*Populus alba*) sourced from Canada, the United Kingdom and Czechoslovakia, to produce a forest tree with a good stem for veneer. Heimburger also grafted conifers and cross pollinated spruce with Eastern white pine (*Pinus strobus*), and purple osier (*Salix purpurea*) with poplar and aspen.

At Hespeler she discussed the local-zone forest station[30] with the superintendent Isaac (Ike) Marritt, who was one of the first foresters in Ontario involved in advisory work for farmers and their woodlots. Marritt demonstrated the operation of a tree planting machine on his woodlot of sugar maple, hickory, and Eastern white pine. The machine required only a tractor driver and one man feeding it to plant seven hundred to eight hundred trees per eight-hour day. Mary also spent time talking with Willard (Bill) Thurston, a forester involved in advising rural landowners and farmers on reforestation and woodlot management.

Mary embarked on a long train trip from Toronto to Indian Head, Saskatchewan, where she was to give a lecture to members of the Canadian Institute of Agriculture. Today, the journey by car is over 1500 miles (2500 kilometres). The train stopped for fifteen minutes at Chapleau where the French author Louis Hémon[31] was struck and killed by a train. It snowed as Mary's train passed through mixed pine and hardwoods, and blocks of pure pine. She wrote her lecture notes and arranged the slides during the trip, and noted in her diary she was in pulp country with stretches of water, aspen and pines, mills and straggling townships. Mr J Walker, superintendent at the Department of Agriculture's Indian Head forest nursery, met Mary at the train station, and in the afternoon introduced her to members of the institute, who told her to "feel at ease". Her lecture was on New Zealand agriculture and forestry, and during the question session she noted the Canadians were struck by New Zealand's annual rainfall and the rapid growth of radiata pine, a species no one there had seen.

The superintendent's house at the Prairie Farm Rehabilitation Administration Centre.
PROVINCIAL ARCHIVES OF SASKATCHEWAN

The barn, greenhouses and meteorological building at the Prairie Farm Rehabilitation Administration. PROVINCIAL ARCHIVES OF SASKATCHEWAN

Mary spent a few days with staff at the Prairie Farm Rehabilitation Administration (PFRA) centre, which produced several million shelter belt trees for the Canadian provinces. The centre's own shelter belts of Scots pine, blue Colorado spruce and Norway spruce were old test plots planted by superintendent Norman Ross, head of the tree planting division at Indian Head in 1905. Caragana hedges were planted between the lined-out beds, and rows of caragana were grown elsewhere; their tops were taken for cuttings at two years. The sample hedges included spruce, Scots pine, balsam fir, and round-leaved hawthorn, and introduced specimens were mostly deciduous trees planted in rows more widely spaced than in New Zealand. Tree breeder Dr William Cram[32] and nursery technician Steve Morgan accompanied Mary to a nursery run by Mr Millen.

Cram was breeding caragana to achieve greater shelter belt height and poplar species for vigour and resistance to frost and wind. He was interested in the experiments on seedling use and wrenching Mary conducted for the New Zealand Forest Service, so she promised to send the information. In the evening over supper with the Walkers she discussed African violets and cyclamens, and vegetation differences between New Zealand and Canada.

The next morning she talked about tree distribution with Mr Crookshanks[33] and met with an entomologist[34] before visiting the PFRA laboratory. Cram's caragana seed had a bug infestation, so he sent a specimen to the lab for identification.

The Walkers drove Mary through prairie parkland country and over the re-making of the Western Highway to Regina, where she met with New Zealand expatriate Dr Leonard Thomson, who was director general of PFRA[35] and chair of the Prairie Provinces Water Board. Thomson arranged for Mary to tour the experimental farm near Outlook, and on the trip she made a detour to visit the Royal Canadian Mounted Police Academy where horses were bred; there were about sixty, all black, being broken in and trained.

Three years previously, an irrigation station had been established at Regina on the South Saskatchewan River prior to construction of the Gardiner Dam.[36] Its purpose was to demonstrate technology to farmers while they underwent the transition to irrigation, and PFRA was in the process of improving the alkaline soil and creating a mixed farm with dairy production. When Mary visited it had lots of hay and alfalfa, but no stock. Irrigation water was pumped from the river at no charge. She noted caragana hedges with green ash, and a sunken shed with drive-in triple doors and double wooden roof beams to store potatoes. Its upper sides were concrete and it had hay-bale insulation and an earthen floor.

They made a brief stop at Conquest *en route* to Saskatoon, where the postmaster told Mary about the Shelterbelt Association, established in Lyleton, Manitoba, by locals Baird and Will Murray. They had petitioned PFRA for an association following the 1935 Prairie Farm Rehabilitation Act. Mary met Les Kerr at

Saskatoon, who showed her around the Sutherland Forest Nursery Station where he was superintendent.[37,38] The station had been designed by Norman Ross in 1913 to supplement the first one built at Indian Head in 1903. As well as growing shelter belt trees, the nursery also carried out horticultural research. She inspected the various evergreen belts and observed an undercutting machine working on Norway spruce.

On the train to Banff she noted fields of millet, mixed bush, aspen, tamarisk and spruce as it passed by Edmonton, Alberta, and balsam fir and poplar near Wetaskiwin. The farms were small with wooden buildings sloping from the north-west. Further south past Calgary the landscape opened to rolling prairies and gullies along the river, and low hills with large, treeless farms. She also noted that Calgary's water was supplied by a dam at Cochrane, and there was another dam at Morley and a cement works at Exshaw. The evergreen forest spread into the Rocky Mountains of Banff National Park where she stayed a few days.

Nearing the end of her trip she visited Vancouver Island, staying in Victoria with her brother-in-law Howard Clark, his wife Florence and their son Michael. Mary described Victoria's town centre as "peaceful with a leisurely air: very pretty with parks in town. One always seems to be approaching a sea shore." She met with local members of the Federation of University Women, and the Forest Service

Hay bales in the prairies and the Saskatchewan Bryck Farms granary: typical scenes on the train journey from Toronto to Indian Head. T. STOCKLEY

"It is impossible to get far enough away from the trees to photograph their entirety."
Professor John Innes, Faculty of Forestry, University of British Columbia, thinks this is
the stand of Douglas fir at Cathedral Grove, Port Alberni, that Mary visited. "The most
famous stand of Douglas fir was Green Timbers in Surrey, south of Vancouver, which
Empire Forestry Congress delegates visited in 1922. The trees were even bigger than at
Cathedral Grove, but that didn't stop them being felled." In 2018 the British Columbia
government forestry agency was heavily criticised for felling some of the largest remaining
Douglas fir in the world. J. INNES

hosted a trip to Campbell River where they were planting Douglas fir on cutover
land. The trip included a detour near Port Alberni to see the oldest stand of
Douglas fir. She described the trees as "marvellous, standing 200 to 300 feet high
with huge old trunks". On her journey north she observed that Vancouver Island,
with its coastal lumber towns and poor farmland, was more inhabited than she
had expected, and she noted a new mill using waste timber. She caught up with
friends and acquaintances, and stayed overnight with Mrs Llogd, an agricultural
graduate from her alma mater, who left Bangor before Mary.

Her homeward journey began with a ferry crossing in fog to Seattle, where
she was met by a member of the Federation of University Women hospitality
committee. During her stay, the committee ensured she was shown the sights and
entertained, including hosting a dinner where Mary met Judge Evangeline Starr.
By New Zealand standards, Mary wrote, Judge Starr was treated like a justice of
the peace: "She sits on the bench, but does not get Your Honour."

The train to San Francisco travelled through the Shasta Valley, which she
compared to St Gotthard, Switzerland: "The line climbs over a divide then down
through a wonderful engineering feat where it crosses and doubles back on itself,
with snow-capped mountains popping up at intervals." She met several men

and their wives headed to the Lumbermen's Association convention, and the hotel where she stayed was full of lumbermen.[39] They gave her logging books, a presentation copy of *The History of San Francisco* produced for the convention, and a note wishing her "a happy time in our country".[40] A few days later she flew home to New Zealand via Fiji.[41]

Return to New Zealand

In the months Mary was away, the Federation of University Women had welcomed thirty settlers on behalf of the Society for the Oversea Settlement of British Women; 19 were teachers. Mary had interviewed four women while she was in London, and the society was requesting more applicants be placed. No doubt members of the federation would also have been most interested in Mary's reports of meetings with overseas members, and they again elected her as an honorary vice president of the Wellington branch.[42]

Mary returned to work at the Department of Agriculture at the end of 1952. Soon after, eleven clone-2 specimens of Leyland cypress (Leighton Green) arrived from Leighton Hall Estate, Welshpool, Powys.[43] They were to replace canker-affected macrocarpa in Rukuhia, Waikato. It is not known whether she visited the estate

Family and friends on the wharf at Wellington in 1953 to welcome Katherine (Rena) Stewart, Margaret Mackersey's aunt, home from Rhodesia where she had looked after a friend's chicken farm: Godfrey Mackersey, Kate Gray, Mary Sutherland, Margaret, and Kate's daughter Nancy Gray. M. MACKERSEY

or if she imported the trees after arriving home. Mary also resumed writing for the *New Zealand Journal of Agriculture*. Her article 'Gorse smothered by plantations' included a photograph taken in Ashley State Forest showing 5-year-old radiata pines completely choking the gorse.[44] In June 1954, she and engineer Henry Eggers co-authored 'The use of timber in farm buildings'.[45] Soon after its publication, she fell seriously ill with a kidney complaint during a field trip in Central Otago. Frank Hutchinson and other NZIF members visited her in Wellington Hospital; she must have realised her days were numbered, for she told Hutchinson her will contained a bequest to the institute.[46]

Sufficiently recovered to leave hospital, Mary was too weak to manage the stairs at the Grays' Khandallah home, Torphins, so her nephew David Gray and his wife Sheila looked after her at their single-level home in Ngaio. The lounge, a large, carpeted room with a big armchair, fireplace, window seat and a bay window overlooking the valley, became Mary's room. On fine days she would take short walks wrapped in an overcoat and thick scarf. At first she could only cross the road and walk 5 or 6 metres holding on to Sheila's arm: "She would stop on the grass verge and sit on a tiny, metal-framed camp stool she liked to carry. She would sit for a few minutes, watch the world go by, then walk back to the house." Every day Mary walked a little further, slowly regaining her strength: "She was determined. Those outings obviously did her good as she was soon able to go back to her own bed and familiar things." Her health improved sufficiently for her to resume her involvement in the Federation of University Women, but she was never well enough to return to farm forestry work for the Department of Agriculture.

In February 1955 Mary wrote to her niece Frances, who was about to take a hospital position as an occupational therapist at La Guaira, Venezuela.[47] Mary wished her well and hoped she would come to New Zealand after her two-year appointment. Frances's father Howard Clark was holidaying in New Zealand and had visited Northland and Gisborne, and Nan (another niece) was getting married: "They have nice presents and few duplicates." Mary had bathed in the sea for the first time since becoming ill, and missed her bach just when she could make good use of it. Her letter to Frances may well have been her last correspondence. She was admitted to Wellington Hospital and died in March 1955, two months before her 62nd birthday. She had suffered high blood pressure for three years and was in renal failure for three weeks.[48]

A FORESTER'S LEGACY

In memory of her parents, Mary left a bequest to the Pearson Fresh Air Fund, which provided opportunities for British urban children to experience country life. As well as remembering the RSPCA[1] in London, her sisters and their families, she left bequests to the Federation of University Women Fellowship Fund and was the first member to make a bequest to the New Zealand Institute of Foresters.[2]

Tributes to Mary were published in the Wellington Federation of University Women's annual report, the *Evening Post* and the *New Zealand Journal of Forestry*, which also noted the passing of foresters Owen Jones and Roderick Macrae.[3]

In her tribute to Mary, Nell described how her sister gained an intimate knowledge of backwoods life in both islands during her time as forest assistant with the State Forest Service.[4] Mary had travelled widely, sometimes with a packhorse and guide, sometimes in her small car over roads and tracks rarely traversed. Her wide forestry knowledge was appreciated by colleagues and many forestry experts she met overseas. "Forestry colleagues admired her vigorous, forthright nature, and friends and relatives remembered her sincerity, unselfishness, generosity, vitality and zest for life. The width of her interests and her understanding of people brought her many friends. Hers was a loveable personality." As superintendent of the YWCA Woburn hostels: "The fairness and impartiality of her administration made her popular with the girls." Mary's niece Helen Baxter remembered her as the much-loved Aunty Mare of the Gray children.

Frances Glendenning[5] collected information about her aunt Mary including her personal letters and diary of her 1952 overseas trip. When Frances was seeking information about Mary, Lindsay Poole wrote to her: "Mary was a sound influence in the young Forest Service, and fitted in well in those early days when forestry was considered a male preserve, and she did a great deal of good in the early farm forestry days."

Mary Sutherland cleared the first path through the trees for other woman foresters to follow. The extent of her work has largely remained hidden, yet her experimental fieldwork for Leon McIntosh Ellis assisted him to develop and implement his afforestation plan, and helped form the strong foundation of this country's forestry knowledge.

On a trip to the United Kingdom, Frances visited her grandparents' lairs (burial plots) at Torphins Cemetery. Robin Sutherland described its memorial stone as "unusual in the extreme, but highly appropriate for the family that included the first woman forestry graduate. It is in the form of a tree trunk, the granite cut approximately circular and trimmed to give the effect of bark. At seven places around the trunk and at different heights major branches of the tree are cut back almost flush with the trunk. On each of these is recorded the names and dates of individual family members: a real family tree."[6] Mary's name is there, but her remains are in Wellington.

Mary is remembered through her gift to the New Zealand Institute of Foresters, received and invested in 1957. Initially named the Mary Sutherland Bequest, it funded an award to a forest ranger student at the completion of their second year of study.[7] When forestry training changed in 1976 it was awarded at completion of the fourth year of study. In 1997 the awards were again revamped, and the Mary Sutherland Award was made available to final year polytechnic students in a discipline relevant to the forestry profession. Since 1975 more than twenty students have been presented with the award.[8] In December 2011 the award was replaced by the Mary Sutherland Scholarship.[9] Mary would be proud her bequest continues to assist deserving students in their studies of forestry and forestry-related subjects.

In 2016, one hundred years since she graduated, Bangor University[10] honoured her memory by establishing the Mary Sutherland Award for the best female forestry graduate from three programmes: BSc Forestry, MSc Forestry and BSc Conservation with Forestry. A Bangor University forestry student also made a pilgrimage to the memorial plaque in the Redwood Grove, Whakarewarewa Forest, New Zealand — truly a demonstration of the inspiration Mary is to foresters.[11]

Studio portrait taken in the 1950s.
SUTHERLAND/GRAY FAMILY

The memorial stone over David Sutherland's lair (Mary's father)
at Torphins Cemetery, Aberdeenshire, Scotland. SUTHERLAND/GRAY FAMILY

ACKNOWLEDGEMENTS

My special thanks to the Stout Trust and Andrew McEwen, chair of the Zealand Institute of Forestry (NZIF) Foundation, for making this book possible. When he was president of the New Zealand Institute of Forestry, Andrew let me access its historical records, answered questions and provided technical advice on forestry. He confirmed Mary's story needed to be told, and on my behalf found funding for it to be published.

My sincere thanks to the Sutherland and Gray families, who are so proud of their much-loved aunt. Mary's niece Frances (Frankie) Glendenning collected family history and memorabilia, including Mary's personal letters, a diary and photographs. When Frankie died, Michael Clark arranged for these records to be left with John Gray, who kindly loaned them to me. Family members willingly shared memories and photos, including Helen Baxter, who provided Mary's graduation photo; Helen's daughter Adrienne Grogan, who contacted family members on my behalf; Sheila Gray and her daughter Hilary King.

Michael Roche, author of 'Mary Sutherland' in the *Dictionary of New Zealand Biography*, provided advice and encouragement. He generously passed on reference material and contact details for people. Claudia Orange and Emma Dewson at the Ministry for Culture and Heritage let me access Michael's research, and Charlotte Macdonald and Bridget Williams gave access to Pip Lynch's research about Mary for the *Book of New Zealand Women*.

This book has been through years of development and some people who assisted are no longer in the roles they held at the time, but they still deserve my thanks. Robyn Burke at the New Zealand Timber Museum, Putaruru, helped me locate the person responsible for Mary's memorial plaque in the Whakarewarewa Forest. John Kininmonth answered my question to say that Chriss Taylor was that person. Te Amorangi Trust Museum held a file on Mary, which Bryon Somervell let me examine and Bruce Chapman located the photo of Mary wearing her forestry gear. Scion archivist Tiena Jordan and librarian Pauline Siegfried gave me access to the State Forest Service records. Information management adviser Jan Lindsay provided help with references and photos, assisted by Sierra de la Croix.

Chris Ecroyd, curator at the National Forestry Herbarium, commented on Mary's microscopic pine species identification study. Staff from Archives New Zealand and the Alexander Turnbull Library helped find elusive files and provided material.

Geoff Willacy helped in the search for elusive first names. At Te Papa Tongarewa, archivist Jennifer Twist gave me access to the Dominion Museum records and provided research assistance; botany curator Pat Brownsey provided information on Te Papa's plant collection database and described his time working at the Dominion Museum herbarium; botany curator Carlos Lehnebach helped unravel the mystery of a tree Mary referred to in a newspaper report and spent a huge amount of time checking my tree and plant names glossary; Ross O'Rourke shared his knowledge about people at the Dominion Museum; and Kirstie Ross directed me to the forestry in schools programme files. Mary Smart, liaison librarian for knowledge and information at Te Aka Matua Research Library, located the pamphlet on Mary's radio talk, which is now at the National Library. Stephanie Smith at Tauranga Library provided research assistance.

Biologist Mike Wilcox contacted me after he found a book on eucalypts that had once belonged to Mary, which he donated to the Scion archives.[1] Rob McNaughton, grandson of former NZIF member Frank Hutchinson, obtained comment on Boy Scout forestry camps from his mother Moera. Elizabeth Flint, who helped Mary collect a vegetable sheep for the Dominion Museum, wrote to me. Margaret Mackersey loaned me the diary and photograph album of her aunt Marion (Marie) Stewart, who voyaged through Fiordland with Mary on the MV *Alert*. John Groome recalled childhood memories of the Depression and meeting Mary in the Kaingaroa Forest. Chas Kerr remembered Mary talking to cadets at the Forest Research Institute in the 1950s.

I am grateful for the information about Mary's education and career in Britain from staff at Bangor University: Einion Thomas, Lynette Delyth Hunter and Marc Duggan of the Library and Archives Service, and Nicola Jane Wallis of the School of Environment, Natural Resources and Geography. Jo Darrow, a daughter of New Zealand friends, kindly undertook research at the UK National Archives, where Michael McGrady provided advice on searching their forestry records. Nancy Sharp, reference specialist at the Canadian Agriculture Library, Ottawa, located information about people Mary met in Canada, and Anne Godbout and John Watson from the Morgan Arboretum answered my question on Robert James Watson.

My thanks to Lynn Peck and Julia Millen of Writes Hill Press for turning my manuscript into a finished book. Lastly, thanks to my sons Shaun and Mike, and to my partner Trevor Hoff for his forbearance.

~ *Vivien Edwards*

CREDITS AND ACKNOWLEDGEMENTS

PHOTOS and ILLUSTRATIONS

Title page: Mary Sutherland in Kaingaroa Forest, 1932. 719/34a 18/2a. National Forestry Library, Scion.

Frontispiece: Kauri tree. 1/2-C-22695-F. /records/22855987. Date and photographer unknown. Alexander Turnbull Library, Wellington, New Zealand.

p. 6　The Mary Sutherland memorial plaque in Whakarewarewa Forest, Rotorua, 2009, Photo: Vivien Edwards.

p. 9　Sutherland family, 1893. Sutherland/Gray family records.

p. 12　Mary Sutherland: portrait, 1930. Sutherland/Gray family records

p. 16　Birthplace of Mary Sutherland. Sutherland/Gray family records.

Mary Sutherland, 1910. Sutherland/Gray family records.

p. 17　Bridge House, Torphins postcard. Sutherland/Gray family records.

p. 18　Mary Sutherland with sister Nancy and friends. Sutherland/Gray family records.

p. 19　Sutherland family, 1909. Sutherland/Gray family records.

Mary Sutherland on her graduation day, 1916. Sutherland/Gray family records.

p. 21　Women of the Forestry Corps directing the fall of a tree. Photo: Horace Nicholls. Q30693 © Imperial War Museum.

Nellie Wright and friends, information and photo supplied by Nellie Wright's grandson Wayne Finch.

p. 24　Map of the Loch Ossian plantations, adapted from John Stirling-Maxwell, 'Loch Ossian Plantations: An essay in afforesting high moorland', 1929, pp. 140-141.

Thinnings of Scots pine planted by John Boyd in 1895, near the Boathouse Plantation, Corrour Estate, 1934, © Crown copyright Forestry Commission, Forest Research, Roslin, B2258, with help from Glen Brearley and Norman Davidson.

p. 27　Belt of kauri trees. Photographer unknown. 1/2-C-22696-F. Records/22852070. c.1925. Alexander Turnbull Library, Wellington, New Zealand.

p. 31　Reafforestation in New Zealand: The State Forest Service in the Rotorua district, 1928. Supplement to the *Auckland Weekly News*, 14 June 1928. AWNS 19280614-39-1, Auckland Heritage Collections.

p. 35　1924 Whakarewarewa rangers school. National Forestry Library, Scion. People identified from the photograph published in *Tree People*, by Peter Berg, John Halkett and Brian Mackrell. Forestry Corporation 1987.

Harrods advertisement for Women's Land Army outfits that appeared in the *Daily Mail*, 1918. © exclusivepix.co.nz

Mary Sutherland kitted out in her 'reliable land outfit'. Te Amorangi Museum Trust.

p. 36 State Forest Service personnel at the 1924 rangers school, Whakarewarewa. AAQA 6395 W3347/5 M10517. Archives NZ.

p. 38 Methods of packing nursery stock. Consignment in benzene cans, banana cases, and trays. Eucalypt seedlings have been packed in the trays. M. Sutherland, 'Forestation Manual', 1928. 737/33b PR 048. National Forestry Library, Scion.

Consignment of nursery stock ready for railway transportation. M. Sutherland, 'Forestation Manual', 1928. 737/33b PR 048. National Forestry Library, Scion.

p. 40 Forestry in schools: children preparing to plant trees in an allocated area of Golden Downs Forest, Nelson Conservancy, 1920s–30s. Photo supplied by Peter Berg.

NZ State Forest Service, Circular No. 16. School forestry and plantations by PM Page, forest extension officer, 1924. National Forestry Library, Scion.

p. 47 Planet multiple seeder drawn by a Caterpillar tractor. 3373. National Forestry Library, Scion.

Old iron tank oven used for seed extraction, Hanmer. 926. National Forestry Library, Scion.

p. 48 Use of Hauck burner in burning off firebreaks, Hanmer. 2693, M. Sutherland, 'Forestation Manual', p. 185. 737/33b. PR 048. National Forestry Library, Scion

Portable pacific fire pump for fire protection. 3303, M. Sutherland, 'Forestation Manual', p. 282. 737/33b. PR 048. National Forestry Library, Scion.

p. 53 Lining out seedlings, Whakarewarewa nursery plantation, 1924. National Forestry Library, Scion.

Sequoia sempervirens a year after being lined out. National Forestry Library, Scion.

p. 58 Creating government timber reserves, 1925. Supplement to the *Auckland Weekly News*, 6 August 1925. ID-AWNS – 19250806-45-1, Auckland Libraries Heritage Collections.

p. 62 Constructing the road through the Waipoua kauri forest. Workers and photographer unknown. c.1920s. PAColl-6585-56. Alexander Turnbull Library, Wellington, New Zealand.

Beginnings of the road through Waipoua Forest, mid 1920s. Photo: William Roy McGregor, consultant to the State Forest Service on Waipoua Forest, and lecturer in Forestry, Auckland University College. The Kauri Museum, Matakohe.

p. 64 Climbing a kauri tree in wooden-soled, toe-spiked boots and using handheld grappling irons, 1935. Photo: Tudor Collins, The Kauri Museum, Matakohe.

Neatly spaced taps for extracting resin from a kauri with a 48 foot centre girth, Waipoua's largest tree at the time. Year and photographer not recorded. National Forestry Library, Scion.

p. 66 1928 State Forest Service Conference. In front, Edward Phillips Turner with beard; to the right, Mary Sutherland walks between Leon MacIntosh Ellis and Arnold Hansson. Photo originally given to Frances Glendenning by Lindsay Poole. Sutherland/Gray family records.

First AGM of the New Zealand Institute of Foresters. 1928. Sutherland/Gray family records.

p. 68 Preparing seedbeds, Whakarewarewa nursery, 1928. National Forestry Library, Scion.

p. 70 M. Sutherland, 'Forestation Manual' 737/33b. PR 048. National Forestry Library, Scion.

p. 73 The equipment used in Mary Sutherland's experiment to create an identification key to pine species, for use in conjunction with macroscopic features. *Transactions and Proceedings of the Royal Society of New Zealand.* vol. 63, pt 4. P517-569. 1934. www.paperspast.natlib.govt.nz/periodicals/TPRSNZ 1934-63.2.6.8

p. 76 Mary Sutherland's Austin 10, loaded with debris after a working bee. Sutherland/Gray family records.

Millicent Brooke, the only female forestry student at Auckland University College. 1929. Supplement to the *Auckland Weekly News.* p. 49. 26 June 1929. AWNS-19290626-49-5. Auckland Libraries Heritage Collections.

p. 78 Receipt for the rubber stamp of the New Zealand Institute of Foresters' official seal, taken from Mary Sutherland's design. NZIF records. Photo: Vivien Edwards.

p. 81 Mary Sutherland in compartment D7, Kaingaroa Forest, taking a measurement after light thinning of *Pinus laricio* during sample plot maintenance, 1932. 719/34a 18/2a. National Forestry Library, Scion.

Mary Sutherland in nursery beds, c.1932. Archives NZ, AAQA 6393/W3347/1 H817

p. 83 The Urewera, 1927. Photo: WC Bergman. Auckland Libraries Glass Plates Heritage Collections, 1370 652-02.

p. 85 Unemployment relief work in the North Island. Supplement to the *Auckland Weekly News*, 23 August 1933. AWNS-19330823-37-1. Auckland Libraries Heritage Collections.

p. 88 The Colonial Museum, Wellington, 1934. Photo: Leslie Adkin, gifted by G L Adkin family estate, 1964. A.005434. Te Papa Tongarewa.

p. 90 Colonial Museum interior, Museum Street, Thorndon, Wellington, c.1910. PAColl-3114-2. /records/22869801. Alexander Turnbull Library, Wellington, New Zealand.

Dominion Museum staff, 1932. Photo: John Salmon. MA_B.000838. Te Papa Archives.

p. 92 Mary Sutherland, Don Brooker, and John Salmon and with the 'vegetable sheep'. Photo: Ellen Heine, CA001026/001/002/0016. Te Papa Archives.

A trip in the Fox Glacier region when Mary Sutherland was working at the Dominion Museum. Photographer unknown, but possibly Ellen Heine. Sutherland/Gray family records John Gray/Sutherland family.

p. 95 National War Memorial with the Dominion Museum and National Art Gallery. PAColl-5932-21. /records/22318018 Alexander Turnbull Library, Wellington, New Zealand.

Frank Peat's kauri gum collection. Dominion Museum, Buckle Street, Wellington. *Evening Post*: Photographic negatives and prints of the *Evening Post*. Ref: PAColl-6301-39. /records/22834637. Alexander Turnbull Library, Wellington, New Zealand.

Display cabinets containing Maori artefacts in the Dominion Museum, Wellington, c.1936. PAColl-6301-27. Alexander Turnbull Library, Wellington, New Zealand.

p. 97 Dominion Museum in 'Educational Broadcasts to Schools', September to December 1936, 2YA Wellington, 4YA Dunedin, pp. 33–38, National Library of New Zealand, Wellington.

p. 100 The Raumati bach and Mary Sutherland in the garden. Sutherland/Gray family records.

p. 105 Mary Sutherland with staff from the Botany Division at Waiwhetu, examining a linum crop: Ruth Mason, Dr Harry Allan, David Cairns, Lai-Yung Li, Lucy Moore, Dr Hamilton, Mary, Arthur Healy and George Briggs, 1942. Reprinted from E J Godley, 1980, 'The First Fifty Years: 1928–1978', Botany Division, Department of Scientific and Industrial Research, Triennial Report 1976–78, pp. 5–16, Christchurch: The Caxton Press, with permission from Manaaki Whenua — Landcare Research.

p. 107 Mary Sutherland at Torphins, Jubilee Road, Khandallah, Christmas 1942. Sutherland/Gray family records.

p. 109 The YWCA Woburn hostel. Ref. 3297. Hutt City Libraries. Petone. © Fairfax

Mary Sutherland, in her early 50s, wearing the YWCA hostel uniform during her war service. Sutherland/Gray family records.

p. 111 Mrs Roosevelt visits a hostel built for women munition workers. With her is J.W.A. Heenan, undersecretary of Internal Affairs, who managed E Roosevelt's 1943 tour, and Violet Macmillan, supervisor at the Woburn hostel. John Pascoe Collection. F534 i/4. Alexander Turnbull Library, Wellington, New Zealand.

Workers in a Wellington munitions factory, 30 August 1943. Photo: John Pascoe. PA-Group-00197. Ref: 1/4-000958-F. Alexander Turnbull Library, Wellington, New Zealand.

p. 113 Mary Sutherland at her YWCA Woburn hostel farewell tea, 1946. Sutherland/Gray family records.

p. 122 Stall at a trade fair advertising and displaying the work done by the Department of Agriculture, 1930. Price Collection: 1/2-000265-G. Alexander Turnbull Library, Wellington, New Zealand.

The Sutherland sisters, Kate, Nancy and Mary, at Torphins, Khandallah, c.1950. Sutherland/Gray family records.

p. 124 Aboard the *Alert*. Marie Stewart with Mary Sutherland and fellow passengers. Photo courtesy of Margaret Mackersey.

p. 125 Map: Emma Muirhead: Caption www.fiordland.org.nz > about – fiordland > fiordland – national – park

p. 127 Puysegur Point lighthouse, c.1940. PAColl-8550-19. Negatives and prints from the Making New Zealand Centennial collection. Alexander Turnbull Library, Wellington, New Zealand.

p. 131 Homer tunnel entrance, c. early 1960s. PA-Group-00131. GG-09-058. Gladys M Goodall Collection, Alexander Turnbull Library, Wellington, New Zealand.

Donald and Elizabeth Sutherland, owners of the guest house The Chalet, with their maid and a guide at Milford, c.1900. Photo: A C Gifford. 1/2-041846-F. Alexander Turnbull Library, Wellington, New Zealand.

p. 133 Mary Sutherland's articles on homestead shelter planting. Sutherland/Gray family records.

p. 136 Map illustrated by Emma Muirhead. Caption abridged from Wikipedia information; en.wikipedia.org › wiki › Geography_of_Scotland > wiki > 1952 > in Scotland > Scotland

p. 137 NC2234: Kylesku Ferry at Kylestrome, mid-1950s. Photo: © the late Dr P E G Clements and licensed for reuse under the Creative Commons Licence. Attribution – Share Alike 2.0 Generic (CC BY-SA 2.0).

p. 139   Foresters at Corrour: back row:
Maxwell Macdonald (district officer in
south-west Scotland); A M Mackenzie
(mensuration officer); J F Macintyre
(retired head forester, Newcastleton
District); A M Fraser (Forest of AE);
A G Morris (forester at Ayr County
Council Waterworks, Glen Alton).
Seated: Simon Cameron (head forester,
Corrour); Sir John Stirling-Maxwell
of Corrour (forestry commissioner);
J A B Macdonald (conservator South
Scotland). Seated on the ground, Rust
the Labrador. Taken at Corrour Lodge
1932 or 1933. © Crown copyright
Forestry Commission. Thanks to Forest
Research Photo Library, Mr Bell and
Norman Davidson.

The Caledonian Sleeper at Corrour
Station, 2015. Photo: Andrew, 2015.
Licensed under the Creative Commons
Attribution 2.0 – Share Alike
Generic. The coloured image has been
desaturated. Caledonian Sleeper at
Corrour Station (17738023599).jpg

Scotland's Corrour Station.jpg by
Stephen Duhig, USA. 1982. Licensed
under the Creative Commons
Attribution - Share Alike 2.0 Generic.

p. 142   Map: Emma Muirhead. Caption
sources en.wikipedia.org > wiki >
1952_in_norway
www.tandfonline.com > doi > abs
www.washingtonpost.com > longterm
> olympics 1998 > history > years

p. 144   Bodø from a scenic lookout, 1956.
Mittet & Co. As/L.S. URN_NBN_no-
nb_digifoto_20170824_00068_NB_
MIT_KNR_00780.jpg National
Library of Norway/Nasjonalbiblioteket,
Oslo, Norway.

Bergen in 1950. URN_NBN_no-
nb_digifoto_20190906_00148_NB_
NKF_B_01_078.jpg. Normannes
Kunstforlag. National Library of
Norway/Nasjonalbiblioteket, Oslo,
Norway

p. 145   Sámi in traditional winter clothing,
1962. Creators unknown. Institution,
Riksarkivet Arkivnavn: Billedbladet
NÅ. The National Archives of Norway.
File name: Barn I samedrakter.
File reference: RA/PA-0797/U/Ua/
L0011/0215b.

p. 149   Map: Emma Muirhead. Caption
source: www.cpr.ca > about-cp >
our-history; en.wikipedia.org >wiki >
Canadian_Pacific_Railway

p. 151   The superintendent's house at
the Prairie Farm Rehabilitation
Administration (PFRA) Centre.
R_A13255_2 Provincial Archives of
Saskatchewan.

The barn, greenhouses and
meteorological building at the Prairie
Farm Rehabilitation Administration
(PFRA) Centre. R_A13255_4 Provincial
Archives of Saskatchewan.

p. 153   Hay bales in the prairies, and the
Saskatchewan Bryck Farms granary:
typical scenes on the train journey
from Toronto to Indian Head. Photos:
Trish Stockley, 2018.

p. 154   Stand of Douglas fir at Cathedral
Grove, Port Alberni. Photo courtesy
of Professor John Innes, dean of the
Faculty of Forestry, University of
British Columbia.

p. 155   Godfrey Mackersey, Kate Gray, Mary
Sutherland, Margaret Mackersey and
Kate's daughter Nancy Gray, 1953.
Photo: Margaret Mackersey.

p. 158   Mary Sutherland, studio portrait,
1950s. S.P. Andrew & Sons. Sutherland/
Gray family records.

p. 159   The memorial stone over David
Sutherland's lair at Torphins Cemetery,
Aberdeenshire, Scotland. Sutherland/
Gray family records.

PLANT GLOSSARY

COMMON NAME	SCIENTIFIC NAME
Angelica (NZ native, kohepiro)	*Angelica rosaefolia,* now *Scandia rosifolia*
Aspen: Big tooth	*Populus grandidentata*
Aspen: Quaking, trembling	*Populus tremuloides*
Barley	*Hordeum vulgare*
Beech: Silver	*Nothofagus menziesii,* synonym *Lophozonia menziesii*
Birch family	*Betulaceae*
Blackberry: European	*Rubus fruticosus*
Blackberry: Himalayan, Armenian	*Rubus discolor*
Broom, NZ	*Carmichaelia sp.*
Cacao	*Theobroma cacao*
Cannabis	*Cannabis indica*
Caragana, pea shrub	*Caragana arborescens*
Cedar: Japanese	*Cryptomeria japonica*
Cedar: Western red	*Thuja plicata*
Coprosma	*Coprosma sp.*
Cotton	*Gossypium hirsutum*
Cypress: Lawson's	*Chamaecyparis lawsoniana*
Cypress: Leyland (Leighton green) clone-2	*Cupressus x leylandii*
Cypress: Macrocarpa, Monterey	*Cupressus macrocarpa*
Daisy (NZ native, tikumu)	*Asteraceae* (*Celmisia semicordata, C. coriacea*)
Duckweed (NZ native, karearea)	*Lemna disperma, L. minor*
Ergot	*Claviceps purpurea*
Eucalyptus	*Eucalypt sp.*
Fir: Balsam	*Abies balsamea*
Fir: Noble	*Abies nobilis*
Fir: Douglas, Oregon pine	*Pseudotsuga menziesii*
Fir: White	*Abies concolor*
Five finger, whauwhaupaku	*Pseudopanax arboreus*
Foxglove, mountain	*Ourisia macrophylla*
Fuchsia (NZ native, kotukutuku)	*Fuchsia sp. (F. excorticata)*
Gorse	*Ulex europaeus*
Grasses	*Gramineae*
Green wattle	*Acacia decurrens*
Guaranta	*Esenbeckia leiocarpa*
Hawthorn	*Crataegus sp.*
Ipê, Brazilian walnut	*Hydroanthus,* formerly *Tabebuia* genus
Kahikatea (NZ native white pine)	*Podocarpus dacrydioides,* now *Dacrycarpus dacrydioides*
Kamahi (NZ native black birch)	*Weinmannia racemosa*
Kauri (NZ native)	*Agathis australis*

Kawaka (NZ native)	*Libocedrus plumosa*
Kirk's pine	*Dacrydium kirkii* now *Halocarpus kirkii*
Kohekohe (NZ native mahogany)	*Dysoxylum spectabile*
Kowhai (NZ native)	*Sophora microphylla*
Lacebark (NZ native, houhere)	*Hoheria populnea, H. sexstylosa*
Lacebark, mountain (NZ native, houhere)	*Hoheria glabrata, H. lyallii*
Larch: European	*Larix europaea,* now *Larix decidua*
Larch: Hybrid	*Larix eurolepis*
Larch: Japanese	*Larix leptolepis,* synonym for *Larix kaempferi*
Larch: Western North American	*Larix occidentalis*
Leatherwood (NZ native, tupare)	*Olearia colensoi*
Lichen: bloodstain	*Haematomma alpinum*
Lupin, blue	*Lupinus angustifolius*
Mamaku (NZ native, black tree fern)	*Cyathea medullaris*
Manuka (NZ native, a.k.a. kahikatoa)	*Leptospermum scoparium var. scoparium*
Manuka (NZ native)	*Leptospermum scoparium var. incanum*
Maple: Sugar (Canada)	*Acer saccharum*
Marram grass	*Ammophila arenaria*
Matai (NZ native, black pine)	*Prumnopitys taxifolia*
Miro (NZ native brown pine)	*Podocarpus ferrugineus* now *Prumnopitys ferruginea*
Mistletoe, green (NZ native, pitita)	*Ileostylus micranthus*
Monkey puzzle	*Araucaria araucana*
Mustard: black	*Brassica nigra*
Mustard: white	*Brassica alba*
Nikau (NZ native palm)	*Rhopalostylis sapida*
Oat, common	*Avena sativa*
Oregon pine, Douglas Fir:	*Pseudotsuga menziesii*
Paraná pine	*Araucaria angustifolia*
Peanut	*Arachis hypogaea*
Pine: Austrian, black	*Pinus austriaca,* now *Pinus nigra* subspecies *nigra*
Pine: Big cone	*Pinus coulteri*
Pine: Bishop	*Pinus muricata*
Pine: Canary Island	*Pinus canariensis*
Pine: Corsican	*Pinus laricio,* now *Pinus nigra* subspecies *laricio*
Pine: Eastern White/Weymouth	*Pinus strobus*
Pine: Japanese five-needle	*Pinus pentaphylla*
Pine: Maritime	*Pinus pinaster*
Pine: Mexican weeping	*Pinus patula*
Pine: Ponderosa, western yellow pine	*Pinus ponderosa*
Pine: Radiata, Monterey	*Pinus insignis, P. radiata*
Pine: Scots	*Pinus sylvestris*
Pohutukawa (NZ native)	*Metrosideros excelsa*
Poplar	*Populus sp.*
Poplar: silver, white	*Populus alba*
Primrose, Scottish	*Primula scotica*
Purple osier	*Salix purpurea*
Rata: Northern (NZ native)	*Metrosideros robusta*
Rata: Southern (NZ native)	*Metrosideros umbellata*
Raupo (NZ native, bullrush)	*Typha orientalis*
Redwood: California	*Sequoia sempervirens*
Redwood: Giant	*Sequoia gigantean,* now *Sequoiadendron giganteum*

Rimu (NZ native, red pine)	*Dacrydium cupressinum*
Rubber, Castilla	*Castilla elastica*
Rubber, India	*Ficus elastica*
Rubber, Para	*Hevea brasiliensis*
Rubber, Guayule, desert	*Parthenium argentatum*
Rubber, silk	*Funtumia elastica*
Rye	*Lolium sp.*
Sand sedge (NZ native)	*Carex pumila*
Sausage tree	*Kigelia africana*
Swamp sawgrass	*Cladium mariscus*
Sedge: square (NZ native)	*Lepidosperma australe*
Sedge: sword-sedge (NZ native)	*Lepidosperma laterale*
Sedge: fountain (NZ native)	*Lepidosperma neozelandicum*
Silver pine (NZ native, manoao)	*Dacrydium colensoi,* now *Manoao colensoi*
Silvery sand grass	*Spinifex hirsutus*
Spruce: Blue Colorado	*Picea pungens*
Spruce: Engelmann	*Picea engelmannii*
Spruce: Norway	*Picea abies*
Sugar cane – Badila (NG15)	*Saccharum officinarum*
Sugar cane – Malabar (yellow Caledonia)	*Saccharum officinarum*
Sugar cane – Pompey (7R425)	*Saccharum officinarum x S. spontanium*
Tanekaha (NZ native, celery pine)	*Phyllocladus trichomanoides*
Tawa (NZ native)	*Beilschmiedia tawa*
Tea	*Camellia sinensis*
Titoki (NZ native ash)	*Alectryon excelsus*
Totara (NZ native)	*Podocarpus totara var. totara*
Totara, Westland (NZ native)	*Podocarpus totara var. waihoensis*
Vegetable sheep	*Raoulia eximia*
Wheat	*Triticum sp.*
Wild buckwheat	*Eriogonum sp.*
Wineberry (NZ native, makomako)	*Aristotelia serrata*

ENDNOTES

ABBREVIATIONS

AGM   Annual general meeting

AJHR   Appendix to the Journals of the House of Representatives

ANZAAS   Australian and New Zealand Association for the Advancement of Science

BAFK   Code for NZ Forest Service, Rotorua Conservancy

DSIR   Department of Scientific and Industrial Research

LLO   Lady Liverpool's Own

NZFUW   New Zealand Federation of University Women

NZIF   New Zealand Institute of Foresters/Forestry

PFRA   Prairie Farm Rehabilitation Administration

SOSBW – the Society for the Oversea Settlement of British Women

INTRODUCTION

1   Michael Roche, 'Sutherland, Mary', *Dictionary of New Zealand Biography*, first published in 1998, *Te Ara: The Encyclopaedia of New Zealand*, teara.govt.nz/en/biographies/4s58/sutherland-mary

2   'Leave of absence up: Organiser for war workers' hostels', *Hutt News*, 2 February 1944. paperspast.natlib.govt.nz/

CHAPTER 1: FORESTRY in BRITAIN

1   Now known as Bangor University.

2   Sir David Emrys Evans, 'Reichel, Sir Harry (Henry Rudolf) (1856–1931), first principal of University College, Bangor'. *Dictionary of Welsh Biography*. https://biography.wales/article/s-REIC-HAR-1856

3   The Sutherland family records were initially collected by Mary's niece Frances (Frankie) Glendenning.

4   M Sutherland, curriculum vitae. Sutherland family records.

5   Family education. Sutherland family records.

6   'Bangor University'. www.bangor.ac.uk 'Administrative/biographical history of the University College of North Wales', *Records of the University College of North Wales*. https://archiveshub.jisc.ac.uk/search/archives/1e969a54-e7e1-34a3-b113-28b926d7c51a

7   John Hetherington, *The Forestry Department at Bangor, 1904 to 2004: A personal account*. Bangor: University of Wales Bangor, School of Agriculture and Forest Sciences, 2004. Archives and Library Service, Bangor University.

8   Professor Eric Mobbs, 'Thomas Thomson: Obituary', *Forestry: An International Journal of Forest Research*, 32(2), 1959, pp. 216–217. doi.org/10.1093/forestry/32.2.216

9   M Sutherland to Johannes Rafu, Copenhagen, 13 March 1924. Forest investigations file R17274587 F 1/277 10/1/28 part 1. Archives NZ.

10 Jan Oosthoek, 'The colonial origins of scientific forestry in Britain', June 25, 2007, *Environmental History Resources*. www.eh-resources.org/colonial-origins-scientific-forestry/

11 'A brief history of the Forestry Commission', by Peter, *woodlands.co.uk blog*, 18 January 2015. www.woodlands.co.uk/blog/woodland-economics/a-brief-history-of-the-forestry-commission/

12 Report of the senate, UCNW council minutes, 2 February 1916. Archives and Library Service, Bangor University.

13 UCNW student register 1912, Archives and Library Service, Bangor University.

14 R G White, reference for Mary Sutherland, 26 September 1916. Sutherland family records.

15 Sir Harry Reichel, reference for Mary Sutherland, 22 November 1916. Sutherland family records.

16 Mary Sutherland, curriculum vitae. Sutherland family records.

17 *Wanganui Chronicle* 5 June 1919. paperspast.natlib.govt.nz/

18 Mary's sister Nell wrote years later that as part of her Land Army service Mary took on the role of supervisor.

19 womenslandarmy.co.uk

20 Article in *Land and Water Extra*. April 1919, reprinted in *Lumberjills: Britain's Forgotten Army*, by Joanna Foat. The History Press, 2019

21 'Nellie Wright (later Evans) and the Women's Forestry Service,' by Wayne Finch, 2016, using information from the Great War Forum website www.greatwarforum.org

22 'Sutherland, David', *Aberdeenshire almanac & register*, 1916. Sutherland family records.

23 Sir John Stirling-Maxwell, 'Scotland's forests 1854–1953', in Royal Society of Scottish Forestry, *Scottish Forestry, Centenary*, vols 8–10, pp. 192–3, 1954. Sutherland family records.

24 Sir William Stirling-Maxwell 9th Baronet, *The University of Glasgow story*, University of Glasgow. www.universitystory.gla.ac.uk/biography/?id=WH1106&type=P

25 M Sutherland, diary of 1952 overseas trip, Sutherland family records.

26 J.S.M. (John Stirling-Maxwell), 'Loch Ossian Plantations: An essay in afforesting High Moorland', 1929, pp. 79, 80.

27 Mary Sutherland, 'Women's labour in forestry', *Transactions of the Royal Scottish Aboricultural Society*, 32(1), p81-84, 1918.

28 'Future of forestry. Sir John Stirling-Maxwell and war developments. Recommendations to Reconstruction Committee.' *The Scotsman*, 8 August 1917. Sutherland family records.

29 Mary Sutherland, *op. cit.* 1918.

30 'Delamere Woods staff, employment of nursery forewomen', National Archives UK. F8/89.

31 The letter to James Simpson, temporary woodsman, has an unclear signature of initials only. Its origin is uncertain; possibly the nursery,

32 Roy Robinson served with Sir John Stirling-Maxwell on the Acland Committee.

33 Letter to J Simpson, 18 January 1918. National Archives UK. F8/89.

34 Letter to R Robinson, 2 March 1918. National Archives UK. F8/89.

35 The Landes forest is the largest man-made woodland in Western Europe, situated on the Atlantic coast of South France. https://en.wikipedia.org/wiki/Landes_forest

36 Mary Sutherland, 'Notes on nursery practice in relation to drought', *Quarterly Journal of Forestry*, XVI, 1922. Archives and Library Service, Bangor University.

37 Untitled item, *Auckland Star*, 30 October 1922, p. 7---. paperspast.natlib.govt.nz/

38 *The Gentlewoman: An Illustrated Weekly Journal for Gentlewomen*. Published in London, 1890–1926.

39 SOSBW connected professional women with work opportunities in South Africa, Canada, Australia and New Zealand, and provided financial assistance for emigration. Bonnie White, *The Society for the Oversea Settlement of British Women, 1919–1964*, Switzerland: Palgave Macmillan. 2019.

40 However, no letter to the NZ State Forest Service was located.

41 J Sutherland to Rt Hon William Massey, 30 June 1923. Sutherland family records.

42   H E Dale to F S Pope, Department of Agriculture, 6 July 1923. Higher forestry education, school of forestry general file, volume 1, September 1919–December 1924. R17277770. ADSQ 17639 F1 552 / 45/9/1 1. Archives NZ.

43   F S Pope to H E Dale, Ministry of Agriculture & Fisheries, London, 24 August 1923, higher forestry education, school of forestry general file, volume 1, September 1919–Dec 1924. R17277770. ADSQ 17639 F1 552 / 45/9/1 1. Archives NZ.

44   *The History of Kauri.* https://www. kauri2000.co.nz/2017/03/11/the-history-of-kauri/

45   Rollo Arnold, *New Zealand's Burning: The Settlers' World in the Mid 1880s.'* Victoria University Press, Wellington NZ, 1994.

CHAPTER 2: FORESTRY in NZ

1   'Immigrants arrive', *New Zealand Herald*, 25 August 1923. paperspast.natlib.govt.nz

2   'Local and general news', *New Zealand Herald*, 25 August 1923. paperspast.natlib. govt.nz

3   'The influenza epidemic: A period of stress', in *A history of buildings and endowments*, Auckland Hospital Board, 1919. Philson Library, University of Auckland Medical School.

4   'Report of the Influenza Epidemic Commission', *Appendix to the Journals of the House of Representatives* (*AJHR*), 1919. H-31a. atojs.natlib.govt.nz

5   'Centenary of the 1918 flu pandemic', New Zealand Parliament, 22 November 2018. https://www.parliament.nz/en/get-involved/features/centenary-of-the-1918-flu-pandemic/

6   'Wanted sympathy', *Evening Post*, 22 August 1923, paperspast.natlib.govt.nz

7   Correspondence with Theodore (Dory) Gray's grandson, John Gray.

8   'Mental hospitals ancient and modern. A lecture by Dr Gray', *Nelson Evening Mail*, 21 November 1923. paperspast.natlib.govt. nz

9   M Sutherland, 'Forestry. Blazing the trail', extracts from the *National Council of Women News*, New Zealand, July 1924, reprinted in *The Imperial Colonist*, April 1925. Sutherland family records.

10   Leon McIntosh Ellis, curriculum vitae, permanent records, National Forestry Library, Scion.

11   Mary Sutherland, Forestry Staff – Stern to Vuletic, R692741 BBQ1 11140 17/. Archives NZ.

12   J R Martin, 'Entrican, Alexander Robert, 1898–1965'. teara.govt.nz/en/biographies/5e9/entrican-alexander-robert

13   The article said that Estella Florence Dodge was newly graduated from the University of Washington's forestry school. 'In other lands', *Australian Forestry Journal*, 15 March 1924, p. 82. National Forestry Library, Scion.

14   'Girl graduates in forestry', *Australian Forestry Journal*, 15 August 1924. p. 224. National Forestry Library, Scion.

15   M Sutherland, 'Forestry. Blazing the trail', April 1925. *op. cit.*

16   John A Kininmonth, *A History of Forestry Research in New Zealand*, New Zealand Forest Research Institute, 1997. National Forestry Library, Scion.

17   The State Forest Service annual report for the year ended 1924, *AJHR*, 1924 Session 1. C-03.

18   Mary Sutherland, Forestry Staff – Stern to Vuletic, R692741 BBQ1 11140 17/. Archives NZ.

19   Correspondence with Michael Roche, forest historian and professor of geography at Massey University.

20   Leon McIntosh Ellis to Mr Goudie, co-ordination study and nursery plantation research, 15 March 1924. Forest investigations file. R17274587 F 1/277 10/1/28 part 1. Archives NZ.

21   Professional and non-professional members list. NZIF records.

22   *Te Karere o Tane*, III(3), p. 27, 1924. Macmillan Brown Library.

23   'Paparoa passenger list', *Evening Post*, 21 August 1923. paperspast.natlib.govt.nz/

24 E M Waller, postcard to Mary Sutherland, 1924, found loose in a copy of the *Empire Forestry Journal*, 5(1) 1926, by Michael Roche. Massey University Agricultural Library.

25 'The Bungalow', http://rotorua.kete.net. nz/site/topics/show/316-the-australia-inn-c1980-1991

26 H A Goudie to the director, 21 June 1924. Forest investigations file. R17274587 F 1/277 10/1/28 part 1. Archives NZ.

27 Leon McIntosh Ellis to the conservator, Rotorua, 26 June 1924. Forest investigations file. R17274587 F 1/277 10/1/28 part 1. Archives NZ.

28 M Sutherland, 'Experimental methods in forestry', *Te Karere o Tane*, III(6), pp. 5–11, July 1924. Macmillan Brown Library.

29 Leon McIntosh Ellis to Miss Sutherland, 28 June 1924. Forest investigations file F 1/277 10/1/28 part. 1. Archives NZ.

30 'Arnold, Maria Hansson' teara.govt.nz/en/ biographies/4h15/hansson-arnold-maria

31 F E Hutchinson, 'Mary Sutherland: An appreciation', *NZIF Newsletter*, 8(3), July 1976. National Forestry Library, Scion.

32 'Hansson & Foster's departure', *Te Karere o Tane* III(7), p. 25, 1924. Macmillan Brown Library.

33 'Rangers' instruction school', *Te Karere o Tane*, III(8), pp. 1–19, 1924. National Forestry Library, Scion.

34 'Cruise records', Rangers' school 1924–26, R1856192 BAFK 1466 287/c 45/10/1. Archives NZ.

35 'Maori women tree planters', *Evening Post*, 12 September 1924. paperspast.natlib.govt.nz

36 M Sutherland to chief clerk, State Forest Service, Rotorua 6 August 1924. Forest investigations file. R17274587 F 1/277 10/1/28 part 1. Archives NZ.

37 'Woman forester. Impressions of Dominion. Visit to Hanmer Springs', *Nelson Evening Mail*, 30 August 1924. paperspast.natlib.govt.nz A clipping is held in the Sutherland family records.

38 'Canterbury–Otago Region: Canterbury Notes', *Te Karere o Tane*, III(9), September 1924. National Forestry Library, Scion.

39 *Te Karere o Tane,* III(10), October 1924. National Forestry Library, Scion.

40 M Sutherland, draft untitled report on forest walk with Hanmer Springs schoolchildren. Forestry in Schools 1924. R 17 277 831. 45/32 1. Archives NZ.

41 The director to M Sutherland, 23 October 1924. Forest investigations file F1/277 10/1/28 part 1. Archives NZ.

42 M Sutherland to the director, 8 and 9 December 1924. Forest investigations file F1/277 10/1/28. Archives NZ.

43 State Forest Service, annual reports to years ended 31 March 1923 & 1924. National Forestry Library, Scion.

44 'Forestry', *Evening Post*, 5 March 1925 (Lyceum Club), 10 March 1925 (Pioneer Club), 8 September 1925. (FUW), 19 September 1925, (WEA). paperspast. natlib.govt.nz/

45 'Scouts and forestry', *Brisbane Courier*, 9 July 1925. Archives NZ. Forestry in Schools 1924. R 17 277 829. 45/32 3. trove.nla.gov.au/ newspaper/article/20941572/1630295

46 M Sutherland, 'Forests and their protection', *School Journal*, XVIII(6), part 3, pp. 162–171. July 1924. National Library Serials.

47 'Rotorua Region. Forestry in Schools', *Te Karere o Tane*, IV(1), 1924, pp.5-6. National Forestry Library, Scion.

48 M Sutherland to the director, School forestry camps, 18 October 1924. Forestry in Schools 1924. R 17 277 831. 45/32 1 Archives NZ.

49 L O Hooker to Leon McIntosh Ellis, 29 January 1925. Forestry in Schools 1924. R 17 277 829. 45/32 3. Archives NZ.

50 P M Page, State Forest Service monthly report. Forestry in Schools 1924. R 17 277 831. 45/32 1. Archives NZ.

51 'Save the forest: Education in schools', Conference report. Forestry in Schools 1924. R 17 277 829. 45/32 3 Archives NZ.

52 M Sutherland to the director of forestry, Forestry in Schools Conference, 9 February 1925. Forestry in Schools 1924. R 17 277 829. 45/32 3. Archives NZ.

53 M Sutherland. 'The power of the forests', *School Journal*, 19(6), part 3, July 1925. National Library.

54   M Sutherland to conservators of state forests, 19 March 1925. Forestry in Schools 1924. R 17 277 829. 45/32 3. Archives NZ.

55   M Sutherland to the director, Forestry in Schools teaching syllabus, 26 March 1925. Forestry in Schools 1924. R 17 277 829. 45/32 3. Archives NZ.

56   State Forest Service annual report to year ended 1925. National Forestry Library, Scion.

57   M Sutherland, 'Exchange column: Seeds, cuttings etc of plants and trees', *Education Gazette*, 22 April 1925. Forestry in Schools 1924. R 17 277 829. 45/32 3. Archives NZ.

58   'State forestry', *New Zealand Life, 4*, 15 May 1925, pp. 15–16. NZ Serials Collection, National Library.

59   M Sutherland to the director, Forestry in Schools, draft speech, 20 June 1925. Forestry in Schools 1924. R 17 277 829. 45/32 3. Archives NZ.

60   R Heaton Rhodes, commissioner of State Forests, 'Letter to boys & girls', *Education Gazette*, 24 June 1925. Forestry in Schools 1924. R 17 277 829. 45/32 3. Archives NZ.

61   'Scouts and forestry', *Brisbane Courier*, 9 July 1925. *op. cit.*

62   Leon McIntosh Ellis to M Sutherland, Hanmer Springs, 17 July 1925. Forestry in Schools 1924. R 17 277 829. 45/32 3. Archives NZ.

63   M Sutherland to the director, State Forest Service, schools forestry, 29 July 1925. Forestry in Schools 1924. R 17 277 829. 45/32 3. Archives NZ.

64   M Sutherland, school forestry camps. Forestry in Schools 1924. R 17 277 829. 45/32 3. Archives NZ.

65   Leon McIntosh Ellis to the conservator of forests, Christchurch, re school forestry camps, 10 August 1925. Forestry in Schools 1924. R 17 277 829. 45/32 3. Archives NZ.

66   M Sutherland to the director of forestry, school plantation endowment scheme, 9 November 1925. Forestry in Schools 1924. R 17 277 829. 45/32 3. Archives NZ.

67   Rotorua proposals 1925–26, operational programme 1924–53. R1853828 BAFK 1466 4/b 1/13. Archives NZ.

68   Leon McIntosh Ellis to conservator, Rotorua, 12 June 1925. Forest investigations file. R17274587 F 1/277 10/1/28 part 1. Archives. NZ.

69   'Hanmer 1925 rangers' instructional school', *Te Karere o Tane*, iv(7), 1925, pp.21–22. Macmillan Brown Library.

70   NZ species classed in the 1920s as taxads have since been reclassified as *Podocarpaceae*: personal comment by Leon Perrie, botany curator, Te Papa Tongariro; *Manual of the New Zealand Flora,* Thomas F Cheeseman, 2nd edition revised and enlarged by the author, edited by W R B Oliver. Wellington, NZ: W A G Skinner, 1925. n.p.

71   Conversation with Mary's niece Helen Baxter.

72   'Local and general', *Evening Post*, 18 August 1925. paperspast.natlib.govt.nz/

73   'New Zealand – the timber farm of Australasia', *New Zealand Life*, iv(6), 15 October 1925, p. 7. NZ Serials Collection, National Library.

74   M Sutherland, 'Afforestation methods in New Zealand', *Empire Forestry Journal*, 4(1), pp. 1–6. July 1925. Sutherland/Gray family archives. [misdated December 1925 on family copy]

75   'Maoris as foresters', *Evening Post*, 17 June 1926. paperspast.natlib.govt.nz

76   'Sea of waving green', *Evening Post*, 5 December 1925. paperspast.natlib.govt.nz

77   F E Hutchinson, 'A historical review of forestry education in New Zealand' in *NZJF, 11*(2), pp. 106–110, 1966.

78   'Afforestation companies: Forestry director's advice', *New Zealand Life*, iv(7), pp. 9–10. 16 November 1925. NZ Serials Collection, National Library.

79   M Sutherland, staff classification card. *BBQI* 1140. Archives NZ.

80   M Sutherland, co-ordination report on Rotorua and Waipoua nursery work, 1925. Forest investigations file. R17274587 F 1/277 10/1/28 part 1. Archives NZ.

81 M Sutherland, report on the use of mechanical devices at Hanmer, 1926. Forest investigations file. R17274587 F 1/277 10/1/28 part 1. Archives NZ.

82 Frederic Truby King, telegram to Forest Department, Wellington, 10 April 1926. Forest investigations file F 1/277 10/1/28 part1. Archives NZ.

83 M Sutherland to the director of forestry, 1926 schools forestry programme, Forestry in Schools 1925-1926. R 277 828. 45/32 4. Archives NZ.

84 Leon McIntosh Ellis, director of NZIF, to R M Somerville, secretary of Te Kuiti Chamber of Commerce. 1 February 1926. Forestry in Schools 1925-1926. R 277 828. 45/32 4. Archives NZ.

85 Arthur W V Reeve, 'St Matthew's LLO Scout Group. Scouting in Christchurch, New Zealand'. Stmatts.co.nz

86 Correspondence with Frank Hutchinson's daughter Moera McNaughton.

87 Rob McNaughton, email to Vivien Edwards, 11 December 2010.

CHAPTER 3: THE CONSOLIDATION YEARS

1 'The beech forests: Dr L Cockayne's new investigation', *New Zealand Life*, 5(6), p 15. 1 June 1926. NZ Serials Collection, National Library.

2 M Sutherland, 'The beech families of our forest', *School Journal*, 10,(3), pp. 163–173. July 1926. National Library.

3 When this baby grew up, she came to New Zealand where she married Peter Glendenning. Frances (Frankie) collected the Sutherland family history, including Mary's letters and diary of her 1952 overseas trip.

4 'A long journey: Rising to the occasion. Our Plunket nurse methods', *Auckland Star*, 27 December 1926. Sutherland family records. paperspast.natlib.govt.nz/newspapers/AS19261227.2.42

5 'Forestry abroad: Trip to Argentine. Green hills of Rio: Contrast with Wellington', *Evening Post*, 12 January 1927. https://paperspast.natlib.govt.nz/newspapers/EP19270112.2.88

6 'Experiment in Brazil: Producing wood pulp for paper: Chemical process', *NZ Times*, 27 December 1926.

7 *ibid.*

8 *Databook on endangered tree and shrub species and provenances, FAO Forestry Paper 77*, Food and Agriculture Organization of the United Nations, Rome 1986. A copy of this book is available at books.google.co.nz/books?id=293chErmYEYC&lpg=PA255&ots=kBIb_xOMoz&dq=Guaranta%20tree&pg=PP1#v=onepage&q=Guaranta%20tree&f=false

9 M Sutherland to Mrs Cole Hamilton, November 1926. Sutherland family records.

10 L B Strong for the director of education to the director of forestry, 1926. Forestry in Schools 1926–28. R 17 277 827 45/32 5. Archives NZ.

11 L O Hooker to Hon O Hawken, minister in charge, State Forest Service. 26 January 1927. Forestry in Schools 1926–28. R 17 277 827 45/32 5. Archives NZ.

12 Secretary of forestry to Miss M Sutherland, 28 January 1927. Forestry in Schools 1926–28. R 17 277 827 45/32 5. Archives NZ.

13 M Sutherland to the secretary, State Forest Service, 'School forestry', 2 February 1927. 45/32 5. Archives NZ.

14 'Now We Must Plant', *New Zealand Life*, 5(4), p. 17. NZ Serials Collection, National Library.

15 'A valuable immigrant: Redwoods in New Zealand', photo of Goudie. *New Zealand Life*, 5(7), p 15. 1 July 1926. NZ Serials Collection, National Library.

16 Leon McIntosh Ellis to M Sutherland, 26 January 1927, Forest investigations file F 1/277 10/1/28 part 1. Archives NZ.

17 'Officers promoted', *New Zealand Gazette*, 10. p. 530. 10 February 1927. Hard copy accessed 2011.

18 M Sutherland, Proposed action plan, 9 February 1927. Forest investigations file F 1/277 10/1/28 part 1. Archives NZ.

19 M Sutherland, Plan: Experimental nursery block 8, Whakarewarewa. Forest investigations file Archives NZ Forest Investigations F 1/282 10/1/28 A.

20   L M Ellis, Memo to all conservators, February 1927. Forest investigations file F 1/277 10/1/28 part 1. Archives NZ.

21   Director of forestry to the conservator of forests, Rotorua, 10 February 1927. Forest investigations file F 1/277 10/1/28 part 1. Archives NZ.

22   A Hansson to L M Ellis, 15 February 1927. Forest investigations file F 1/277 10/1/28 part 1. Archives NZ.

23   L M Ellis to M Sutherland, 18 February 1927. Forest investigations file F 1/277 10/1/28 part 1. Archives NZ.

24   M Sutherland, General report for period ending 28 February 1927. Forest investigations file F 1/277 10/1/28 part 1. Archives NZ.

25   R B Steele, A review of forest extension work. Forest investigations file F 1/277 10/1/28 part 1. Archives NZ.

26   A Hansson to forest assistant Sutherland, 22 February 1927. Forest Investigations 1927–1932. R17 274 628. F 1/282 10/1/28 part 2. Archives NZ.

27   M Sutherland to the director, for attention of chief inspector, 3 March 1927. Forest investigations file F 1/277 10/1/28 part 1. Archives NZ.

28   M Sutherland to the director, for attention of chief inspector, 9 March 1927. Forest investigations file F 1/277 10/1/28 part 1. Archives NZ.

29   A Hansson to M Sutherland, 5 April 1927. Forest investigations file F 1/277 10/1/28 part 1. Archives NZ.

30   L M Ellis, to all conservators, 6 April 1927. Forest investigations file F 1/277 10/1/28 part 1. Archives NZ.

31   History and Development of the School. *Te Kura Ngahere*, 1(1) 1925.

32   Harry Reichel & Frank Tate, 'Report of the Royal Commission on University Education in New Zealand, 1925', *Appendices to the Journals of the House of Representatives (AJHR)*, 1925. E-7A, p. 9. https://atojs.natlib.govt.nz/cgi-bin/atojs?a=d&d=AJHR1925-I.2.2.4.8&l=mi&e=-------10--1------0--

33   F E Hutchinson, 'A historical review of forestry education in New Zealand' in *NZJF, 11*(2), pp. 106–110, 1966.

34   O Jones to Professor H H Corbin, 24 March 1927. NZIF records.

35   Meeting to consider preliminary matters in connection with forming an association of professional foresters in New Zealand, 6 April 1927. NZIF records.

36   M Sutherland, General report for period ending 30 April 1927. Forest investigations file F 1/277 10/1/28 part 1. Archives NZ.

37   F W Foster, minutes of the inaugural meeting, 28 April 1927. NZIF records.

38   L M Ellis to W T Morrison, 6 April 1927. Forest investigations file F 1/277 10/1/28 part 1. Archives NZ.

39   L M Ellis, telegram to the chief inspector, Arnold Hansson, 18 May 1927. Forest investigations file F 1/277 10/1/28 part 1. Archives NZ.

40   M Sutherland, General report ended 30 June 1927. Forest investigations file F 1/277 10/1/28 part 1. Archives NZ

41   L M Ellis to M Sutherland, 9 February 1927. Forest investigations file F 1/277 10/1/28 part 1. Archives NZ.

42   M Sutherland to L M Ellis, 8 June 1927. Forest investigations file F 1/277 10/1/28 part 1. Archives NZ.

43   M Sutherland, Forest investigations programme for period 1927–1935. Forest investigations file F 1/277 10/1/28 part 1. Archives NZ.

44   A Hansson for the Director of Forestry to M Sutherland. 11 July 1927. Forest Investigations R17274587 FI/277 10/1/28 part 1

45   A Hansson to M Sutherland, 11 August 1927. Forest investigations file R17274587 FI/277 10/1/28 part 1. Archives NZ.

46   M Sutherland, Board lining – use of Morrison's patented transplanter. Forest investigations file F 1/277 10/1/28 part 1. Archives NZ.

47   Director of forestry to chief inspector, 21 November 1927. Forest investigations file F 1/277 10/1/28 part 1. Archives NZ.

48   M Sutherland, Investigation work to 30 October 1927, interim report. Forest investigations file F 1/277 10/1/28 part 1. Archives NZ.

49   M Sutherland to the director of forestry,
      Forestry in Schools, 13 August 1927.
      Forestry in Schools 1926-28. R 17 277 827.
      45/32 5. Archives NZ.

50   'School endowment plantations', *Otago
      Daily Times*, 28 November 1927. Forestry
      in Schools 1926-28. R 17 277 827. 45/32 5.
      Archives NZ.

51   List of schools in Taranaki Education
      District that have established plantations
      and approximate area planted to 31
      December 1927. Forestry in Schools
      1928–1929. R17 277 826. 45/32 6. Archives
      NZ.

52   'Waipoua kauri forest', *New Zealand Life*,
      5(9), 1 October 1926. p. 11. NZ Serials
      Collection, National Library.

53   Mary wrote about this trip in a letter to
      family. M Sutherland to Gray family, first
      page missing. Sutherland family records.

54   'Report by W R McGregor, lecturer in
      forestry, Auckland University College',
      New Zealand Life, 5(9), 1 October 1926,
      p. 11. NZ Serials Collection, National
      Library.

55   M Sutherland, monthly report for March
      1928. Forest investigations file F 1/277
      10/1/28 part 1. Archives NZ.

56   'Personal Matters', *Evening Post*, 13 January
      1928. www.paperspast.natlib.govt.nz/

57   'Putting forests in forestry. Interview with
      LM Ellis', *New Zealand Life*, 7(4), 10
      March 1928, p. 39. NZ Serials Collection,
      National Library.

58   First NZIF annual general meeting, 13
      March 1928. NZIF records.

59   E Phillips Turner to F Foster, July 1928.
      ('not official' letter). New Zealand Institute
      of Foresters 1928-1952. F1/561 R17 277 847.
      F1/561 45/74 1. Archives NZ.

60   'Status of foresters: Formation of institute
      professional hallmark', *NZ Herald*,
      24 March 1928. NZIF records.

61   M Sutherland, monthly report, March
      1928. Forest investigations file F 1/277
      10/1/28 part 1. Archives NZ.

62   'State afforestation', *Auckland Star*,
      31 March 1928. www.paperspast.natlib.
      govt.nz

63   Michael Roche, 'Ellis, Leon MacIntosh
      1887–1941', *Dictionary of New Zealand
      Biography*, updated 22 June 2007. www.
      dnzb.govt.nz/

64   A Hansson to M Sutherland, 4 April 1928.
      Forest investigations file F 1/277 10/1/28
      part 1. Archives NZ.

65   M Sutherland, monthly report, April 1928.
      Forest investigations file F 1/277 10/1/28
      part 1. Archives NZ.

66   M Sutherland, 'Bush, berries and birds',
      draft for *School Journal*. Forestry in
      Schools 1928–1929. R17 277 826. 45/32 6.
      1928–1929. Archives NZ.

67   Phillips Turner was also the previous
      secretary of the Forest Service.

68   WT Morrison to the secretary of forestry,
      Article for *School Journal*, 31 May 1928.
      Forestry in Schools 1928–1929. R17 277
      826. 45/32 6. 1928–1929. Archives NZ.

69   L Cockayne and E Phillips Turner,
      The Trees of New Zealand, R E Owen,
      Government Printer, 1950. Original
      edition 1928.

70   M Sutherland, memos 11, 14, 23, 24 & 28
      May 1928. Forest Investigations 1927–1932.
      R17 274 628. F 1/282 10/1/28 part 2.
      Archives NZ.

71   M Sutherland, monthly report, May
      1928. Forest Investigations 1927–1932. R17
      274 628. F 1/282 10/1/28 part 2. Archives
      NZ.

72   M Sutherland, monthly report, June
      1928. Forest Investigations 1927–1932. R17
      274 628. F 1/282 10/1/28 part 2. Archives
      NZ.

73   M Sutherland, monthly report, July 1928.
      Forest Investigations 1927–1932. R17
      274 628. F 1/282 10/1/28 part 2. Archives
      NZ.

74   E Phillips Turner to WT Morrison, 30 July
      1928. Forest Investigations 1927–1932. R17
      274 628. F 1/282 10/1/28 part 2. Archives
      NZ.

75   E Phillips Turner to WT Morrison,
      8 August 1928 (part 2 of manual). Forest
      Investigations 1927–1932. R17 274 628.
      F 1/282 10/1/28 part 2. Archives NZ.

76   WT Morrison to E Phillips Turner,
      30 August 1928. Forest Investigations
      1927–1932. R17 274 628. F 1/282 10/1/28
      part 2. Archives NZ.

77   A Hansson to the director, undated. Forest
      Investigations 1927–1932. R17 274 628. F
      1/282 10/1/28 part 2. Archives NZ.

78   M Sutherland, monthly report, August
      1928. Forest Investigations 1927–1932. R17
      274 628. F 1/282 10/1/28 part 2. Archives
      NZ.

79   M Sutherland to C M Smith, 14 September
      1928. Forest Investigations 1927–1932. R17
      274 628. F 1/282 10/1/28 part 2. Archives
      NZ.

80   A Hansson to Miss Sutherland, 1928.
      Forest Investigations 1927–1932. R17
      274 628. F 1/282 10/1/28 part 2. Archives
      NZ.

CHAPTER 4: A CHANGE of DIRECTION

1   WT Morrison to E Phillips Turner,
      1 October 1928. Forest Investigations
      1927–1932. R17 274 628. F 1/282 10/1/28
      part 2. Archives NZ.

2   'Empire Forestry Conference Tour of New
      Zealand', *New Zealand Life*, *1*(4), p. 17,
      10 November 1928. NZ Serials Collection,
      National Library.

3   'State Forest Service annual report to
      31 March 1929'. National Forestry Library,
      Scion.

4   *The Empire Forestry Handbook*, London:
      The Empire Forestry Association, p. 46,
      1930.

5   E Phillips Turner to the conservator,
      WT Morrison, Rotorua, 9 November
      1928. Forestation Manual, 1927–1929.
      R1854469 BAFK 1466 127a 13/15/1.
      Archives NZ.

6   WT Morrison to E Phillips Turner,
      Rotorua. 15 November 1928. Forest
      Investigations 1927–1932. R17 274 628.
      F 1/282 10/1/28 part 2. Archives NZ.

7   M Sutherland, Forestation manual, 1928.
      737/33b PR 048. National Forestry Library,
      Scion.

8   Conservator of forests, Palmerston North,
      to the conservator of forests, Rotorua,
      8 January 1929. Forest Investigations
      1927–1932. R17 274 628. F 1/282 10/1/28
      part 2. Archives NZ.

9   R D Campbell to the conservator
      of forests, Rotorua, attention Miss
      Sutherland. 2 May 1929. Forest
      Investigations 1927–1932. R17 274 628.
      F 1/282 10/1/28 part 2. Archives NZ.

10   E Phillips Turner to the conservator,
      WT Morrison, Rotorua, 12 January 1929.
      Forest Investigations 1927–1932. R17 274
      628. F 1/282 10/1/28 part 2. Archives NZ.

11   M Sutherland, Report on forestation
      investigations to 31 March 1929. 737/33
      PR22 National Forestry Library, Scion.

12   M Sutherland to the conservator, Rotorua,
      WT Morrison, 24 May 1929. Forest
      Investigations 1928–1932. R17 274 629
      F 1/282 10/1/28A. Archives NZ.

13   M Sutherland, Annual report to 31 March
      1929, sent 1 July 1929, Forest Investigations
      1928–1932. R17 274 629 F 1/282 10/1/28A.
      Archives NZ.

14   WT Morrison to the director of forestry,
      E Phillips Turner, 21 June 1929. Forest
      Investigations 1928–1932. R17 274 629
      F 1/282 10/1/28A. Archives NZ.

15   E Phillips Turner to WT Morrison,
      Afforestation policy, 14 June 1929,
      Forestation Manual, 1927–1929. R1854469
      BAFK 1466 127a 13/15/1. Archives NZ.

16   WT Morrison to E Phillips Turner, 20
      June 1929, Forestation Manual, 1927–1929.
      R1854469 BAFK 1466 127a 13/15/1.
      Archives NZ.

17   The AGM was held on 29 May 1929 and
      reported in the *Dominion*: 'The Research
      Mind', the *Dominion*, 31 May 1929. www.
      paperspast.natlib.govt.nz

18   F Hutchinson, 'An identification scheme
      for exotic coniferae common in New
      Zealand', *Te Karere o Tane*, *3*(8), pp. 20–22,
      1924.

19   M Sutherland to chief inspector, 21 June
      1929. Forest Investigations 1928–1932. R17
      274 629 F 1/282 10/1/28A. Archives NZ.

20   E Phillips Turner to W T Morrison,
     14 September 1929. (1 example) Forest
     Investigations 1928–1932. R17 274 629
     F 1/282 10/1/28A. Archives NZ.

21   M Sutherland, 'A microscopical study of
     the structure of the leaves of the genus
     Pinus', *Transactions and Proceedings of
     the Royal Society of New Zealand*, *63*(4).
     pp. 517–569, 1934. www.paperspast.natlib.
     govt.nz/periodicals/TPRSNZ 1934-63.2.6.8

22   Joyce W Lanyon, *A card key to Pinus, based
     on needle anatomy*, pp. 5, 23–25. Sydney:
     Govt. Printer, 1966.

23   Correspondence with Chris Ecroyd,
     curator at the National Forestry
     Herbarium, Scion.

24   Correspondence with Carlos Lehnebach,
     botany curator at Te Papa Tongarewa.

25   E Phillips Turner, director of forestry to
     the conservator of forests, Rotorua, 23
     December 1929. Forest Investigations
     1927–1932. R17 274 628. F 1/282 10/1/28
     part 2. Archives NZ.

26   According to Mary's niece Helen Baxter,
     when travelling to Johnsonville in Mary's
     Austin, passengers had to get out of the car
     so it could climb the hill.

27   A McGavock for the director to the
     commissioner, 24 December 1929. Forest
     Investigations 1927–1932. R17 274 628.
     F 1/282 10/1/28 part 2. Archives NZ.

28   M Sutherland, 'Notes of underplanting
     of cutover bush areas with exotic species',
     Te Kura Ngahere, 3(2), pp. 77–81. National
     Forestry Library, Scion.

29   A Hansson to M Sutherland, 27 January
     1930. Forest Investigations 1927–1932. R17
     274 628. F 1/282 10/1/28 part 2. Archives
     NZ.

30   M Sutherland to chief inspector, 1
     February 1930. Forest Investigations
     1927–1932. R17 274 628. F 1/282 10/1/28
     part 2.. Archives NZ.

31   Peter Clayworth, 'Located on the
     precipices and pinnacles: A report on the
     Waimarino non-seller blocks and seller
     reserves', commissioned by the Waitangi
     Tribunal, June 2004.

32   M Sutherland to chief inspector, Report
     for February 1930. Forest Investigations
     1927–1932. R17 274 628. F 1/282 10/1/28
     part 2. Archives NZ.

33   M Sutherland, staff classification card,
     State Forest Service. Forestry Staff – Stern
     to Vuletic, R692741 BBQ1 11140 17/.
     Archives NZ.

34   M Sutherland to the silvicultural research
     officer, report for March–April 1930. Forest
     Investigations 1927–1932. R17 274 628.
     F 1/282 10/1/28 part 2. Archives NZ.

35   M Sutherland, A review of sample plot
     work throughout the conservation regions,
     as at 31 March 1930. 737/33A, PR008.
     National Forestry Library, Scion.

36   F E Hutchinson, 'Mary Sutherland: An
     appreciation', *NZIF Newsletter 8*(3), July
     1976. National Forestry Library, Scion.

37   F Hutchinson to M Sutherland, 28 June
     1930. NZIF records.

38   C E Foweraker, 'Progress report on ecology
     and regeneration of the taxad rain forest
     of the Westland botanical district of New
     Zealand.' State Forest Service, July 1921.
     Permanent records 737/33C. PR 079.
     National Forestry Library, Scion.

39   F Hutchinson, 'An approach to the
     management of the rimu forests', State
     Forest Service, 1931. Permanent records
     737/33C. PR 053. National Forestry
     Library, Scion.

40   M Sutherland to F Hutchinson, honorary
     secretary NZ Institute of Foresters. 25 July
     1930. NZIF records.

41   F E Hutchinson, 'New Zealand Institute
     of Foresters: The founding years', *New
     Zealand Journal of Forestry*, 1977, p. 191.

42   F E Hutchinson to Alan N Perham, 28
     October 1931. NZIF records.

43   NZIF did not take immediate
     responsibility for publishing *Te Kura
     Ngahere* from Canterbury University
     College. It came about due to the forestry
     school's desire to form a closer link
     with NZIF, the cost of production, the
     economic depression, the school's eventual
     closure and NZIF's wish to expand the
     journal. Correspondence with Andrew
     McEwen.

44   *Te Kura Ngahere, 3*(4) 1934.

45 'Office Bearers', *Te Kura Ngahere* 5(5) 1971.

46 'Chief Inspector of Forestry Appointed', *New Zealand Gazette*, volume 1, 1930, p. 858.

47 F O Buckingham, 'Re C M Smith.' *NZIF Newsletter*, 9(1), April 1977. NZIF records.

48 C M Smith to the director of forestry, E Phillips Turner, 7 October 1930. Forest Investigations 1928–1932. R17 274 629 F 1/282 10/1/28A. Archives NZ.

49 Unsigned, undated memo. Handwriting identified as Phillip Turner's by Vivien Edwards and Michael Roche, using comparison notes. Memo next to Smith's memo. Forest Investigations 1928–1932. R17 274 629 F 1/282 10/1/28A. Archives NZ.

50 C M Smith to M Sutherland, November 1930 (day illegible). Forest Investigations 1928–1932. R17 274 629 F 1/282 10/1/28A. Archives NZ.

51 M Sutherland to the director, E Phillips Turner, 23 December 1930. Forest Investigations 1928–1932. R17 274 629 F 1/282 10/1/28A Archives NZ.

52 M Sutherland, report for February–March 1931, Forest Investigations 1928–1932. R17 274 629 F 1/282 10/1/28A. Archives NZ.

53 'Forestry department, retirement of director, promotion of assistant', *NZ Herald*, 25 March 1931. www.paperspast. natlib.govt.nz/

54 Mary's niece Helen Baxter kept the jodhpurs for a number of years.

55 'Rotorua Notes', *Auckland Star*, 19 February 1932. www.paperspast.natlib. govt.nz/

56 Mary omitted naming them in her letter.

57 'Editorial: Progress in mensuration', Te Kura *Ngahere*, 3(2), 1932, pp. 49–50.

58 'Standardisation of sample plot procedure', *Te Kura Ngahere*, 3(2), 1932, pp. 84–86.

59 New Zealand Official Year Book, 1932. Tauranga Public Library.

60 The New Zealand National Expenditure Commission. *AJHR*, 1932.

61 'Inaugural members', *New Zealand Journal of Forestry*, 7(2), pp. 107–08, 1955.

62 Mary Sutherland, 'Forest Resources of New Zealand', draft paper for Fifth Pacific Science Congress. Victoria and Vancouver. 1–15 June 1933. Heritage Collection 904(931). National Forestry Library, Scion.

63 *Proceedings of the Fifth Pacific Science Congress*, Victoria and Vancouver, 1–15 June 1933, Bishop Museum, Hawaii.

64 Mary Sutherland, staff classification card. State Forest Service, Stern to Vuletic, R692741 BBQ1 11140 17/. Archives NZ.

65 E Phillips Turner to T C Birch, 14 July 1934. NZIF records.

66 Kirstie Ross, 'I am shour we learnt a lot about the trees: The forestry in schools movement', Paper presented at New Zealand Geographical Society Biennial Conference 2010, Christchurch.

67 Maori chewed a mixture of the resin, water and milk from puha (sow thistle, *Sonchus oleraceus*).

CHAPTER 5: FROM FORESTRY to BOTANY

1 In a 1935 letter, Mary wrote that her Forest Service position was 'axed' two years before, and Nell's eulogy says Mary started at the museum in 1933. The date on the museum's staff photograph, 1932, appears to be incorrect, or she was working there part time, which seems unlikely as she did not sign off on the last sample plot record at the Forest Service until 20 December 1932.

2 R K Dell, 'The first hundred years of the Dominion Museum', unpublished manuscript, Dominion Museum, 1965, p. 176. 06920993. Te Aka Matua Research Library Reading Room.

3 Dominion Museum salaries to year ended 31 March 1934 & 35, *New Zealand Gazette*, Internal Affairs Department.

4 The director, Walter Oliver, to the under-secretary, Internal Affairs, 28 December 1934

5 Dominion Museum annual reports to year ended 31 March 1933 & 1934, AJHR H-22 11.

6   Frances M Kell 'Herbarium WELT in New Zealand's National Museum 1865–1997' *Tuhinga*, 12:2001. pp. 1–15. Te Papa Library, Te Papa Tongarewa Museum of New Zealand.

7   *op cit.*

8   The year recorded in the database may be incorrect as both women were in these areas during the same period in 1936.

9   Although Te Papa's collection database was not complete in 2018, a search on keywords 'Mary Sutherland' came up with more than 4200 results, of which nearly 900 related to plants. According to Carlos Lehnebach, curator of plants at Te Papa, many of the database results appear to apply to the correct Mary Sutherland.

10   Plant collection database (WELT), Te Papa Tongarewa Museum of New Zealand.

11   Lindsay Poole, 'Cockayne recalled at NZIF 75th anniversary tree planting', *NZ Journal of Forestry, 48*(2), 2003, pp. 42–43.

12   M Sutherland. 'Dr Leonard Cockayne, CMG', *Forestry, 9*, 1935, p. 67.

13   W Oliver, to the undersecretary, Internal Affairs, 28 December 1934. Staff–general correspondence (librarian's role) 1934–1938. MU000137/003/002. Te Papa Tongarewa Museum of New Zealand.

14   R K Dell, 1965, *op. cit.*

15   'Home for art and science', *Evening Post*, 29 July 1936. www.paperspast.natlib.govt. nz/

16   More information about Frank Peat and his Treasure House and Hotel Titirangi is available at lopdellprecinct.org.nz/our-history/

17   M Sutherland, telegram to Bigges, Forestry, Donnelly's Crossing. 4 December. 1935. MU000002-008-0007. Te Papa Archives.

18   *Raoulia eximia* is a species of aster endemic to New Zealand, commonly known as tutāhuna, or 'vegetable sheep' because it resembles a sheep at a distance.

19   'Mt Torlesse expedition', Miscellaneous expeditions by members of museum staff 1935–54. MU000002/009/0010. Te Papa Archives.

20   Lucy Cranwell. en.wikipedia.org/wiki/Lucy_Cranwell.

21   'Elizabeth Flint', Royal Society Te Aparangi. royalsociety.org.nz/150th-anniversary/150-women-in-150-words/1918-1967/elizabeth-flint

22   J T Salmon to Ms M A Robinson, 27 January 1985, Mary Sutherland file. Te Amorangi Trust Museum.

23   Mary's niece Helen Baxter remembers seeing the sheep in the Grays' living room at Khandallah, Wellington, where it became a talking point for visitors.

24   According to Pat Brownsey, botany curator at Te Papa, the sheep deteriorated in the 1980s and was deaccessioned. Te Papa has another sheep on display.

25   An example of the lichen can be seen in Te Papa's collection; collections.tepapa.govt. nz/object/846790

26   'Mt. Torlesse expedition', Miscellaneous expeditions by members of museum staff 1935–54. MU000002/009/0010. Te Papa Archives.

27   M Sutherland to curator of the herbarium, Department of Botany, University of California. 4 September 1935. Exchanges with University of California. MU000002/037/006. Te Papa Archives.

28   Dominion Museum correspondence relating to *Kigelia africana.* 5 December 1935 to 31 March 1936. Native Plant Exhibition 1937. MU000133/005/0002. Te Papa Archives.

29   Dominion Museum correspondence relating to rubber, 13 April 1935 to 23 August 1936. Economic Botany-Rubber. MU000133/004/0017. Te Papa Archives.

30   Sutherland M to Mr E S Newton. Agricultural Department, Apia, 31 March 1936. Native Plant Exhibition 1937. MU000133/005/0002. Te Papa Archives.

31   Dominion Museum correspondence relating to rubber. 13 April 1935 to 23 August 1936. *Op. cit.*

32   M Sutherland to the conservator of forests (Morrison) Rotorua, 15 Jue. 1936. (MU000133/005/0002. Te Papa Archives.

33   G Fowlie to Miss Sutherland, 28 April 1936 and 19 May 1936. MU000133/005/0002. Te Papa Archives.

34 M Sutherland, Dominion Museum correspondence to and from Herbert L Mason, associate curator of the Herbarium, University of California, 12 December. 1935 and 7 May to 17 July 1936. MU000002/037/0006. Te Papa Archives.

35 M Sutherland to Mr E S Newton, Agricultural Department, Apia, 31 March 1936. *Op. cit.*

36 M Sutherland, Dominion Museum correspondence to and from Albert E Butler, American Museum of Natural History, 4 June & 8 September 1936, Native Plant Exhibition 1937. MU000133/005/0002. Te Papa Archives.

37 Dominion Museum annual report, year ending 31 March 1936. AJHR H-22 11.

38 Dominion Museum, overtime worked by officers. (weeks ending 4, 11, 18, 25 July and 1 August 1936). MU000137/003/002 Staff- General Correspondence, Te Papa Archives.

39 Art Gallery and Museum official opening ceremony. *Evening Post*, 1 August 1936, p. 10. www.paperspast.natlib.govt.nz

40 'The New Dominion Museum', *Evening Post*, 31 July 1936. www.paperspast.natlib.govt.nz

41 Pat Brownsey, botany curator at Te Papa Musuem, worked in the National Museum herbarium from 1975. When he arrived, the herbarium was crammed with unsorted material. 'We stored some in filing cabinets and in the corridor, but I doubt that would have been the case in Mary Sutherland's day.'

42 Dominion Museum correspondence relating to Sugar, 20 April 1935 to 22 October 1936, economic botany – sugar. MU000133/004/0023. Te Papa Archives.

43 Dominion Museum correspondence relating to tea, 21 October 1935 to 27 June 1936, economic botany – tea. MU000133/004/0018. Te Papa Archives.

44 Dominion Museum correspondence relating to mustard and cereals, 10 August 1935 to 9 January 1937, economic botany – cereals. MU000133/004/0020. Te Papa Archives.

45 The Dominion Museum, in Educational Broadcasts to Schools (2YA Wellington, 4YA Dunedin): September to December 1936, pp. 33–38, (pamphlet). National Library, New Zealand.

46 'Membership list of the Wellington Philosophical Society, Biological Section' in *Transactions and Proceedings of the Royal Society of New Zealand*, 64, p. 449. Magazines and Journals, paperspast.natlib.govt.nz; 'A Brief History of the Royal Society of New Zealand Wellington Branch', royalsociety.org.nz/assets/documents/Wellington-history.pdf

47 Record of officers and membership in 'New Zealand Institute of Foresters Incorporated. Officers, 1935–36', *Te Kura Ngahere*, 3(5), pp. 236–237, 1935.

48 'NZ Forestry League. Election of Officers. A Difficult Year. Watershed Conservation', *Evening Post*, 3 July 1936. paperspast.natlib.govt.nz/

49 NZFUW Wellington, branch and committee meetings March 1931 to April 1940, minute book 3, and office holders list. New Zealand Federation of Graduate Women, Wellington Branch: Records; MS-Group 0237/90-233-1/7, Turnbull Library.

50 'Bennett, Agnes Elizabeth Lloyd', *Te Ara: The Encyclopedia of New Zealand*. teara.govt.nz/en/biographies/3b28/bennett-agnes-elizabeth-lloyd

51 'University Women. Visitor Entertained', *Evening Post*, 7 November 1936. paperspast.natlib.govt.nz/

52 'Edgar, Kate Milligan', *Te Ara: The Encyclopedia of New Zealand*. teara.govt.nz/en/biographies/2e3/edger-kate-milligan

53 Olga Hardy, 'Highlights from the First Fifty Years', NZFUW Wellington. New Zealand Federation of Graduate Women, Wellington Branch: Records; MS-Group 0237/90-233-1/4, Turnbull Library.

54 Wellington Girls' College. en.wikipedia.org/wiki/Wellington_Girls%27_College

55 NZFUW Wellington branch annual report year ended 31 December 1936. New Zealand Federation of Graduate Women, Wellington Branch: Records; MS-Group 0237/90-233-1/7. Turnbull Library.

56 Marion Stewart was a member of the Scientific Poultry Breeders Association, the Poultry Science Association and had a large poultry farm in Tauranga. For more information see teara.govt.nz/en/biographies/5s46/stewart-marion-watson

57 'Bell, Kathrine McAllister'. *Te Ara: The Encyclopedia of New Zealand*. teara.govt.nz/en/biographies/5b21/bell-kathrine-mcallister

58 M Sutherland, undated family letter. Sutherland family records.

59 Correspondence with Mary's niece Helen Baxter. The bach is gone now.

60 M Sutherland, undated family letter. Sutherland family records.

61 L Yen & Co, invoice for one old *Pinus pentaphylla*, 28 April 1937, native plant exhibition, 1937, MU000133/005/0002, Te Papa Archives.

62 A C Clive to M Sutherland, 17 July 1937, native plant exhibition, 1937. MU000133/005/0002, Te Papa Archives.

63 Samuel Guernsey & Theodore Pitman Dioramas. cs.finescale.com/fsm/modeling_subjects/f/19/t/154053.aspx

64 Roger Walpole to Dr [Walter] Oliver, 5 [May deleted and April added] 1937. Staff – General Correspondence – MU000133/004/0017, Te Papa Archives.

65 Correspondence with Helen Baxter. When Helen was a schoolgirl she often visited her aunt at the museum.

66 Interview with Ross O'Rourke.

67 F E Hutchinson, 'Mary Sutherland: An Appreciation', *NZIF Newsletter, 8*(3), July 1976. National Forestry Library

68 Mary mentions attending and presenting a paper at the ANZAAS meeting in a family letter. Sutherland family records, Scion.

69 'Report of the twenty-third meeting of the Australian and New Zealand Association for the Advancement of Science', edited by F J A Brogan, DSIR, Wellington. Published by the Association in Sydney. January 1937. Sladden Collection. Tauranga Library Archives.

70 (a) The director, W R B Oliver, correspondence to Miss M Sutherland enclosing a form to apply for further sick leave, 28 October, 1937, native plant exhibition, 1937. MU000133/005/0002. Te Papa Archives.
(b) The director to the board of trustees, National Art Gallery & Dominion Museum. 5 Aug 1940. MU000014/007/0015, Te Papa Archives.

71 The director, Walter Oliver, to Miss M Sutherland, 28 October 1937, native plant exhibition, 1937. National Art Gallery and Dominion Museum –Trustees meetings. MU000014/007/0015, Te Papa Archives.

72 E J Godley, 'Biographical Notes (23): John Scott Thomson FLZ, FCS, HON FRNZIF (1882–1943)', *New Zealand Botanical Society Newsletter, 45*, September 1996. www.nzbotanicalsociety.org.nz/newsletter/NZBotSoc-1996-45.pdf.

73 The director to the secretary, National Art Gallery & Dominion Museum, 7 January 1938. MU000014/007/0015, Te Papa Archives.

74 Frances M Kell, 'Herbarium WELT in New Zealand's National Museum 1865–1997', *Tuhinga, 12*, 2001, pp. 1–15. Te Papa Library.

75 W J Phillips to the secretary, National Art Gallery & Dominion Museum Board of Trustees, 3 May 1938. National Art Gallery and Dominion Museum – Trustees meetings. MU000014/007/0015, Te Papa Archives.

76 The director, correspondence re Miss Valerie Norman's resignation, 5 December 1938. National Art Gallery and Dominion Museum – Trustees meetings. MU000014/007/0015, Te Papa Archives.

77 The director to the secretary, National Art Gallery & Dominion Museum Board of Trustees, 23 December 1938. National Art Gallery and Dominion Museum – Trustees meetings. MU000014/007/0015, Te Papa Archives.

78 John Salmon to Ms M A Robinson, 27 January 1985. Mary Sutherland file, Te Amorangi Trust Museum.

79   W R B [Walter] Oliver, *New Zealand Birds*, Wellington: AH & AW Reed, 1930.

80   NZFUW Wellington, branch and committee meetings March 1931–1940; minute book No 3(a) report and discussion, 6 April 1937; meeting, 4 August 1937. New Zealand Federation of Graduate Women, Wellington Branch: Records; MS-Group 0237/90-233-1/4, Turnbull Library.

81   NZFUW Wellington, office holders list; committee meetings 16 November 1937, 1 March 1938, 4 April 1938, 12 July 1938; *News sheet*, 9, May 1938; 18th annual report. New Zealand Federation of Graduate Women, Wellington Branch: Records; MS-Group 0237/90-233-1/7. Turnbull Library.

82   W R B [Walter] Oliver to the secretary, National Art Gallery & Dominion Museum Board of Trustees, 6 March 1939. MU000014/007/0015, Te Papa Archives.

83   A paper shortage during World War Two led to regulations to curb paper use. Confetti was prohibited, so maybe stamps were too. 'Chapter 16 — The shoe pinches', *The Home Front Volume II*, p. 756. Historical Publications Branch, Wellington, 1986.

84   M Sutherland to Mr Owen Fletcher, Otago Museum, 21 October 1940, annual native plant exhibition 1940. MU000133/005/003, Te Papa Archives.

85   Owen Fletcher to Miss M Sutherland, 14 November 1940, annual native plant exhibition 1940. MU000133/005/003, Te Papa Archives.

86   M Sutherland to Herbert Mason, associate curator of the University of California Herbarium, 12 November 1940, exchanges with University of California. MU000002/037/0006, Te Papa Archives.

87   Mary wrote *N. pinaceae*, however, Carlos Lehnebach, botany curator at Te Papa, believes Mary meant *NZ pinaceae* (the 'Z' having been omitted).

88   The director to the secretary, National Art Gallery & Dominion Museum Board of Trustees, 17 December 1940. National Art Gallery and Dominion Museum – Trustees meetings. MU000014/007/0015, Te Papa Archives.

89   Information for the *New Zealand Gazette*, 'National Art Gallery and Dominion Museum', November 13, 1940. National Art Gallery and Dominion Museum – Trustees meetings. MU000014/007/0015. Te Papa Archives.

CHAPTER 6: WAR WORK and AGRICULTURE

1   NZIF council meetings, 27 November 1941 and 18 March 1942. NZIF records.

2   Te Papa's plant collection database. collections.tepapa.govt.nz/topic/577

3   M Sutherland, 1942 Dominion Museum correspondence on sugar cane in Opotiki, economic botany – sugar. MU000133/004/0023, Te Papa Archives.

4   Most of the 500 specimens at Te Papa Tongarewa collected by Joseph Banks and Daniel Solander during Captain James Cook's 1769–70 expedition can be viewed online at collections.tepapa.govt.nz/topic/2152.

5   Dominion Museum annual report year ending 31 March 1941. *AJHR* – AtoJs online, atojs.natlib.govt.nz

6   M Sutherland, Dominion Museum correspondence with Lincoln Agricultural College staff – Professor Eric Hudson, J W Calder, and Ian Blair – December 1941 to February 1942, economic botany – cereals. MU000133/004/0020, Te Papa Archives.

7   'Ira Waddill Clokey.' en.wikipedia.org/wiki/Ira_Waddell_Clokey

8   M Sutherland, Dominion Museum correspondence with Lincoln Constance about exchanges with the University of California, Berkeley, 1942. MU000002/037/0006, Te Papa Archives.

9   Vivienne Cassie Cooper, 'Victor Willhelm Lindauer (1888–1964): his life and works', *Tuhinga*, *1*, pp. 1–14. Collections Online, Museum of New Zealand Te Papa Tongarewa. collections.tepapa.govt.nz/document/3405

10 W A Scarfe – notebook. Collections Online, Museum of New Zealand Te Papa Tongarewa. collections.tepapa.govt.nz/object/246719

11 'Moore, Lucy Beatrice.' *Te Ara: The Encyclopedia of New Zealand*. teara.govt.nz/en/biographies/5m55/moore-lucy-beatrice

12 E [Eric] J Godley, 'The First Fifty Years: 1928–1978', Botany Division, DSIR, Triennial Report 1976–78, pp. 5–16, Christchurch: The Caxton Press, 1980.

13 Lucy M Cranwell to M Sutherland, 3 June 1942. MU000208-002-0008, Te Papa Archives.

14 Dominion Museum annual report year ending 31 March 1942. *AJHR* – AtoJs online, https://atojs.natlib.govt.nz

15 William Colenso collected a variety of New Zealand plants and was particularly interested in discovering new species. Colenso collection: Collections Online, Museum of New Zealand Te Papa Tongarewa. collections.tepapa.govt.nz/topic/1295

16 Te Papa has 4443 specimens collected by Colenso in their database. Botony collectors: Collections Online, Museum of New Zealand Te Papa Tongarewa. collections.tepapa.govt.nz/topic/2008

17 It is not clear whether it was Victoria College of Wellington or one of the many other Victoria colleges around the world.

18 Richard Dell, *The First 100 years of the Dominion Museum.* Dominion Museum 1966. 06920993. Te Aka Matua Research Library Reading Room.

19 M Sutherland to Miss Perry, 2YC quiz session, 21 July 1942. MU000208-002-0008, Te Papa Archives.

20 'Kirk, Thomas.' *Te Ara: The Encyclopedia of New Zealand*. teara.govt.nz/en/biographies/2k10/kirk-thomas

21 H H Allan, *A Handbook of the Naturalized Flora of New Zealand*, Wellington: Government Printer, 1940.

22 E J Godley, 'Biographical Notes (28): George Simpson. FLS, FRSNZ, FNZIV (1880–1952)', *New Zealand Botanical Society Newsletter*, *50*, December 1997, pp. 19–22. www.nzbotanicalsociety.org.nz/newsletter/NZBotSoc-1997-50.pdf

23 M Sutherland, Dominion Museum correspondence with George Simpson. Dominion Museum – WRB Oliver miscellaneous files; 1935–1952. MU000208/003/0004. Te Papa Archives.

24 Dominion Museum annual report year ended 31 March 1943. Te Papa Archives.

25 Correspondence with Mary's niece Helen Baxter.

26 Nancy Taylor, 'Chapter 15: Manpower is directed' in *The official history of New Zealand in the Second World War 1939–1945*, Wellington: Historical Publications Branch, 1986. nzetc.victoria.ac.nz/tm/scholarly/tei-WH2-2Hom-c15.html

27 Ethel Law, *Down the years: A record of the past for the women of the present and the future*, YWCA, printed by Taranaki Newspapers, 1964. National Library 267.5 LAW 1964.

28 B Angus, 'Women war workers hostels', 1949. WAII 21 55c, Archives NZ.

29 Notes by Frankie Glendenning, Sutherland Family records.

30 Lady Newall speaking. nzhistory.govt.nz/media/sound/lady-newall-1946

31 'For war workers Lady Newall praises', *Evening Post*, 10 April 1943. www.paperspast.natlib.govt.nz/

32 M Sutherland, Review of Woburn hostels for period 1943–1946. WAII 21 55c. Archives NZ.

33 'Woburn Hostel', *Parliamentary debates: House of Representatives, 263.* 22 July 1943.

34 M Sutherland, 'Review of Woburn hostels for period 1943–1946'. WAII 21 55c. Archives NZ.

35 'On the run. Mrs Roosevelt a smiling tourist', *Auckland Star*, 31 August 1943. paperspast.natlib.govt.nz/

36   In the United Kingdom, ascribing the title 'Lady' indicates a woman holds a hereditary title in her own right; it is considered incorrect usage by the wife of a knight. There are no hereditary peerages in New Zealand, so this convention is not always observed; 'Lady' may be used on occasions where the courtesy title is considered appropriate.

37   'Work appreciated. Hostels organised', *Evening Post*, 27 January 1944. paperspast. natlib.govt.nz/

38   'Fire in Hostel', *Evening Post*, 17 February 1944. paperspast.natlib.govt.nz/

39   M Sutherland, 'Review of Woburn Hostels for period 1943–1946'. WAII 21 55c. Archives NZ.

40   *ibid.*

41   Marion Bruce (née Fonfère) worked for the YWCA and first met Mary at the Dominion Museum. Marion Bruce, report to Margaret Robinson, State Forest Service, Mary Sutherland file, Te Amorangi Trust Museum.

42   Ethel Law, *Down the years: A record of the past for the women of the present and the future*, YWCA, printed by Taranaki Newspapers, 1964. National Library 267.5 LAW 1964.

43   Te Papa plant collection database.

44   Dominion Museum annual report year ended 31 March 1945. *AJHR* – AtoJs online, atojs.natlib.govt.nz

45   Art Gallery and Dominion Museum staff matters. MU000208-025-0001. Te Papa Archives.

46   Tony Nightingale (editor), *White collars and gumboots. A history of the Ministry of Agriculture and Fisheries 1892–1992*, Dunmore Publishing, 1992.

47   Public Service lists, *New Zealand Gazette*, annually 1946–55, National Library of New Zealand.

48   Department of Agriculture annual report 1946-1947, *AJHR*, H-29.

49   M Sutherland, 'Planting round the homestead', *New Zealand Journal of Agriculture*, 74(3), pp. 267-272 March 1947; 'A working plan for homestead drainage', *New Zealand Journal of Agriculture*, 74(6), pp. 585-597 June 1947; 'The planting of homestead shelter', *New Zealand Journal of Agriculture*, 75(2), pp. 129-139 August 1947; 'Rapid shelter from minor species of trees', *New Zealand Journal of Agriculture*, 75(4), pp. 387-393 October 1947.

50   M Sutherland letter to Frances Clark, 26 June 1947.

51   Edward Cullen, Minister of Agriculture, 'Amalgamation of the Fields and Rural Development Divisions', *New Zealand Journal of Agriculture,* 77(2), 16 August 1948.

52   Department of Agriculture annual reports 1947–48 and 1948–49, *AJHR* – AtoJs online, atojs.natlib.govt.nz

53   M Sutherland, 'Growing tree stocks for shelter planting', *New Zealand Journal of Agriculture*, 76(2), 16 February 1948 and 76(3), pp. 251–254, 15 March 1948; 'Multi-purpose trees for planting on farms', *New Zealand Journal of Agriculture,* 77(1), 15 July 1948.

54   M Sutherland to Nell, Nance, Dave and Helen, 6 October 1948. Sutherland family records.

55   Ted Fussel married Eileen Plank, whom Mary had worked with at the Dominion Museum.

56   The Auckland Museum Herbarium inherited the specimens from the Levin Herbarium, however, the collection date was recorded as 1950 whereas Mary visited Espiritu Santo in 1948.

57   Mary's niece Helen Baxter reported that Barbie's job was kept open.

58   M Sutherland, 'Trees and hedges for the approach to the farm', *New Zealand Journal of Agriculture*, 77(5), November 1948, pp. 489–495 and 77(6), December 1948, pp. 585-587.

CHAPTER 7: FARM SCHOOLS and BOATS

1   Arnold Williams, *Land of the sunrise: Recollections of A B Williams, Puketiti Station, Te Puia, New Zealand*, printed by Gisborne Herald, 1957.

2   M Sutherland, 'Survey of tree planting on an East Coast hill country farm', *New Zealand Journal of Agriculture*, 79(5), 15 November 1949, pp. 465–479.

3   Department of Agriculture annual reports for the years 1948–49 and 1949–50, *AJHR* – AtoJs online, atojs.natlib.govt.nz

4   In 1928, Nicholas Yakas and other bushmen building the road also came across the big tree. www.doc.govt.nz/parks-and-recreation/places-to-go/northland/places/waipoua-forest/things-to-do/tane-mahuta-walk/

5   M Sutherland to Nell, Nancy and family, 15 March 1950. Sutherland family records.

6   In 1831 the Church Missionary Society established a model farm at Waimate North to teach agriculture and trade skills to Maori. nzhistory.govt.nz/keyword/tags-7

7   A 'long orchard' is wild trees growing along a roadside.

8   The Cream Trip was a launch service that delivered mail and supplies, and collected cream from farms around the Bay of Islands. A day cruise, following selected routes of the 1927 service, still runs today. bay-of-islands-nz.com/activities/fullers_boi/cream_trip.shtml

9   Zane Gray, an American dentist and author of Westerns, documented saltwater and freshwater fishing in *Tales of the angler's eldorado: New Zealand*. Zane Mirfin, 'Mystique and Misbehaviour of Zane Grey' stuff, 2009. stuff.co.nz/nelson-mail/opinion/columnists/3041490/Mystique-and-misbehaviour-of-Zane-Grey

10 Paul Shellinger and Robert Salkin, 'Vernon Herbert Reed', *International Dictionary of Historic Places: Volume 5, Asia and Oceania*, 1996, p. 861. London: Routledge.

11 Williams Memorial Church of St Paul (Anglican) www.heritage.org.nz

12 'Mission House'. en.wikipedia.org/wiki/Mission_House

13 Department of Agriculture annual reports for years 1948–49 and 1949–50. *AJHS* – AtoJs online, atojs.natlib.govt.nz

14 M Sutherland, 'Native vegetation' in *Farming in New Zealand*, volume 1, Department of Agriculture, 1950. S471 Far. Auckland Institute and Museum Library.

15 'Stewart, Marion Watson'. *Te Ara: The Encyclopedia of New Zealand*. teara.govt.nz/en/biographies/5s46/stewart-marion-watson

16 Correspondence with Marion (Marie) Stewart's niece Margaret Mackersey who recalled that Mary 'often wore trousers or a tweed skirt and brogues'.

17 Marion Stewart's diary, Bluff to Milford, November 1950, borrowed from Margaret Mackersey.

18 Mary Sutherland, letter to Khandallah & Anerley from the MV *Alert*, Breaksea Sound, 19 November 1950. Sutherland family records.

19 'Launch Alert return to Dunedin', *Otago Daily Times*, 11 February 1948; 'Rough Trip. Sounds visited', *Otago Daily Times*, 12 May 1948. paperspast.natlib.govt.nz

20 Douglas Bawden is listed as principal keeper, NZ Lighthouses, Puysegur Point. www.newzealandlighthouses.com/puysegur_point.htm

21 Maritime New Zealand reports this occurred in 1942.

22 Jock Phillips, 'Sealing — The rise and fall of sealing', *Te Ara – the Encyclopedia of New Zealand*, www.TeAra.govt.nz/en/interactive/6220/map-of-sealing-places (accessed 21 May 2019)

23 'Richard Treacy Henry'. en.wikipedia.org/wiki/Richard_Treacy_Henry

24 'Historic Astronomer's Point'. www.doc.govt.nz/parks-and-recreation/places-to-go/fiordland/places/fiordland-national-park/heritage-sites/astronomers-point/

25 There are a number of *Apiacea sp.* plants along the Fiordland coast formerly known as "Angelica" (an old synonym). It is possible that Marie meant *Angelica rosaefolia* (now known as *Scandia rosifolia*), but actually saw *Anisotome lyallii* (Lyalls carrot), which looks similar, is endemic to the south, and would have been easily spotted from a boat. Source: email to the publisher from Ines Schonberger, Herbarium Manager, Manaaki Whenua – Landcare Research, April 2020.

26 J W Smith was second mate on board the *Acheron* that surveyed Fiordland in 1851. Part of Doubtful Sound was once known as Smith Sound, then Malaspina Sound. Both names have since dissappeared from Fiordland geography. See John Hall-Jones, *Fiordland Explored: An illustrated history,* 1976.

27 Dimp is a topical insect repellent used since the late 1940s.

28 This would have been the 1949 New Zealand–American Fiordland expedition to research introduced wapiti deer. rsnz.natlib.govt.nz/volume/rsnz_79/rsnz_79_01_001700.html

29 The Homer Tunnel officially opened in 1954. 'Home Tunnel' from *An Encyclopaedia of New Zealand*, edited by A. H. McLintock, originally published in 1966. *Te Ara — the Encyclopedia of New Zealand* www.TeAra.govt.nz/en/1966/homer-tunnel (accessed 13 Jul 2020)

30 'Sutherland, Donald'. *Te Ara: The Encyclopedia of New Zealand.* teara.govt.nz/en/biographies/2s53/sutherland-donald

31 Mary Sutherland, letter to Khandallah & Anerley, from the mv *Alert*, Breaksea Sound, 19 November 1950. Sutherland family records.

CHAPTER 8: EUROPE and CANADA 1952

1 A P Thomson, NZIF secretary, to Mr Loue, secretary of the Canadian Institute of Forestry, 20 March 1952. NZIF archives.

2 M Sutherland, diary of 1952 overseas trip. Sutherland family records.

3 M Sutherland, 'Homestead shelter planting', Bulletin No. 346, NZ Department of Agriculture, 1951.

4 M Sutherland, 'Farm tree planting'; 'Forest Taxation in Europe and New Zealand', *New Zealand Journal of Agriculture, 84*(3), 15 March 1952.

5 M Sutherland, diary of 1952 overseas trip. Sutherland family records.

6 *ibid.*

7 For more about the Gully Gully Man, see www.theedge-uk.com/view/the-gully-man

8 In her diary, Mary calls the church the Sainte Marie de la Garde. M Sutherland, diary of 1952 overseas trip. Sutherland family records.

9 'The Science Museum and the Leonardo da Vinci Quincentenary Exhibition of 1952.' www.informalscience.org/science-museum-and-leonardo-da-vinci-quincentenary-exhibition-1952

10 Crosby Hall, Bishopsgate, was a residential hall for professional women at the time. en.wikipedia.org/wiki/Crosby_Hall,_London#British_Federation_of_University_Women

11 Now the Nottinghamshire County Show.

12 Lord Bledisloe was the Governor General of New Zealand, 1930–35.

13 The history of the castle can be read at www.castlesfortsbattles.co.uk/highland/ardvreck_castle.html

14 Gaelic place names have various English translations. This book uses Stronchrubie for Sron Chrubaidh, while acknowledging the alternative, Stronechrubie.

15 The UK National Archives holds records to the 1952 conference.

16 M Sutherland, diary of 1952 overseas trip. Sutherland family records.

17 *ibid.*

18 *ibid.*

19 Carlos Lehnebach, botany curator at Te Papa, suggests it may have been a Canadian species, smooth alder (*Alnus undulata,* synonym of *Alnus serrulata*), but was more likely the grey or speckled alder (*Alnus incana*) that grows in Norway in bogs and nutrient-rich swamps that match the site Mary visited.

20 The Vardøhus fortress was built by soldiers from Bergen in 1734–38 to protect Norway's north-eastern realm and fisheries. It has a collection of 18th- and 19th-century wooden buildings. In 1769, a Jesuit priest lodged there to observe the transit of Venus. nordnorge.com/en/artikkel/vardohus-fortress-is-found-in-far-north-eastern-norway/

21 The *Fram* was built for explorer Fridtjof Nansen's attempt to reach the geographic North Pole. Roald Amundsen also used the ship from 1910–1914. He planned to drift over the Arctic Ocean as Nansen had done, but first tackled the South Pole, arriving before Robert Scott. en.wikipedia.org/wiki/Fridtjof_Nansen https://en.wikipedia.org/wiki/Roald_Amundsen

22 M Sutherland, diary of 1952 overseas trip. Sutherland family records.

23 Canadian Forest Service. en.wikipedia.wiki>Canadian_Forest_Service

24 Norman Mackenzie Ross, 'Tree Planting on the Prairies of Manitoba, Saskatchewan and Alberta'. Classic reprint published by Forgotten Books. 7 August 2018. ISBN 10 0265575893. ISBN13:9780265575895.

25 More information about the Morgan Arboretum and Bob Watson's involvement is available at en.wikipedia.org/wiki/Morgan_Arboretum

26 Anne Godbout at the arboretum confirmed that this was Robert (Bob) Watson, but she was unable to locate any record of seed exchange with New Zealand.

27 'Central Experimental Farm' en.wikipedia.org/wiki/Central_Experimental_Farm

28 'Miller, David.' *Te Ara: The Encyclopedia of New Zealand*. teara.govt.nz/en/biographies/5m48/miller-david

29 Ottawa Rewind, 'What's up with that island off Parliament Hill?', provides a pictorial history of this little island, now known as Hull Island. ottawarewind.com/2018/04/10/whats-up-with-that-island-off-parliament-hill/

30 Forest zones are defined by a biogeoclimatic ecosystem classification. Understanding the entire range of ecosystems enables better forest management. Over half of Ontario has boreal forest where undergrowth is almost non-existent. There is only a small layer of soil above the permafrost because of long winters below freezing point and short summers.

31 Louis Hémon wrote *Maria Chapdelaine*. Hémon is buried at Chapleau.

32 Mary names him as Dr Cromb, however, Nancy Sharp, reference specialist at the Canadian Agriculture Library in Ottawa, believes he would have been Dr William Cram who superseded J Walker as supervisor of the Tree Nursery Division at Indian Head. *The Forestry Chronicle*, p. 292. pubs.cif-ifc.org/doi/pdf/10.5558/tfc45392-6

33 Mary spelt his name Cruikshanks, but Nancy Sharp believes he would have been A W Crookshanks, who is listed in the Departmental Directory of Personnel, 1958.

34 Mary tentatively named him as Dr Brandon, but no record of an entomologist named Brandon was found. He could have been from the Research Station at Brandon, Manitoba, one of the five original experimental farms.

35 Dr Leonard Baden Thomson was director general of PFRA, 1948–1956. Under his leadership PFRA developed and promoted soil conservation practices that minimised severe wind erosion on the prairies. Since 1987 a conservation award has been presented in his name. soilcc.ca/saskatchewan-farmers-named-2018-l-b-thomson-conservation-award

36 A brief history of the centre is available at www.agr.gc.ca/eng/about-us/offices-and-locations/canada-saskatchewan-irrigation-diversification-centre/about-the-canada-saskatchewan-irrigation-diversification-centre/?id=1186152258980

37 The Sutherland Forest Nursery Station. www.fffh.ca/sutherland-forest-nursery-station

38   Les Kerr. http://www.fffh.ca/sutherland-forest-nursery-station/superintendents/les-kerr

39   This hotel was probably the Beresford. Mike Roche found a pamphlet from there in an *Empire Forestry Journal* that once belonged to Mary, which is now held in the Massey University Department of Agriculture library.

40   M Sutherland, diary of 1952 overseas trip. Sutherland family records.

41   A letter from Mary to Nell & Nance, dated 28 November 1952, was written on paper from the Lautoka Hotel, Fiji. Sutherland family records.

42   Federation of University Women annual report 1953, National Library of New Zealand.

43   The 1888 clone 1 was a cross-fertilisation of Nootka cypress (modern taxonomy *Cupressus nootkatensis)* cones with Monterey cypress (*Cupressus macrocarpa*) pollen. Twenty years later clone 2 came from Monterey cypress cones fertilised by Nootka cypress pollen.

44   M Sutherland, 'Gorse smothered by plantations', *NZ Journal of Agriculture*, *88*(2), 1954.

45   H W T Eggers & M Sutherland, 'The use of timber in farm buildings', *NZ Journal of Agriculture*, *88*(6), 15 June 1954.

46   F E Hutchinson, 'Mary Sutherland: An appreciation'. *NZIF Newsletter*, *8*(3), July 1976.

47   Mary Sutherland, letter to Frances Clark, 4 February 1955. Sutherland family records.

48   Mary Sutherland, death certificate. Sutherland family records.

POSTSCRIPT: A FORESTER'S LEGACY

1   RSPCA: Royal Society for the Prevention of Cruelty to Animals.

2   Wellington Probate Files (Third Sequence) – Mary Sutherland. R23051664 AAOM 6031 W3265 227/ 0213/55. Archives NZ.

3   Federation of University Women annual report 1955; 'Obituary Miss M. Sutherland', *Evening Post*, 15 March 1955; 'Obituary Miss Mary Sutherland', *NZ Journal of Forestry*, *7*(1), p. 8, 1954; 'Tribute and a plea', *NZ Journal of Forestry, 7*(1), 1954 (the publication date is before Mary's death, but the journal was not issued till June 1955).

4   Helen St Clair Sutherland, Mary Sutherland, 1956. Sutherland family records.

5   Frances was the New Zealand commissioner for the Clan Sutherland Society, and also researched and gathered information on Sutherland genealogy outside the immediate family.

6   Robin Sutherland, 'Mary Sutherland, the first woman forestry graduate'. *Newsletter of Clan Sutherland Society in Scotland*, December 1995.

7   Paul Smale, 'Proposed revamp of NZIF awards', *NZ Journal of Forestry*, *42*(3), pp. 33–35, 1997.

8   Recipients of Mary Sutherland's bequest. Dr Andrew McEwen, chair, NZIF Foundation.

9   Mary Sutherland Scholarship. www.nzif.org.nz/about-us/nzif-foundation/student-scholarships-3/

10   Previously the University College of North Wales.

11   Nicky Wallis, recruitment and events administrator at Bangor University.

ACKNOWLEDGEMENTS

1   *Trees from other lands for shelter and timber in New Zealand: Eucalypts*, by J H Simmonds, held at the National Forestry Library, Scion.

BIBLIOGRAPHY

PUBLISHED SOURCES

Books, pamphlets, journal articles

Allan, H H. *A handbook of the naturalized flora of New Zealand*. Wellington, NZ: Government Printer, 1940.

ANZAAS. *Report of the twenty-third meeting of the Australian and New Zealand Association for the Advancement of Science: Auckland meeting, January, 1937*, edited by F J A Brogan. Wellington, NZ: Government Printer, 1937.

Auckland Hospital and Charitable Aid Board. 'The influenza epidemic: A period of stress', in *A history of its buildings and endowments*. Auckland, NZ: Whitcombe & Tombs, 1919.

'Bledisloe, Viscount Charles Bathurst (1867–1958)' In *Bateman NZ Encyclopedia*, 3rd edition. New Zealand: David Bateman Ltd, 1992

Buckingham, F O. 'Re C M Smith.' *NZIF Newsletter* 9(1), April 1977.

Canterbury College School of Forestry, Forestry Club / NZ Institute of Foresters. Christchurch, NZ. *Te Kura Ngahere*
— 'Editorial: progress in mensuration', 3(2), 1932.
— 'Notes of underplanting of cutover bush areas with exotic species', M Sutherland, 3(2), 1932.
— 'Standardisation of sample plot procedure', 3(2), 1932.
— 'New Zealand Institute of Foresters record of officers and membership', 3(5), 1935.

Cockayne, L, and E Phillips Turner. *The Trees of New Zealand*. Wellington, NZ: Government Printer, 1950 (first published 1928).

Department of Agriculture, NZ.
New Zealand Journal of Agriculture [*Journal of the Department of Agriculture of New Zealand*]
— 'A working plan for homestead shelter', M Sutherland. 74(6), June 1947.
— 'Amalgamation of the Fields and Rural Development divisions' Edward Cullen, Minister of Agriculture. 77(2), August 1948.
— 'Farm tree planting', M Sutherland, 84(3), March 1952.
— 'Forest taxation in Europe and New Zealand', M Sutherland, 84(3), March 1952.
— 'Gorse smothered by plantations', M Sutherland, 88(2) 1954.
— 'Growing tree stocks for shelter planting', M Sutherland, 76(2), February 1948; 76(3), March 1948.
— 'Multi-purpose trees for planting on farms.' M Sutherland, 77(1), July 1948.
— 'The use of timber in farm buildings', H W T Eggers & M Sutherland, 88(6), June 1954.

Department of Education, NZ.
School Journal
— 'Forests and their protection', M Sutherland, 18(6), part 3, July 1924, pp. 162–171.
— 'The beech families of our forest', M Sutherland, 20(6), part 3, July 1926.
— 'The power of the forests', M Sutherland, 19(6), part 3, July 1925.

Department of Internal Affairs, NZ.
The New Zealand Gazette
— 'Chief inspector of forestry appointed', Vol.1, 1930, p. 858.
— 'Officers promoted', 10 February 1927. p. 35.
— 'Salaries to year ended March 1934', supplement February 22, 1935, p. 421.

Desmond, Ray, & Christine Elwood. *Dictionary of British and Irish botanists and horticulturalists*. London, UK: Natural History Museum, 1994.

Farrar, J L. 'Some historical notes on forest tree breeding in Canada', *The Forestry Chronicle*, 45(6), 1969, pp. 392-394.

Federation of University Women. Annual report, 1953 and 1955. National Library of New Zealand.

Forestry Commission, New South Wales. *Australian Forestry Journal*
— 'In other lands', 15 March 1924.
— 'Forestry in schools: Pupils' plantations', 7(8), 15 August 1924.
— 'Girl graduates in forestry', 15 August 1924.

Godley, E J. 'The first fifty years: 1928–1978', in *Triennial Report 1976–78/Department of Scientific Research, New Zealand, Botany Division.* Christchurch, NZ: The division, 1978.

Halkett, John, Peter Berg and Brian Mackrell. *Tree people: Forest Service memoirs.* Wellington, NZ: NZ Forestry Corporation, 1992.

Harrison, Brian. (Editor). *The history of the University of Oxford: Volume* VIII: *The twentieth century.* Oxford UK: Oxford University Press, 1994.

Hutchinson, F E. 'Mary Sutherland: An appreciation', *NZIF Newsletter, 8*(3), July 1976.

Kell, Frances M. 'Herbarium WELT in New Zealand's national museum 1865–1997', *Tuhinga 12,* 2001, pp. 1–15.

Kininmonth, John A. *A history of forestry research in New Zealand.* Rotorua, NZ: New Zealand Forest Research Institute, 1997.

Lanyon, Joyce W. *A card key to Pinus based on needle anatomy.* Sydney, Australia: Government Printer, 1966.

Law, Ethel. *Down the years: A record of the past for the women of the present and the future.* New Plymouth, NZ: Printed by Taranaki Newspapers, 1964.

Nelson, W A, L E Phillips and N M Adams. 'Algal type material and historical phycological collections in the herbarium at Museum of New Zealand Te Papa Tongarewa', *Tuhinga 10,* 1998, pp. 63–85. Wellington: Te Papa Museum of New Zealand. collections.tepapa.govt.nz/document/3375

New Zealand Broadcasting Board. 'The Dominion Museum', in *Educational broadcasts to schools: September–December 1936.* 2YA Wellington.

New Zealand Institute of Foresters. *New Zealand Journal of Forestry*
— 'Cockayne recalled at NZIF 75th anniversary tree planting', Lindsay Poole, *48*(2), 2003, pp. 42–43.
— 'Inaugural members', *7*(2), 1955, pp. 107–108.
— '… The founding years', F E Hutchinson, *22*(2), 1977, pp. 187–193.
— 'A historical review of forestry education in New Zealand.' F E Hutchinson, *11*(2), 1966, pp. 106–110.
— 'Proposed revamp of NZIF awards', Paul Smale, *42*(3), 1997, pp. 33–35.
— 'Obituary: Miss Mary Sutherland', A D McKinnon, *7*(1), 1954, p. 8.
— 'Leyland cypress introductions to New Zealand', J W Sturrock, *34*(3), 1989.

New Zealand Life.
— 'Afforestation companies: Forestry director's advice', *4*(7), November 1925.
— 'A valuable immigrant: Redwoods in New Zealand', photo of Goudie, *5*(7), July 1926.

— 'Empire Forestry Conference tour of New Zealand', *1*(4), November 1928.
— 'New Zealand — The timber farm of Australasia', *4*(6), October 1925.
— 'Now we must plant', *5*(4), April 1926.
— 'Putting forests in forestry. Interview with L Ellis', *7*(4), March 1928.
— 'Report by W R McGregor, lecturer in forestry. Auckland University College', *5*(9), October 1926.
— 'State Forestry', *4*, 15 May 1925.
— 'The beech forests. Dr L Cockayne's new investigation', *5*(6), June 1926.
— 'Waipoua Kauri Forest', *5*(9) October 1926.
— 'A Canadian view of New Zealand forestry', *5*(10), November 1926.
— 'A great forester. Memorial to the late Sir William Schlich', *5*(7), July 1926.
— 'Forestry news & views. Auckland Forestry School', *6*(1), December 1926.
— 'Forestry notes & news. Afforestation companies', *6*(2), January 1927.
— 'Bush and Birds', *5*(9), October; *5*(10), November 1926.
— 'Forestry and soil', *6*(1), December 1926.
— 'Forestry. Save trees and plant trees', *4*(6), October 1925.
— 'Making new forests: 33,888 acres in a year', *5*(9), October 1926.
— 'The late Sir David Hutchins', *4*(4), August 1925.
— 'The New Zealand Forestry League', *5*(9), October 1926.
— 'Town forests wanted', *5*(10), November 1926.
— 'Trees and forestry', *4*(4), August 1925.
— 'Tree topics', *6*(1), December 1926.
— 'What afforestation companies are doing. New Zealand Timberlands Ltd', *5*(6), June 1926.

New Zealand State Forest Service.
Te Karere o Tane: A monthly newsletter issued by the personnel of the State Forest Service, NZ.
— 'Canterbury–Otago region: Canterbury notes', *3*(9), September 1924.
— 'Children's forest walk, Hanmer', *3*(10), October 1924.
— 'Hanmer 1925 rangers instructional school', *4*(7), October 1925.
— 'Hansson & Foster's departure', *3*(7), August 1924.
— 'An identification scheme for exotic coniferae common in New Zealand', F Hutchinson, *3*(8) & *3*(9), September 1924.
— 'Miss Sutherland to be in Rotorua compiling history', *3*(3), March 1924.
— 'Rangers instruction school', *3*(8), 1924.

— 'Rotorua region. Forestry in schools', *4*(1), January–February 1925.

— 'Experimental methods in forestry', M Sutherland, *3*(6), July 1924.

Nightingale, Tony (Editor). *White collars and gumboots: A history of the Ministry of Agriculture and Fisheries 1892–1992*. Palmerston North, NZ: Dunmore Publishing, 1992.

Oliver, W R B. *New Zealand Birds.* Wellington, NZ: A H & A W Reed, 1930.

Pacific Science Congress Victoria and Vancouver BC, National Research Council of Canada and Pacific Science Association. *Proceedings for the fifth Pacific Science Congress, Canada.* Toronto, Canada: University of Toronto Press, 1934.

Parke, Ruth. *A fence around the cuckoo.* Ringwood, Victoria: Viking Australia, 1992.

Perlin, John. *A forest journey: The story of wood and civilization.* Cambridge, Mass.: Harvard University Press, 1991.

Public Service Commission, NZ.

— List of persons employed in the Public Service 1946–1950.

— List of persons employed in the Public Service on the 31st day of March 1945–1946; 1946–1947, 1947–1948. The Department of Internal Affairs, National Art Gallery and Dominion Museum Bulletin.

— List of persons employed in the Public Service 1948–1949, Department of Agriculture, Sutherland, M, 1948–1955

Roche, Michael. *History of New Zealand forestry.* Wellington NZ: New Zealand Forestry Corporation, 1990.

Ross, Kirstie. 'I am shour we learnt a lot about the trees: The forestry in schools movement.' Paper presented at the New Zealand Geographical Society Biennial Conference, Christchurch, NZ, 2010.

Schellinger, Paul E, and Robert M Salkin (Editors). 'Reed, Vernon Herbert', in *International Dictionary of Historic Places: Volume 5 Asia and Oceania.* New York, USA: Routledge, 1996.

Stirling-Maxwell, Sir John. *Loch Ossian plantations: An essay in afforesting high moorland.* Private publication, 1929, pp. 79, 80. Available at Forest Memories, www.forestry-memories.org.uk/ picture/number3356/

Stitt, James W. *Joint industrial councils in British History: Inception, adoption, and utilization, 1917– 1939.* Connecticut, USA: Praeger Publishing, 2006.

Sutherland, M. 'Forestry. Blazing the trail', *The National Council of Women News,* July 1924.

Sutherland, M. 'Native vegetation', in *Farming in New Zealand: Volume 1.* Wellington, NZ: Department of Agriculture, 1950.

Sutherland, M. '*Homestead shelter planting*', Bulletin No. 346. Wellington, NZ: Department of Agriculture, 1951.

Sutherland, M. 'Notes on nursery practice in relation to drought', *Quarterly Journal of Forestry,* 16, 1922.

Sutherland, M. 'Dr Leonard Cockayne CMG', *Forestry 9,* 1935.

Sutherland, Robin. 'Mary Sutherland, the first woman forestry graduate', *Newsletter of Clan Sutherland Society in Scotland,* December 1995.

Whakatane District Museum & Gallery. *Hihita & Hoani: Missionaries in Tuhoeland.* Whakatane, NZ: Author, 2008.

Williams, A B, and Gordon Jones. *Land of the sunrise: Recollections of A B Williams, Puketiti Station, Te Puia, New Zealand.* Gisborne, NZ: A B Williams, 1957.

Woolsey Jr Theodore S. *Studies in French forestry.* New York: John Wiley & Sons, 1920.

Electronic sources

Appendix to the Journal of the House of Representatives. AtoJs online, atojs.natlib.govt.nz

— Department of Agriculture annual reports: 1946–1947, 1948–1949, 1949–1950. H-29.

— National Art Gallery and Dominion Museum report of the board of trustees for the years ending 31 March 1933, 1934, 1936, 1941, 1942,1943, 1945. H-22.

— Report of the Influenza Epidemic Commission, 1919. H-31a.

— Report of the Royal Commission on University Education in New Zealand, 1925. H Reichel and F Tate, p. 9. E-7A.

— State Forest Service annual report of the director of forestry, years ended 31 March 1923, 1924, 1929. C-03.

— State Forest Service first quinquennial review of the operation of the National Forest Policy, together with the annual report of the director of forestry for the year ended 31 March 1925. C-03.

— The New Zealand National Expenditure Commission, 1932.

Australian Dictionary of Biography. adb.anu.edu.au

— 'Forde, Francis Michael (Frank) 1890–1983.'

— 'Tate, Frank (1864–1939).'

Clan Sutherland Society in Scotland. www.clansutherland.org.uk

Clayworth, Peter. 'Located on the precipices and pinnacles. A report on the Waimarino non-seller blocks and seller reserves.' A report commissioned by the Waitangi Tribunal. June 2004. forms.justice.govt.nz/search/Documents/ WT/wt_DOC_94586775/Wai%20903%2C%20 A055.pdf

Council of the Royal Society of New Zealand. *Transactions and proceedings of the Royal Society of New Zealand*. paperspast.natlib.govt.nz/periodicals
— 'Membership list of the Wellington Philosophical Society, Biological Section', Vol. 64, 1934, p. 449.
— 'A microscopical study of the structure of the leaves of the genus *Pinus*', M Sutherland, Vol. 63, Part 4, 1934, pp. 517–569.
— 'Flora and vegetation of the Caswell and George Sounds district: Area covered by the New Zealand–American Fiordland expedition, Vol. 79. 1951.

Dictionary of New Zealand Biography. dnzb.govt.nz/
— 'Ellis, Leon MacIntosh 1887-1941', Michael Roche, updated 22 June 2007.

Encyclopaedia Britannica. 'Edith Summerskill, British politician and physician.' www.britannica.com/biography/Edith-Summerskill

Environmental History Resources. 'The colonial origins of scientific forestry in Britain', Jan Oosthoek, June 2007. www.eh-resources.org/colonial-origins-scientific-forestry/

FineScale Modeler. 'Samuel Guernsey and Theodore Pitman Dioramas', April 29, 2013. cs.finescale.com/fsm/modeling_subjects/f/19/t/154053.aspx

Forestry Memories Image Library. 'Forestry officials at Corrour Lodge.' www.forestry-memories.org.uk/picture/number180.asp

Informal Science. www.informalscience.org
— 'The Science Museum and the Leonardo da Vinci Quincentenary Exhibition of 1952.' www.informalscience.org/science-museum-and-leonardo-da-vinci-quincentenary-exhibition-1952

Lincoln University: *Living Heritage*. livingheritage.lincoln.ac.nz/
— 'I D (Ian) Blair: In memoriam.'
— 'Eric R Hudson.'

Mobbs, E.C. 'Thomas Thomson: Obituary', *in Forestry: An international journal of forest research* 32(2), 1959. pp. 216–217. doi.org/10.1093/forestry/32.2.216

Museum of New Zealand Te Papa Tongarewa.
— Banks and Solander specimens. collections.tepapa.govt.nz/topic/2152
— Botany collectors. collections.tepapa.govt.nz/topic/2008
— WA Scarfe — notebook. collections.tepapa.govt.nz/object/246719
— 'Victor Willhelm Lindauer (1888-1964): his life and works', Vivienne Cooper, Tuhinga: Records of the Museum of New Zealand Te Papa Tongarewa, No. 1, 1995. pp. 1–14. collections.tepapa.govt.nz/document/3405
— Plant collection database (WELT) collections.tepapa.govt.nz/search/plant%20collection%20database%20WELT/results

National Trust, UK. www.nationaltrust.org.uk
— 'Who was Wilfrid Fox?'
— '… History of Polesden Lacey.'
— '… History of Winkworth Arboretum.'

New Zealand Botanical Society. www.nzbotanicalsociety.org.nz/newsletter/newsletters.html
— 'Biographical notes (23): John Scott Thomson FLS, FCS, HON. FRNZIH (1882–1943)', E J Godley, No. 45, September 1996. pp. 11–14
— 'Biographical Notes (28): George Simpson FLS FRSNZ FNZIV (1880–1952)', E J Godley, No. 50, December 1997. pp. 19–20.
— 'Obituary: Godley, Eric: A visionary botanist (1919–2010)', D Galloway, No. 101, September 2010. pp. 14–18; 'Eric Godley – recollections', pp. 18–24.

New Zealand history Nga korero a ipurangi o Aotearoa. nzhistory.govt.nz
— 'Rua Kenana.' nzhistory.govt.nz/keyword/rua-kenana
— 'Lady Newall Speaking.' nzhistory.govt.nz/media/sound/lady-newall-1946

New Zealand Parliament. Historical Hansard. Woburn Hostel, 22 July 1943. www.parliament.nz/en/pb/hansard-debates/historical-hansard/#1940

Royal Society Te Apārangi. 'Elizabeth Flint: Freshwater algae scientist (1909–2011)' royalsociety.org.nz/150th-anniversary/150-women-in-150-words/1918-1967/elizabeth-flint/

St Matthew's LLO Scout Group. www.Stmatts.co.nz 'History.'

Saskatchewan Agricultural Hall of Fame. Leonard Baden Thomson. sahf.ca/inductees/t/leonard_Thomson.html

Sutherland Forest Nursery Station, Canada. Les Kerr & Norman Ross. www.fffh.ca/sutherland-forest-nursery-station

Taylor, Nancy M. 'Manpower is directed', in *The home front, Vol. II: The official history of New Zealand in the Second World War 1939–1945*. Wellington, NZ: Historical Publications Branch. New Zealand Electronic Text Collection/Te Pūhikotuhi o Aotearoa, 1986. nzetc.victoria.ac.nz/tm/scholarly/tei-WH2-2Hom-c15.html.

Tauranga Memories: Katikati History. 'Violet Adela Marie Macmillan, (1902-1981).' tauranga.kete. net.nz/katikati_history/topics/show/728-violet-adela-marie-macmillan-1902-1981

Te Ara — The Encyclopedia of New Zealand.
— 'Story: Sandflies and mosquitos: Dealing with bites.' teara.govt.nz/en/sandflies-and-mosquitoes/page
— 'Story: Sealing, Page 1. The rise and fall of sealing.' teara.govt.nz/en/sealing/page-1

Te Ara — The Encyclopedia of New Zealand Biographies. teara.govt.nz/en/biographies/ 'Allan, Harry Howard Barton', 'Bell, Kathrine McAllister', 'Bennett, Agnes Elizabeth Lloyd', 'Bledisloe, Charles Bathurst', 'Cunningham, Gordon Herriot', 'Dell, Richard', 'Entrican, Alexander Robert', 'Falla, Robert Alexander', 'Hansson, Arnold Maria', 'Kirk, Harry Borer', 'Kirk, Thomas', 'Langstone, Frank', 'McLagan, Angus', 'Mason, Henry Greathead Rex', 'Miller, David', 'Moore, Lucy Beatrice', 'Oliver, Walter Reginald Brook', 'Rhodes, Robert Heaton', 'Stewart, Marion Watson', 'Sullivan, Daniel Giles', 'Sutherland, Donald', 'Sutherland, Mary', 'Woodhouse, Philip Randal', 'Zotov, Victor Dmitrievich',

Theological College of Lanka. Revd Basil Jackson. www.wikipedia.org/wiki/Theological_College_of_Lanka

University of Glasgow. www.universitystory.gla.ac.uk/
— Sir William Stirling Maxwell, 9th Baronet.
— Sir John Stirling Maxwell, 10th Baronet.

White, Bonnie. *The Society for the Oversea Settlement of British Women, 1919–1964.* Cham, Switzerland: Palgrave Macmillan, 2019. www.palgrave.com/gp/book/9783030133474

Wikipedia. en.wikipedia.org/wiki/ 'Amundsen, Roald', 'Champion, Harry George', 'Clokey, Ira Waddill', 'Constance, Lincoln', 'Cranwell, Lucy', 'Darling, Frank Fraser', 'Dass, Petter', 'Eaton, Lotty May', 'Farrer, Dame Frances Margaret', 'Fraser, Simon 14th Lord Lovat', 'The Gentlewoman', 'Gray, Zane', 'Greville, Margaret', 'Grieg, Edvard', 'Hawken, Oswald James', 'Hémon, Louis', 'Henry, Richard Treacy', 'Heyerdahl, Thor', 'Hore-Ruthven, Zara. Countess of Gowrie', 'MacKenzie, Osgood Hanbury', 'The Ministry of Agriculture, Fisheries and Food (United Kingdom)', 'Nansen, Fridtjof', 'RCMP Academy, Depot Division', 'Riddell, Walter Alexander', 'Roosevelt, Eleanor', 'Scott, Robert Falcon', 'King, Frederic Truby',

woodlands.co.uk, Blog. 'A brief history of the Forestry Commission.' by Peter, www. woodlands.co.uk/blog/woodland-economics/a-brief-history-of-the-forestry-commission/

NEWSPAPERS

www.paperspast.natlib.govt.nz

Auckland Star: 'A long journey. Rising to the occasion. New Zealand methods', 27 December 1926; 'State afforestation', 31 March 1928; 'Rotorua notes', 19 February 1932; 'On the run. Mrs Roosevelt a smiling tourist', 31 August 1943.

Dominion: 'The research mind', 31 May 1929.

Evening Post: 'Women's war work: Forestry service', 19 June 1919; 'Paparoa passenger list', 21 August 1923; 'Wanted sympathy', 22 August 1923; 'Maori women tree planters', 12 September 1924; 'Forestry', 5 March 1925 (Lyceum Club), 10 March 1925 (Pioneer Club), 8 September 1925 (FUW), 19 September 1925 (WEA); 'Sea of waving green', 5 December 1925; 'Forestry abroad. Trip to Argentine. Green hills of Rio', 12 January 1927; 'Personal matters', 13 January 1928; 'Here and there. A forestry tribute', 8 August 1931; 'NZ Forestry League. Election of officers. A difficult year. Watershed conservation', 3 July 1936; 'Home for art and science', 29 July 1936; 'The new Dominion Museum', 31 July 1936; 'Art Gallery and Museum official opening ceremony, 1 August 1936; 'University Women. Visitor entertained', 7 November 1936; 'For war workers Lady Newall praises', 10 April 1943; 'Work appreciated. Hostels organised', 27 January 1944; 'Fire in hostel', 17 February 1944; 'Obituary Miss M Sutherland', 15 March 1955.

Hutt News: 'Leave of absence up', 2 February 1944.

Nelson Evening Mail: 'Mental hospitals ancient and modern. Lecture by Dr. Gray', 21 November 1923.

New Zealand Herald: 'Immigrants arrive', 25 August 1923; 'Local and general news', 25 August 1923; 'Status of foresters: Formation of institute professional hallmark', 24 March 1928; 'Forestry Department. Retirement of director. Promotion of assistant', 25 March 1931.

New Zealand Times: 'Arbor Day; schools' observance', 7 February 1925. 'Experiment in Brazil: Producing wood pulp for paper: Chemical process', 27 December 1926.

New Zealand Truth: 'John Caughley: State-managing the young idea', 5 August 1926.

Otago Daily Times: 'Dimp advertisement', 21 December 1946; 'Launch Alert return to Dunedin', 11 February 1948; 'Rough trip. Sounds visited', 12 May 1948.

ARCHIVES, PERSONAL PAPERS, UNPUBLISHED MANUSCRIPTS

Alexander Turnbull Library
— Dell, Richard Kenneth. 'The First Hundred Years of the Dominion Museum: 1865–1966'. Wellington, NZ: Dominion Museum, 1966.

— NZ Federation of University Women –
  Wellington. MS Group. 90-233 Box 3.
  — Number 3 minute book.
  — Branch and committee meetings, March
    1931–April 1940.
  — Hardy, Miss Olga. 'Highlights from the first
    fifty years.' NZFUW – Wellington Branch.
  — NZFUW office holders' list'
  — NZFUW Wellington, 18th annual report.'
Archives New Zealand
  Auckland office
  — Afforestation manual 1927–1929. R1854469
    BAFK 1466 127a 13/15/1 Text.
  — Operational programme, 1924–1953.
    R1853828 BAFK 1466 4/b 1/13 Text.
  — Rangers school, 1924–26. R1856192 BAFK
    1466 287/c 45/10/1 Text.
  — Forestry staff –Stern to Vuletic. R692741
    BBQ1 11140 17/ Text
  Wellington office
  — Angus, B. 'Women in industry – women war
    workers in hostels.' 1949. R12677438 WAII
    21 55c
  — Forest investigations. R17 274 587. F 1/277
    10/1/28 part 1, 1924–1927; R17 274 628.
    F 1/282 10/1/28 part 2, 1927–1932; R17 274
    629. F 1/282 10/1/28A, 1928–1932.
  — Forestry in schools. R 17 277 831. 45/32 1,
    1924; R 17 277 829. 45/32 3, 1924; R 277 828.
    45/32 4. 1925–1926. R 17 277 827. 45/32 5,
    1926–28; R17 277 826. 45/32 6, 1928–1929;
  — Higher forestry education. School of
    Forestry general file, volume 1, September
    1919–December 1924. R17277770. ADSQ
    17639 F1 552 / 45/9/1 1
  — New Zealand Institute of Foresters,
    1928–1952. R17 277 847. F1/561 45/74 1.
  — Wellington probate files (third sequence) —
    Mary Sutherland. R23051664 AAOM 6031
    W3265 227/ 0213/55.
Bangor University archives and library service
  — Report of departments as to national
    service. University College of North Wales
    papers relating to the First World War.
    BMSS/39688.
  — Report of the senate. University College of
    North Wales council minutes, 2 February
    1916. (unreferenced)
  — 'UCNW student register 1912.'
    (unreferenced)
National Archives UK
  — Delamere Woods staff. Employment of
    nursery forewomen. F8/89.
New Zealand Federation of University Women.
  Wellington branch: Records; MS-Group-0237
  90-233-1/7

— New Zealand Federation of University Women,
  the annual reports for the Wellington branch for
  the years ending 31 December 1931, 1932, 1936,
  1937, 1938 and 1939.
— New Zealand Federation of University Women
  Four-yearly report of the Wellington branch
  1932–1935.
— New Zealand Federation of University Women
  Wellington office holders list 1921–1954;
  1954–1979.
— Minute book 3 — Branch and committee; 90-
  233-1/4 March 1931–April 1940.
New Zealand Institute of Forestry (uncatalogued)
  — First NZIF annual general meeting, 13 March
    1928.
  — Foster, F W. Minutes, inaugural meeting, 28
    April 1927.
  — Hutchinson, F to M Sutherland, 28 June
    1930.
  — Submitted designs for official seals, 1930
  — Hutchinson, F to Allan N Perham, 28
    October 1931.
  — Jones, O to Professor H H Corbin, 24
    March 1927.
  — Meeting to consider preliminary matters
    in connection with forming an association
    of professional foresters in New Zealand, 6
    April 1927.
  — New Zealand Institute of Foresters council
    meetings 27 November 1941 and 18 March
    1942.
  — Phillips Turner, E to T C Birch, 14 July 1934.
  — Professional and non-professional members
    list.
  — Sutherland, M to F Hutchinson, honourable
    secretary, New Zealand Institute of Foresters,
    25 July 1930.
  — Thomson, A P, NZIF secretary, to Mr Loue,
    secretary, Canadian Institute of Forestry.
    20 March 1952.
Sutherland family records
  — Reichel, Harry R, reference for Mary
    Sutherland, 22 November 1916.
  — Sutherland family's education.
  — Sutherland, Helen St C, tribute to Mary
    Sutherland, 1956.
  — Sutherland, M, diary of 1952 overseas trip.
  — Sutherland, M to Frances Clark. 26 June
    1947; 4 February 1955.
  — Sutherland, M to Khandallah & Anerley
    from MV Alert, Breaksea Sound, 19
    November 1950.
  — Sutherland, M to Nell, Nance, Dave &
    Helen, 6 October 1948.
  — Sutherland, M to Nell & Nance, 28
    November 1952.
  — Sutherland, M to Nell & Nancy etc, 15
    March 1950.

— Sutherland, J to Right Honourable William Ferguson Massey, 30 June 1923.
— Sutherland, M to Mrs Cole Hamilton, November 1926.
— Sutherland, M to the Gray family, 1928. (Front page missing).
— Sutherland, M, undated family letter, 1937.
— White, R G reference for Mary Sutherland, 26 September 1916.

Te Amorangi Trust Museum
— Mary Sutherland file. (Uncatalogued)

Te Papa Tongarewa Archives, Dominion Museum references
— Annual native plant exhibition 1940. MU000133/005/003.
— Art Gallery and Dominion Museum staff matters. MU000208-025-0001.
— Economic botany – rubber. MU000133/004/0017.
— Economic botany – cereals. MU000133/004/0020.
— 'Economic botany – sugar. MU000133/004/0023.
— Economic botany – tea. MU000133/004/0018.
— Exchanges with University of California, Berkeley. MU000002/037/0006.
— Miscellaneous expeditions by members of Museum staff 1935-54. MU000002/009/0010.
— Dominion Museum expeditions, 1918–1935.' MU000002-008-0007.
— National Art Gallery and Dominion Museum – Trustees meetings etc. MU000014/007/0015.
— Native plant exhibition 1937. MU000133/005/0002.
— Staff – general correspondence.' MU000137/003/002.
— W R B Oliver miscellaneous files; 1929-1942. MU000208-002-0008.

The National Forestry Library, Scion, Rotorua: New Zealand State Forest Service permanent records.
— Foweraker, C E. 'Progress report on ecology and regeneration of the taxad rain forest of the Westland botanical district of New Zealand. Progress reports 1921–1925.' 737/33c. PR 079.
— Hutchinson, F. 'An approach to the management of the rimu forests', 1931. State Forest Service permanent records. 737/33c/ PR 053. National Forestry Library, Scion, Rotorua, NZ.
— Sutherland, M. 'Afforestation investigations – summary of projects which will be started in 1927 – by region, 1927. 737/33b PR 031.

— Sutherland, M. 'A review of sample plot work throughout the conservation regions as at March 1930.' 737/33a PR 008.
— Sutherland, M. 'Co-ordination study, Hanmer Station.' 737/33d PR 117.
— Sutherland, M. 'Forestation manual', 1928. 737/33b. PR 048.
— Sutherland, M. 'Forestation investigations: report to 31/03/1929.' 737/33b PR 22
— Sutherland, M. 'Report on underplanting plots – S F No. 37, mamaku. Project VI. A2 and 7, 1928. 737/33b PR021.

Mackersey family records
— Stewart, Marion. 'Diary: Bluff to Milford, November 1950'. Loaned by Margaret Mackersey.

Personal communications

Emails: Adrienne Grogan, 2009, 9 November 2018, 2019; Andrew McEwen, 20 November 2010, 4 and 20 December 2010, 18 January 2011, February 2014, 14 September 2015, 28 and 29 October 2015, 4 November 2017, 24 May 2018, 10 April 2019, 26 April 2019; Bruce Chapman, 2019; Carlos Lehnebach, 26 July 2018, 23 January 2019, 14 February (9); Catherine Glover, 27 and 28 March 2019; Chris Eckland; Dr John Morgan, 2019; Dr Paul Brassley, 2019; Hannah O'Dwyer, 26 and 27 June (2) 2019; Harley Couper, 2019; Jan Lindsay, 2019 (13); Joanne Darrow, 7 April 2014; Joe Gray, 14 February 2014; John Groome, 9 December 2010; Kirstie Ross, 3. December 2010, 19 December 2010; Lynette Delyth Hunter, 16, 23, 24 and 28 January 2014; Marc Duggan, 5 and 13 February 2014, 2019; Michael Clark, 2009, 2010; Michael Roche, 17, 18 and 23 March 2009, April 2009, 3 June 2009, 2019; Murray Darroch, 2012; Nicola Jane Wallis, 28 and 31 January 2014, 12, 13 and 21 February 2014, 26 March 2019; NZ Sugar Chelsea Team, 21 January 2019; Palma, Ricardo; Pat Brownsey; Paul Brassley, 28 March 2019; Ray Hewitt, 4 April 2019; Ross O'Rourke; Sierra De La Croix, 1 April, 1 May, and 6 June 2019.

Interviews/discussions: Adrienne Grogan; Andrew McEwen; Bryon Somervell; Chas Kerr; John Gray, 2010, 2012, 2018, 2019; Margaret Mackersey; Professor Michael Roche; Sheila Gray.

Letters: Dr Elizabeth Flint, 2011; Helen Baxter; Michael Clark.

Telephone: Chriss Taylor; Helen Baxter, 2009–2019; John Gray; John Kininmonth; Tony Grayburn; Margaret Mackersey.

INDEX